Living Wisdom

BY THE SAME AUTHOR

Looking into Mind

Standing in Your Own Way

Living Wisdom

RE-VISIONING
THE PHILOSOPHIC
QUEST

ANTHONY DAMIANI

PUBLISHED FOR THE PAUL BRUNTON
PHILOSOPHIC FOUNDATION BY

LARSON PUBLICATIONS

International Standard Book Number: 0-943914-78-7
Library of Congress Catalog Card Number: 96-78529

Published for the Paul Brunton Philosophic Foundation by
Larson Publications
4936 NYS Route 414
Burdett, New York 14818 USA

03 02 01 00 99 98 97 96

10 9 8 7 6 5 4 3 2 1

"THOSE OF US who love philosophy, cultivate it, and understand something about it, after a while will feel as though we are dissolving in that wonder, in that awe. It's inevitable. You don't even have to bring in self-abnegation, because it will happen very naturally if you truly cultivate philosophy."

—Anthony Damiani

Contents

Editors' Foreword

Is it possible to understand who and what we truly are, to understand our relationship to the universe and to the Intelligence it expresses, and to live according to this vision?

Here is a book that can help us understand and reach such a goal.

By developing all our human faculties, by attending to the guidance of the Idea that unfolds in and as this world, by realizing in experience that we and the world are ongoing expressions of the eternal divine vision of universal Mind, we realize the philosophic goal.

When this is accomplished, life is transformed. From then on we will live with a new wisdom, an all-encompassing compassion, reverence and a sense of beauty, and a full commitment to a life of service that flows from the highest and most durable conception of goodness. Underlying all this will be the permanent awareness of the Divine Mind that pervades and stands behind all.

This is the love wisdom engenders. This is living wisdom.

Living Wisdom is an edited transcript of a series of profoundly inspiring classes given by Anthony Damiani from November of 1982 until shortly before his passing in October of 1984. In these classes, which were given at Wisdom's Goldenrod Center for Philosophic Studies in Valois, New York, Anthony offered generous commentary and his own developments on notes in the What Is Philosophy? section of Paul Brunton's *Notebooks.* The transcripts have been carefully edited by students who attended the classes and are still associated with the continuing program of philosophic studies at Wisdom's Goldenrod.

Most terms with which readers are unfamiliar should become adequately clear in context by simply reading further or consulting the chapter endnotes. In some cases, however, the glossary at the end of the book may be more helpful. We welcome your suggestions as to whether it should be expanded in future printings.

Living Wisdom

1

Introduction to the Philosophic Life

IT MAY BE ASKED why I insist on using the word "philosophy" as a self-sufficient name without prefixing it by some descriptive term or person's name when it has held different meanings in different centuries, or been associated with different points of view ranging from the most materialistic to the most spiritualist. The question is well asked, although the answer may not be quite satisfactory. I do so because I want to restore this word to its ancient dignity. I want it used for the highest kind of insight into the Truth of things, which means into the Truth of the unique Reality. I want the philosopher to be equated with the sage, the man [*sic*] who not only knows this Truth, has this insight, and experiences this Reality in meditation, but also, although in a modified form, in action amid the world's turmoil.

(v13, 20:1.127 and *Perspectives,* p. 250)

ANTHONY: PB is not going to call you a philosopher if you haven't experienced the higher states of consciousness. A theoretician or metaphysician who hasn't experienced these states is not a philosopher. That's the one distinction he's making here.

IT IS PERHAPS the amplitude and symmetry of the philosophic approach which make it so completely satisfying.

For this is the only approach which honours reason and appreciates beauty, cultivates intuition and respects mystical experience, fosters reverence and teaches true prayer, enjoins action and promotes morality. It is the spiritual life fully grown.

(v13, 20:1.22 and *Perspectives,* p. 261)

ANTHONY: Philosophy is broad-based, as big as life itself. It finds proper due for all the different aspects in life. It finds their proper evaluation or their proper place.

There's not only precision and accuracy in PB's writing, but there's beauty in what he's saying. You see, the doctrine has to be beautiful also. It can't be only good and true; it must be beautiful.

THE ESOTERIC MEANING of the star is "Philosophic Man," that is, one who has travelled the complete fivefold path and brought its results into proper balance. This path consists of religious veneration, mystical meditation, rational reflection, moral re-education, and altruistic service. The esoteric meaning of the circle, when situated within the very centre of the star, is the Divine Overself-atom within the human heart.

(v13, 20:1.23 and *Perspectives,* p. 260)

ANTHONY: Draw a five-pointed star and put a circle in the middle. The esoteric meaning of the star is "the Philosopher," symbolized by this five-pointed star. Why? Look at each one of those points. Under the auspices of the Overself, the person has been put through a program of moral re-education, mystical meditation, religious veneration, rational reflection, and altruistic service. One, two, three, four, five. The Overself atom is in the center. This five-fold path is something which is brought to completion by the radiation coming from the Overself. The completion will not take place without that. Without that higher point of view, the relativity of morals is obvious; anyone who studies any anthropology will see that. And it's hardly likely that you'll know what religious veneration truly is or mystical meditation unless the Overself guides you in these things.

AH: Is the suggestion that none of those things would be possible without the Overself's grace?

ANTHONY: They're possible to some degree, yes, but certainly not in the completed sense that he's speaking about here: that of the philosopher whose morality is derived from within, from the heart-center. Mystical meditation will not really proceed very far unless there's the blessing or the encouragement from your own higher Self, and likewise with the others. So very obviously, the philosopher is one who's been taken under tutelage by the higher Self and put through this five-fold path. It has to be brought to completion, and all these things have to be balanced with one another.

> THERE IS A KIND of understanding combined with feeling which is not a common one here in the West, indeed uncommon enough to seem more discoverable and less puzzling in the Asiatic regions. It is puzzling for four reasons. One is that it cannot be attributed to the intellect alone, nor to the emotional nature alone. Another is that it provides an experience so difficult to describe that it is preferable not to discuss it at all. A third is that although the most reverent it is not allied to religion. A fourth point is that it is outside any precise labelling as for instance a metaphysics or cult which could really belong to it. Yet it is neither anything new or old. It is nameless. But because there is only one way to deal with it honestly—the way of utter silence, speechless when in contact with other humans, perfectly still when in the secrecy of a closed room—we may renew the Pythagorean appellation of "philosophy" for it is truly the love of wisdom-knowledge.
>
> (v13, 20:1.129 and *Perspectives,* p. 253)

ANTHONY: Here we stand in the face of the Silence. Sometimes we try to grasp this by sitting outside and watching the sunset, and I tell you, "Reduce yourself to two-dimensional being, keep quiet, try to feel that stillness." If you do, there's nothing you can talk about; there's nothing there that you can say anything about. But you begin to like it, little by little, more and more.

> PHILOSOPHY OVERCOMES the mystic's fear of worldly life and the worldling's fear of mystical life by bringing them together and reconciling their demands under the transforming light of a new synthesis.
>
> (v13, 20:1.8)

ANTHONY: And in our age that's absolutely necessary. Never before has there been such a demand on people to combine both the spiritual and material, to stop separating them.

> THOSE WHO WOULD assign philosophy the role of a leisurely pastime for a few people who have nothing better to do, are greatly mistaken. Philosophy, correctly understood, involves living as well as being. Its value is not merely intellectual, not merely to stimulate thought, but also to guide action. Its ideas and ideals are not left suspended in mid-air, as it were, unable to come down to earth in practical and practicable forms. It can be put to the test in daily living. It can be applied to all personal and social problems without exception. It shows us how to achieve a balanced existence in an unbalanced society. It is truth made workable. The study of and practice of philosophy are particularly valuable to men and women who follow certain professions, such as physicians, lawyers, and teachers, or who hold a certain social status, such as business executives, political administrators, and leaders of organizations. Those who have been placed by character or destiny or by both where their authority touches the lives of numerous others, or where their influence affects the minds of many more, who occupy positions of responsibility or superior status, will find in its principles that which will enable them to direct others wisely and in a manner conducive to the ultimate happiness of all. In the end it can only justify its name if it dynamically

> inspires its votaries to a wise altruistic and untiring activity, both in self-development and social development.
>
> (v13, 20:1.177 and *Perspectives,* p. 255)

ANTHONY: It really comes down to this: Philosophy is not only the supremely precious and the most beautiful, but also the most practical.

DB: Philosophy allows one to live in harmony with the unfoldment of the World-Idea.

ANTHONY: What could be more practical than discovering the laws that are imprinted on the cosmos by the World-Mind and working in harmony with them? That actually leads to a cessation of suffering and pain.

> WE WHO HONOUR philosophy so highly cannot afford to be other than honest with ourselves. We have to acknowledge that the end of all our striving is surrender. No human being can do other than this—an utterly humble prostration, where we dissolve, lose the ego, lose ourselves—the rest is paradox and mystery.
>
> (v13, 20:5.11)

AH: Anthony, I don't understand this quote, would you help?

ANTHONY: Well, it's a very beautiful quote. He's saying those of us who love philosophy, cultivate it, and understand it, are brought to wonder and awe and dissolve in that. . . . And then of course, what follows will be mysteries and paradoxes, but that would be philosophic understanding.

AH: So the "we" here is students of philosophy, lovers of philosophy?

ANTHONY: Those who love philosophy—that's what philosophy is, "lovers of wisdom." Those of us who love philosophy, cultivate it, and understand something about it, after a while will feel as though we are dissolving in that wonder, in that awe. It's inevitable. You don't even have to bring in self-abnegation, because it will happen very naturally if you truly cultivate philosophy.

KD: Is it because you're brought out of your personal being? Is it thinking itself that draws you out, so that, for example, trying to understand metaphysical principles somehow brings you out of the personal?

ANTHONY: Yes, it brings you out of the personal. You don't live in a world of action and reaction. You get to understand the *fact* that *is,* and not your reactions to it. There's a fact, there's a *what,* and you try to understand that, and that means you have to eliminate your reactions to it. If you eliminate your reactions to it, you eliminate the whole dualistic process of thinking, you get into the depths of philosophy, and then the wonder and the awe of it all begins to dawn on you.

KD: Why?

ANTHONY: Well, when you get rid of the little ego, then the rest comes in. The rest can't come in unless you get rid of the ego. You get some of that now and then, don't you? When you are listening very intensely to a piece of music there is no choice but to *deny* the self, so that, through identity, you might properly appreciate that music. In a similar way, to properly appreciate the wonder of the ideas, some of the things that are explained in philosophy, it is necessary to get rid of your "I." And in philosophy, if a person is truly in love with the things that are being understood, it's inevitable that an abnegation of the [ego-]self will take place. And all of those will eventually lead to that self-abnegation. You can't get into philosophy if you're full of yourself.

TRUTH EXISTED before the churches began to spire their way upwards into the sky, and it will continue to exist after the last academy of philosophy has been battered down. Nothing can still the primal need of it in man. Priesthoods can be exterminated until not one vestige is left in the land; mystic hermitages can be broken until they are but dust; philosophical books can be burnt out of existence by culture-hating tyrants, yet this subterranean sense in man which demands the understanding of its own existence will one day rise again with an urgent claim and create a new expression of itself.

(v13, 20:5.262 and *Perspectives*, p. 254)

ANTHONY: Some of his notes are really statements. This is what the truth is, period. No commentary is going to change it or explain it. Discussion isn't necessary, a simple recognition is enough.

A SCHOOL SHOULD EXIST not only to teach but also to investigate, not to formulate prematurely a finalized system but to remain creative, to go on testing theories by applying them and validating ideas by experience.

(v2, 1:4.111 and *Perspectives*, p. 12)

ANTHONY: This is why we do not restrict ourselves to any one school. It is not possible to come down with a final chapter on answering a question. When you understand philosophy, you understand that that can't be done.

2

Philosophic Development

STAGES OF DEVELOPMENT

THE PURSUIT of moral excellence is immeasurably better than the pursuit of mystical sensations. Its gains are more durable, more indispensable, and more valuable.

(v5, 6:1.52 and *Perspectives,* p. 67)

THERE ARE five ways in which the human being progressively views his own self and consequently five graduated ethical stages on his quest. First, as an ignorant materialist he lives entirely within his personality and hence for personal benefit regardless of much hurt caused to others in order to secure this benefit. Second, as an enlightened materialist he is wrapped in his own fortunes but does not seek them at the expense of others. Third, as a religionist he perceives the impermanence of the ego and, with a sense of sacrifice, he denies his self-will. Fourth, as a mystic he acknowledges the existence of a higher power, God, but finds it only within himself. Fifth, as a philosopher he recognizes the universality and oneness of being in others and practises altruism with joy.

(v5, 6:1.53 and *Perspectives,* p. 67)

DB: The point in the first quote was that ethical development is in some sense immeasurably more valuable than any one of the mystical states. It is longer lasting, more efficacious, more indispensable. It seems you might get familiar with a lot of ideas, and even have some sort of mystical experiences, and still have the character of a snake. In PB's definition of spiritual unfoldment, the ethical part is primary.

ANTHONY: Do you think a person will undertake that ethical development without being given some guidance from within? And if that's so, then which would you give priority to?

JB: The guidance from within comes first?

ANTHONY: If you don't get a glimpse or some kind of intuitive guidance from within that this is the right thing to do, you won't do it. So now which would you give priority to—to the stage of ethical development and character unfoldment, or to the glimpse, which is almost a necessary prerequisite to bring that about? Or can you show me instances where a person undertook ethical development without a glimpse, or without some inner enlightenment?

SD: How would you get that glimpse if you didn't work for it? Don't you meditate and work towards getting a glimpse?

ANTHONY: Yes.

SD: And you have to live a certain way in order to be able to receive that glimpse?

ANTHONY: Well, take someone like Brother Lawrence, who was a soldier of fortune, or Ignatius Loyola: They didn't exactly live an exemplary life—and a glimpse came to them and they changed their ways.

SD: Well, they weren't criminals—

ANTHONY: Soldiers of fortune? They were mercenaries! I was just asking a question. I'm not proposing to answer it.

SD: Well, what you're saying there is that you can do anything.

ANTHONY: Well, we do, don't we? [*laughter*]

SD: Well, pretty much, and we don't get very far, either.

ANTHONY: The reason is that we don't have intuitive guidance.

SD: Maybe if we follow some of the doctrines that are laid down—

ANTHONY: That already presupposes some kind of grace has been shed, or you're not going to follow a doctrine.

> THE INITIATION into wisdom—if it is to be lasting—is not suddenly given by any master; it is slowly grown by the experiences and reflection of life. Thought is gradually converted into habit, and habit is gradually merged into high character. The philosophic attitude, if it is to be genuine, will pass into the student's nerves and move his muscles.
>
> (v13, 20:3.193)

AC: Do you think that's a process of evolution of the quester?

RC: "Thought is gradually converted into habit" means that you consciously develop good *vasanas* [tendencies, attitudes, dispositions] and then those good *vasanas* make it possible for you to have a more transparent receptivity to the guidance of the higher soul.

AC: Literally, all your actions are dictated by the higher.

ANTHONY: Philosophy becomes corporealized, in the body.

LR: You say that it moves into the nerves, and then moves the muscles?

ANTHONY: It becomes corporealized, *literally.* You become that, your body becomes that attitude.

HS: What does it mean that philosophy is in the nerves?

ANTHONY: PB's saying there that the philosophic ideal that you're reading and studying has to be actualized in your character, in your very being. That's all he's saying. Don't worry about the nerve pushing the arms.

> TO THE DEGREE that we are able to transcend the world-thought within our consciousness, to that degree we are able to transcend the gravitational force of worldly desire itself. But this presupposes a knowledge of the mentalistic

doctrine. Therefore, even in the sphere of ethics can be seen the usefulness of such knowledge.

(v13, 21:5.32)

ANTHONY: What does PB mean by "transcend the world-thought"?

BS: To see it as a projection from the mind.

ANTHONY: Yes. In other words, to understand it. To understand it means that you recognize that it's an incessant repetition of an idea. And if it's an incessant repetition, like a cinematic film, then you will not believe that it has reality. As long as your I-thought, or the ego, covers that interval that exists between two of these thoughts, then the world will appear as a solid real thing to you. In other words, it will appear as reality to you; and if it appears as reality to you, it's going to have a lot of glamour. You're going to want it. Now in mentalism you understand that that's not the case. You understand that the world-thought is a projection, instant by instant, of a thought. And in that sense, if you can understand it, you transcend it. You don't rise above it, you don't go up to the heavenly spheres. You understand thoroughly, then you transcend it.

PERCEIVE THESE TWO things now: the dreamlike character of life in the world, and the illusory character of the personal ego. Hence the need of the "What am I?" enquiry, that the illusion of the ego may be dispelled. When you can see these things clearly, then you may be still and undisturbed, unentangled, and unillusioned amid the struggle of life. You will be wise, free, impervious to the petty persecution of men—their lies, malice, and injuries—for being no longer identified with the personality, you are no longer their target.

(v13, 21:5.4)

ANTHONY: "Perceive these two"—the dreamlike thought and the illusory character of the ego. Well, if you understood the premise before, that the world is an incessant duplication, then naturally the ego would have to be of that illusory nature as well as the world-thought, wouldn't it?

LD: Isn't that saying the same thing as the first part of the last quote, where PB speaks about transcending the World-Idea? When you see the world as a dream, and the ego as illusory, isn't that seeing the World-Idea, which includes the ego, as mental?

ANTHONY: So now you're transcending both of them.

LD: Transcending?

ANTHONY: The way I just explained transcendence, as when you understand something. For instance, you see a mirage, but you no longer go over there expecting to get a drink of water. You've transcended that. It doesn't mean you've taken a balloon and gone up high.

LD: It more or less means transcending your conception of it.

ANTHONY: Transcending your conception of your ignorance. . . .

PB points out elsewhere that in the East they've been constantly preoccupied with trying to understand "Who am I?" and that that's legitimate, that's part of philosophy. But PB, being a Westerner, always found that that was only half the answer, because the other half of the answer was "What am I?" and the "What" is necessarily included as part of the World-Idea. So the Westerners were preoccupied with an inquiry into the nature of the world. Not only what is the nature of the "I" but what is the nature of the world. So he came in with the "*What* am I?" to complement the "*Who* am I?" and these two together would give us a complete picture of philosophy.

AH: In the "Who am I?" exercise, what do you see?

ANTHONY: The "Who am I?" exercise leads you to the subjective Logos that's operative within you, and will not give you an explanation of what the world is.

AH: Will it show you the illusory quality of the ego?

ANTHONY: No, it would lead you to the subjective Logos which is within you; it shows you what the real I is. So it would *not* explain what the nature of the World-Idea is.

RC: These two exercises seem to correspond also to the fourth and fifth levels of the earlier quote (p. 18) where PB pointed out that we conceive of ourselves progressively and that there are corresponding levels of ethical development. In the fourth you perceive the divinity but perceive it only within yourself.

ANTHONY: Yes, you could make that correlation.

RC: And with the ethics corresponding to the fifth level, the person "practises altruism with joy," which is a very different ethical ideal than renunciation of the world.

> THERE ARE THREE things man needs to know to make him a spiritually educated man: the truth about himself, his world, and his God. The mystic who thinks it is enough to know the first alone and to leave out the last two, is satisfied to be half-educated.
>
> (v13, 20:4.95 and *Perspectives*, p. 257)

ANTHONY: The word *self* is not capitalized, right? The truth about that uncapitalized self is that it is illusory, that you have to realize the non-existence of the ego. But even with that insight, with that understanding, you're still only one-third of the way. The next thing is to understand the nature of the World-Idea. Then, the third thing is the identification with your I AM, with your God.

RC: What is it about the possession of the first that would make a person a mystic?

ANTHONY: That you can see through the illusory nature of your ego makes you a mystic. I don't think that's available to you if you're a non-mystic. That's an initiation, that's a mystical initiation.

LD: If you see the illusoriness of the ego, doesn't that by implication say that you are seeing from a position other than the ego, which indicates that you're seeing from a higher point of view?

ANTHONY: You may have had a glimpse of the fact that the

ego is illusory, that it doesn't have a reality, but that doesn't mean that you're established in that standpoint. So you could have a glimpse wherein the illusory nature of the ego is revealed. And the consequence is that from then on you identify with the ego less and less. But it is a mystical experience. Ordinary people just don't come up with the realization that their ego is illusory.

Now what is the truth about your God? There he's talking about *your* God, *your* Overself.

PC: And knowing that is really a whole different thing from knowing the illusoriness of the ego.

ANTHONY: Yes.

RC: Would you say that your world is the world that appears as the objective pole presented to the ego? Is the person to know that as a false construction by the false ego?

ANTHONY: When the nature of the illusory ego is seen, the world that's concomitant with it collapses. It's only after this happens that you can get to know the nature of the World-Idea. You can't know the nature of the World-Idea while you're the ego.

So, the mystic comes to the realization that both the ego and the world that that ego perceives are illusory. That's the first realization as a mystic—the illusory nature of the ego and the concomitant world. Then you have to investigate the Idea of the world that's given to you, and when you do, you find out something about the World-Idea. That would be the second level. And the third level would be your I AM, the God within you. I'm just summarizing what has already been said.

RC: I still have a hard time thinking that seeing the illusoriness of the ego necessarily makes someone a mystic.

ANTHONY: Well, I should have qualified that and added "makes you a mystic or a nut!" [*laughter*]

RC: Or a skeptic or a cynic or a nihilist?

ANTHONY: No, you become a mystic. Because the whole world collapses on you.

RC: Would you accept that a person could become a nihilist on the basis of that?

ANTHONY: No, you don't have that experience of the illusoriness of the ego without the freedom of release.

RC: Does it depend on my individual soul's level of evolution whether or not I'll be able to recognize that that sense of release is the truth about myself?

ANTHONY: Let me try this way. Let's say you were a native or inhabitant of some island where they have no Sanskrit texts, no mystical literature. You have the experience of the illusoriness of the ego, and the release from that ego, and the lifting of the burden. And then, let's say, it comes back again, and again you think of yourself as the ego. You can't go around asking people, "Well, what does this mean?" because you're living on this island.

But I'm going to try to say that the experience is absolutely self-validating and doesn't need a commentary by anyone else, either personally or in a book. Because once the experience occurs, it inevitably has altered your outlook, your attitude towards life. You may have been a person who believed in the material world, that objects exist because sense functioning presents you with them; but after that occasion you'll never accept that, or there'll always be doubts about that.

When the experience occurs, life has reached that level of intelligence in which Self is fulfilling itself. And it doesn't need a text or certification from any source outside of yourself to know that this is the way it is. It will be intrinsic to you as an individual from now on, that the ego is not real, that it is illusory.

RC: Will it also be intrinsic that the ego is not what I really am?

ANTHONY: To say truthfully and factually, "I am not really the ego," refers to an actual mystical experience. Of course there are also other approaches that will make a person a mystic; this is not the only one.

PC: So when a person has that experience, in what sense does that person not yet know the truth of the I AM?

ANTHONY: Because that's a long, arduous, difficult process, maybe twenty, thirty incarnations yet to go.

PC: Would this mean that the ego has gone through a death of some sort but the individual is not yet in any kind of union with the higher Self?

ANTHONY: It was a temporary glimpse. And for whatever length of time it lasted, whether for five minutes or five months, when it's over, it's over. And it's only the beginning. And it might vary. In some people, it might take one or two incarnations to achieve the identity with the Overself, but I would say the average time is pretty long.

AH: We're speaking about the negation of the ego. There's a contradiction between this experience and the ego. After the experience, the ego tries to reclaim what was once its own, and it can't quite do that in the way that it used to.

ANTHONY: Yes.

AH: That fact, that the ego no longer has that kind of blind security in its own autonomy, leads to this long drawn-out process.

ANTHONY: Yes. You have to remember that even if no books were ever written, and there were no gurus, no teachers, no sages, no texts available, no companions to talk to, this still operates. It's a natural process. It operates regardless of whether you have flags flying, books written, or not. This is what I mean when I speak about life reaching out through experience to understand itself. And this is independent even of the cultural mores of the environment. This is a natural process. An apple or a pear on a tree ripens naturally. You don't have to go there and read to it about the genesis of the process of its growth, budding, and maturation! [*laughter*] It just happens. And the pear has no notion that it's Norwegian or Finnish or American, or anything like that.

AH: Some of the mystical experiences that I've read about use the expression "I am not" rather than "I am a grander self." It seems that the notion of a grander self is the conclusion of the philosophic work.

ANTHONY: Yes, it's a very long drawn-out path. But the important thing to understand is that this is a process that's going on in nature. You can be born on an island with nobody to talk to. Everybody would be carrying a stone weighing two hundred pounds and you wouldn't be carrying any.

AH: What about the example of Brother Lawrence's illumination?

ANTHONY: Any example we take will always be in the context of a certain culture, a certain society, nationality, texts that have been written, all these things. I'm saying: Wipe away all of this, and the process of life understanding itself, reaching maturation, goes on just the same. If there's no Buddhism, no Hinduism, no Platonism, etc., it still goes on.

Now that doesn't mean that these traditions are worthless. They're not. They carry their own weight, and they're quite useful because they shorten the path somewhat, and they give us direction and afford a quickening of the pace. But I'm saying that this process would happen just the same.

KD: "This process" refers to life understanding itself?

ANTHONY: Yes, life ripening. Life ripens, just like a pear ripens, or an apple, or a banana. They get ripe. If they're in the sun long enough, they get ripe. So very often people have had so many incarnations that in one of those incarnations they suddenly say, "This is it. No more. I'm not interested. Picture's over. Goodbye."

KD: Then, in other words, it's part of nature itself to have that thought-process begin to investigate itself?

ANTHONY: In the case of people who are over-satiated with experiences of life, it just cuts off. It reaches a point and just cuts off. Just turns around, goes in. Because there's no sense looking out there any more. It's the same picture. It's a rerun.

KD: Life understands—just the fullness of life itself leads to its—

ANTHONY: —its maturation, yes. You have to watch out that you don't get what they call "rotten ripe." [*laughter*]

> THE FIRST STEP is to discover that there is a Presence, a Power, a Life, a Mind, Being, unique, not made or begot, without shape, unseen and unheard, everywhere and always the same. The second step is to discover its relationship to the universe and to oneself.
>
> (v13, 20:4.133 and *Perspectives*, p. 257)

ANTHONY: Tell me, what do you think that Being, that Power, that Life, that Mind, that Presence might be?

AH: I thought it was the realization of Mind, Universal Mind, Mind in Itself, which includes the Overself.

ANTHONY: So then you're saying that insofar as a person is the Overself, that person can have this realization of the World-Mind, and that the quote presupposes that the person is in that situation?

AB: Are you suggesting that when you are in the Overself, you're in a position to realize that Life, Power, Being, Mind which is the World-Mind?

ANTHONY: Yes, the unique Mind.

We would have to say something like this: that the World-Mind, or Mind, the unique Mind, is the same *One* in all Overselves. Or if you want, you could say that each and every Overself is a point within the World-Mind. It is from the position of the Overself where the recognition of this unique Mind can take place. Where else can it take place?

Read the second part again.

> . . . The second step is to discover its relationship to the universe and to oneself.

ANTHONY: So that would be the next step, then?

AB: You realize this unique Mind. Now you have to find out what this unique Mind has to do with you, and what it has to do with your world.

ANTHONY: Yes, primarily what it has to do with the world—that it's the substratum of the world. And then within that you locate your self, self with a small "s."

JB: How could positioning yourself in the Overself be the first step?

ANTHONY: I don't think it's meant chronologically. The only way you can come across the notion of Mind, unique Mind, is when you are situated in the Overself. You certainly can't know of it when you're in the ego.

KD: Please say again what it is that you know when you are in the Overself.

ANTHONY: (*quietly*): You become aware of this immense Power, this unique Being, this unfathomable Mind, this shoreless bottomless ocean, the World-Mind or Mind. You won't discover that Mind unless you are situated in the Overself. You can't know anything about that Mind except from the point of view of being identified with the Overself or being in the Overself. "Being in" makes it sound dualistic, but you know what I mean.

AS: You're saying that the Solar Logos is the knower within all—

ANTHONY: Yes, within all Overselves. This is what all unit souls become aware of.

AS: Sometimes PB distinguishes these two stages: There is Stillness and then he says beyond that there's this Power, there's the experience of Power. In this context, would you say that the Stillness is like being established in that Overself, but then the further stage of the recognition of this Power is of that Solar Logos?

ANTHONY: Yes. It's the arisal of this mighty Presence, a Presence that suffocates you, and you feel as though all the forces of the universe are converging on you, and you can hardly breathe. After a while you begin to get a feeling of this Presence. And for someone who has had the experience of the Overself or has gone into that Stillness, very often, this arises, this Presence of Power.

JG: How can you stand it?

ANTHONY: You'll even like it. You'll even enjoy it. You'll want more. You could stand it. The ego isn't there.

It is not enough to attain knowledge of the soul; any mystic may do that. It is necessary to attain *clear* knowledge. Only the philosophic mystic may do that. This emphasis on clarity is important. It implies a removal of all the obstructions in feeling, the complexes in mind, and obfuscations in ego which prevent it. When this is done, the aspirant beholds truth as it really is.

(v13, 20:4.168 and *Perspectives*, p. 257)

AS: When PB first refers to knowledge of the soul, he doesn't mean a theoretical knowledge, he means the person has experienced it. But that's not a *clear* knowledge. It's not clear, for example, because the person hasn't completely gotten rid of the egoism and so on, and comes back from that and loses it, so it can't really be clear.

ANTHONY: So then the individual has to go through a philosophic discipline.

AS: That individual has to really employ reason, to clear away all of the obstructions to a full clear knowledge of that.

AH: We have to hold the distinction that knowledge of the soul is unique to all other kinds of knowledge, even clear knowledge.

ANTHONY: No, you don't hold to that distinction. The first experience that you might have of the soul is not clear knowledge. Maybe at later times you might have more understanding of what's going on, but it's not clear. Clear knowledge of the soul requires psychological purification, ontological wisdom, and understanding. It requires the whole philosophic discipline. The beginning experience or the first experiences are fitful, and there's a lot of coloration going on.

AS: Like muddy water.

AH: I can't understand how you can have an experience of soul or mind in a partial way. From the point of view of the experience itself, you wouldn't speak of having had insight into partial mind, or muddy mind.

LD: But to the extent that the ego is involved in any experience, to that extent impurity would arise.

AH: But that experience is a negation of the ego.

LD: But going into the experience, there is an ego experiencing presence of mind. In the pure total experience, there's a negation of the ego, but—

AH: I think I have a tendency to see it in a very absolute sense and that's probably incorrect.

ANTHONY: That's your problem right now. You make it very clear, black and white, but it isn't just like that. As a matter of fact, most people who do have a glimpse, the first time they have a glimpse, are just about as confused after the glimpse as they were before.

When you come out after having a glimpse—we're not talking about the glimpse now, but when you come out *after* you have the glimpse—you have knowledge that you have a soul. PB is using the term "knowledge" in that sense.

AH: I see.

ANTHONY: Now you have knowledge of the soul. What kind of knowledge is that?

AH: Knowledge of my absence.

ANTHONY: No, it's not of your absence. That's only one of the aspects of the knowledge that you have, that the ego wasn't there. But you have had this experience, you come out, and you know you've had this experience. Now you try to understand what this is that you experienced. And you will find out that you're very bewildered. That's not a clear knowledge. To clarify and understand what that glimpse of the soul was, when you were identical with the soul, will require a long psychological purification and philosophic discipline.

AH: This quote is referring to *conceptual* knowledge of the soul.

ANTHONY: The way you formulate what happened to you? No. I think it's a little more than conceptual. I mean, if you had a piece of fruit that no one had ever come across, and you ate it, and then you tried to tell me what it was about, I wouldn't say it's a conceptual knowledge. I think there's more than just a concept behind what you're saying.

> WHEN THE MIND withdraws from its creations *after* understanding their mentalness and looks into *itself,* it discovers the final truth. But when it does this prematurely—that is, before such enquiry into the world's nature—it discovers a half-truth: the nature of the "I."
>
> (v13, 20:4.54)

AS: If it hasn't seen the mentalness of the world, if the world to it is something other, then when it finds the truth of itself, it won't be finding the truth of the world. But if it first realizes the world to be mental in nature then when it finds that the source is mentality or mind, it will be finding the source of the world at the same time.

In the final truth, the realized person can remain in the Real whether thinking or not, whether the world is appearing or not. But if you don't realize that the world itself is an emanation of Mind or an experience of Mind, then you won't be able to have the final truth, you'll only have half the truth. You'll only have the truth while in that realized state, in that mystical state or while withdrawn into yourself. You won't be able to have that truth while functioning back in the world, and therefore it is only a half truth. You haven't realized that the world appearing doesn't contradict the nature of Mind, and therefore it's a half truth.

ANTHONY: That's right to the point: nondualism. The truth of nondualism requires the recognition that both sides of the equation are Mind. If you only recognize one side, you don't come up with the ultimate truth. PB is simply saying that the truth of nondualism requires that you recognize that both sides of the equation— "I" and the world —are mental. Leave one out and you only come up with a partial truth.

JL: PB has said elsewhere that the realization of the "I" comes first before the revelation of the mentalness of the world, but are you saying that you can have an insight into the mentalness of the world without the other?

ANTHONY: Well, you'd have to tell me what you mean when you say you could have "an insight into the mentalness of the world." Kant reasoned everything out and came to the conclusion in his reasoning process that the world was thought. Would you say that this was also a conviction?

JL: It wasn't necessarily knowledge.

ANTHONY: Well, that's the point I was getting at. The recognition of oneself as Mind makes it much easier to understand or recognize the fact that the world is a thought of mind. But it's possible to come up rationally with the understanding that the world is a thought, without having the living conviction that would be a mystical experience. Kant did not have mystical experience of the mentalness of the world, but he was utterly convinced that it was mental.

> THE HIDDEN TEACHING starts and finishes with experience. Every man must begin his mental life as a seeker by noting the fact that he is conscious of an external environment. He will proceed in time to discover that it is an ordered one, that Nature is the manifestation of an orderly Mind. He discovers in the end that consciousness of this Mind becomes the profoundest fact of his internal experience.
>
> (v13. 20:4.132 and *Perspectives*, p. 254)

ANTHONY: Don't you feel that the last sentence especially is true for us? For thirty years, twenty years, whatever it is, you go through all these various schools—public school, high school, college, university—you go on, and then, all of a sudden, this man brings to your attention that the profoundest experience is that of your own mind. That's what got you going on the quest: Mentalism.

It's a very exhilarating kind of feeling. All of a sudden you're restored to yourself, whereas when you were going through the educational processes they were alienating you from yourself more and more, more thoroughly, more insidiously.

> IT IS NOT ENOUGH to negate thinking; this may yield a mental blank without content. We have also to transcend it. The first is the way of ordinary yoga; the second is the way of philosophic yoga. In the second way, therefore, we seek strenuously to carry thought to its most abstract and rarefied point, to a critical culminating whereby its whole character changes and it merges of its own accord in the higher source whence it arises. If successful, this produces a pleasant, sometimes ecstatic state—but the ecstasy is not our aim as with ordinary mysticism. With us the reflection must keep loyally to a loftier aim, that of dissolving the ego in its divine source. The metaphysical thinking must work its way, first upwards to a more and more abstract concept and second inwards to a more and more complete absorption from the external world. The consequence is that when illumination results, whether it comes in the form of a mystical trance, ecstasy, or intuition, its character will be unquestionably different and immeasurably superior to that which comes from the mere sterilization of the thinking process which is the method of ordinary yoga.
>
> (v13, 20:4.62 and *Perspectives,* p. 261)

ANTHONY: Remember the example we used where we said there's a piano out there, and you strike a note on it, and it vibrates with a frequency of 440 vibrations per second? You're a few feet away, and an interaction takes place between that so-called material vibratory activity and the physical organ, including the ear, the inner ear, a firing of synapses in the brain and so on. Now, in this simple example, a condition or a state of matter—if I might use that word—arises, and then you say, "That's the note A." Now, who is it that passed a judgment on the modification or the conditions of matter at that moment?

KD: Not the ego, not what we call the empirical subject. It would be that consciousness, or the Witness, that has that one thought, that contains both what we call the empirical subject and that object which would be known.

ANTHONY: Now this Witness-I that you're referring to—can we make it more difficult and say this unperceived Perceiver—can we say it that way? Because we're saying that the Knower, in a sense, is an unperceived Perceiver. But that is who knows; that's the one that knows. In a sense we're saying that the complementarity that exists between the so-called empirical subject and the empirical object is due to the fact that both of these things are objective to the Knower, because the Knower is passing a judgment on that.

So you notice how you made a transition from analyzing your experience of the sensible world? In other words, the activity of the vibratory strings and the inner tympanum which responds to that and the firing of the synapses in the brain, and the arisal of images in the brain, and so on—you notice that all of that is objective to the Knower? But when you try to understand the nature of this Knower, you recognize that, in a sense, you cannot perceive that Perceiver. Now haven't you made a transition from the analysis of the gross and the sensible? Through a process of analysis you've reached a level of abstraction, where you've distinguished the gross, the sensible, from the immaterial principle or the immaterial and the unknown Knower. You noticed that? In your analysis you had to become more and more abstract until you reached the notion of this unperceived Perceiver.

KD: Yes.

ANTHONY: In the process of following me, you had to become more and more abstract in your understanding and this culminated in a very abstract notion: the unperceived Perceiver. And in the process of trying to understand that, you even have to discard the ego. Now if you try to further understand this unperceived Perceiver, and focus your attention on it, there begins a process of inwardizing your consciousness, your attention. Just think for a minute. Just go over what I'm saying. Concentrate now on this notion of the unperceived Perceiver. What happens? You have to leave words behind, concepts, even thoughts. You have to leave them behind, don't you? So your consciousness is getting inwardized.

KD: Yes.

ANTHONY: The first time you heard this, you became very, very happy. Why? For an instant, you entered a thought-free state. Your consciousness was inwardized.

Let's try another example. After a vigorous process of reasoning, we've gone through an analysis of experience, and we suddenly come to the conclusion that *perception is immediate.* Take the dream example: When you're looking at a dream, you don't have a pair of eyes. You see the dream without any eyes. So you understand: Perception is immediate. You don't need any senses to see the dream. Is that true? Perception is immediate. What happened? You had to go through an enormous process of abstraction. You have to practically recognize that the mind which judges is not that which is being judged. What is being judged is the condition of matter: the body and the way it interacts or responds with its environment. These two things, together, constitute a state of matter. And something is judging that state of matter. That something which is judging that state of matter is not the ego. But then who is it? Immediately you're thrown into an abstract situation. What happens is that through the process of thinking vigorously on a certain point, little by little the thought gets so attentuated that it becomes thinner and thinner and then finally it just dissolves. And you can go into *nirvikalpa*—a thought-free state—even if it's just for a second. For that instant you've gone into a thought-free state. And you will very often experience a kind of happiness. But then the next moment, of course, the ego comes back and makes its claims, and you're back in the same habitual patterns of thinking that you were in a minute ago, or before you started the process of intense thinking and reflection.

Now, if you take that theme—the unperceived Perceiver—and just sit down and meditate on it, you'll see that your consciousness gets more and more withdrawn, more and more *in*-drawn. It's as if you've pushed all the faculties of the mind to one corner, and you're just investigating into the nature of knowledge itself; or, thought is thinking about itself. And in that very process it becomes so attenuated that it dissolves.

This is quite different than the ordinary yogi who sits down and says, "I'm going to crush out every thought that comes into my mind until I have no thoughts at all." You can sit down and do that, and you can reach a state that's thought-free. But you don't know what happened. You have no idea what happened. Whereas in philosophic yoga you can actually watch the process of thought dissolving itself into pure Thought.

So if, for example, you have an unlimited supply of will and energy, and you think the problem of epistemology through—now remember, I said an unlimited will, an unlimited energy—what will come to an end will be thought itself. You'll come to a position where you've thought the thing out, and in the very thinking it out, it dissolves. There's nothing further to be thought out, and you go into rest.

KD: When you attempt to think about this unperceived Perceiver—you've withdrawn your attention from the subject-object relationship—is that "thinking turned upon itself"?

ANTHONY: Yes. Now it's turning upon itself and trying to understand its own nature. And in order to do so, it must stop. It comes to a standstill, because it's trying to *grasp* itself. It's trying to understand itself. And if it tries very intensely to understand itself, it will stop working. It will stop thinking.

AH: From the point of view of that thought-free condition, both yogas would be the same, would they not?

ANTHONY: Well, it's one thing to go in through the door of understanding and it's another thing to go in through the door of dogmatism. You know what you're doing in one case; you don't know what you're doing in the other.

AH: Is the distinction at the level of thought? It would seem that it could not be held as distinct from the point of view of the thought-free state.

ANTHONY: No, the distinction is not in the thought-free state; the distinction, of course, is within thought.

AH: So ordinary yoga yields the same result as philosophic yoga?

ANTHONY: No, that's where you're mistaken, when you say "*yields* the same result." The thought-free state would be the same in both cases, but the results would be different. In one case there would be an understanding of what happened. In the other case there would not be.

MB: Is philosophic yoga superior?

ANTHONY: When the yogi who doesn't understand or practice philosophy comes out of a thought-free state, the world again imposes itself on that yogi who is faced with the same perplexity, whereas the yogi who understands philosophically what happens is no longer perplexed. The second would be a superior state. Is understanding nothing? To come out with the understanding as to what happened and to come out with no understanding—is that difference nothing? So of course the philosophic yoga is quite superior.

But you don't have to make it so abstract. The point I was also trying to get at is that these are processes you can observe. And I used a very particular example. You have the 440 vibrations per second, you have the state of matter which is the way the body is conditioned by that interaction. And then when I ask you "Who makes the judgment, 'This is the sound A'?" and you recognize that it is the Knower, this is an intelligent understanding. It isn't a blanking out of any kind. It's an intelligent understanding that the Soul is making a judgment on these two complementary aspects. The seer and what is seen are seen as one; they're both objective to the Knower. In that very process of understanding what I've been talking about, do you notice how you have to drop the ego? In that moment you drop the ego in order to be able to understand that there is a Witness or an unperceived Perceiver who recognizes this situation or this piece of knowledge. And if you're introspective enough, you'll recognize that at that instant you felt a little happy about this piece of knowledge you got, because you dropped the ego. You don't have to be sitting in the Himalayas under a big fir tree. It could happen right here.

THE ACTIVITY of analytic thinking has been banned in most mystical schools. They regard it as an obstacle to the attainment of spiritual consciousness. And ordinarily it is indeed so. For until the intellect can lie perfectly still, such consciousness cannot make itself apparent. The difficulty of making intellect quite passive is however an enormous one. Consequently different concentration techniques have been devised to overcome it. Nearly all of them involve the banishment of thinking and the cessation of reasoning. The philosophical school uses any or all of them where advisable but it also uses a technique peculiarly its own. It makes use of abstract concepts which are concerned with the nature of the mind itself and which are furnished by seers who have developed a deep insight into such nature. It permits the student to work out these concepts in a rational way but leading to subtler and subtler moods until they automatically vanish and thinking ceases as the transcendental state is induced to come of itself. This method is particularly suited either to those who have already got over the elementary difficulties of concentration or to those who regard reasoning power as an asset to be conserved rather than rejected. The conventional mystic, being the victim of external suggestion, will cling to the traditional view of his own school, which usually sees no good at all in reasoned thinking, and aver that spiritual attainment through such a path is psychologically impossible. Never having been instructed in it and never having tried it, he is not really in a position to judge.

(v13, 20:4.65 and *Perspectives*, p. 262)

LR: Does concentration need to be attained before this kind of abstraction process can begin, or can the abstract concepts be a means of bringing about that concentration?

ANTHONY: Some level of concentration is required before a person becomes intrigued by a concept which a seer has devised. For instance, take the phrase "thought is a manifestation of mind." If there isn't a certain level of concentration already available to you, you won't stop at the word "manifestation" and be intrigued and bewildered and perplexed and puzzled and ask yourself, "What does that mean?"

Generally the familiarity with words is of such a nature that unless you have a kind of vigilance built into your attention, you won't stop at the word and question it, but will just assume that you understand it. Familiarity breeds contempt, and in the world of words, utter contempt.

> CONTINUED and constant pondering over the ideas presented herein is itself a part of the yoga of philosophical discernment. Such reflection will as naturally lead the student towards realization of his goal as will the companion and equally necessary activity of suppressing all ideas altogether in mental quiet. This is because these ideas are not mere speculations but are themselves the outcome of a translation from inner experience. While such ideas as are here presented grow under the water of their reflection and the sunshine of their love into fruitful branches of thought, they gradually begin to foster intuition.
>
> (v13, 20:4.66 and *Perspectives*, p. 262)

ANTHONY: Let's start with some examples. Take, for instance, Handel, who wrote the *Messiah*; take Beethoven, the Fifth Symphony; take Bach, the last chorus from the *Saint Matthew Passion*. Handel didn't stir for two weeks. He sat absolutely immobile for two weeks, and his maid thought he was going crazy. He wouldn't eat. He just stayed there, staring into space. He evidently got very quiet, very silent. Then all of a sudden he intuited an aspect of that inner glory, let's call it exaltation, so when you listen to the last chorus you feel exalted. On the other hand, think of Beethoven with the tremendous introvertive concentrative ability he had: he came out with the Fifth Symphony. And there you can hear that that music is charged with victory, a noble victory. Think of Bach, with his pietistic upbringing, and in the silence he received another aspect of that infinite glory, relating to piety and humility. He had to be silent in order for that intuition to come.

You can be silent and an intuition may not come, and you'd be like Handel, sitting there for two weeks. That's a long time to fast! But in all these cases, the intuition did come in the silence and each was about a certain aspect of this infinite glorious reality.

Now what does the composer have to do? The composer has the inner experience and has the technique by which to try to portray that inner experience. The composer knows enough about the material; in this case, knows enough about music. The composer knows about all the forms in music and how to associate certain notes with each other so that they evoke the same *vasanas* [emotionally charged tendencies, deep memory traces] in you that the composer is aware of. And so the composer puts it into this form, and then you listen to it, and there's a duplication, there's a translation of the composer's inner experience reduplicated in your consciousness. And now you reflect on that experience that you go through; that is, you reflect on the ideas that the composer gave you. And *you* start getting bright and cheerful about the intuition *the composer* had. You might even experience that exaltation or that victory or that humility, whichever one is being spoken about.

We're not talking about a sage. An artist is more comprehensible, in the sense that the artist has the inner experience, like a mystic, and then also has the technique by which it is possible to translate that inner experience into a suitable form that can evoke within you something of what the artist experienced.

Now, the sage does something similar. The sage has the experience of the mentalness of all things, that all things are Mind, and then has to find and combine the appropriate words—this is really practicing magic—to organize the different memory traces that you work with in such a way that they will evoke in you an intuition of what the sage experienced. Then if you contemplate, or let's say you reflect on that—and that means that you are very enchanted by these words, they're very meaningful and you reflect on them—then they start growing in you. Because ordinarily it wouldn't be the case that the memory traces, the way they are in our being, would organize themselves in such a way as to portray inner states of being. It's very unlikely that that would ever happen. But the sage *can* use words in such a way that they will evoke the necessary *vasanas* or memory traces in you and produce an intuition. That's, of course, a species of white magic, but the sage can do it.

CDA: If that's white magic, then so is music!

ANTHONY: Music *is* white magic, of course! It's not only white magic, it's a miracle.

KD: What does it mean that the sage knows how to elicit those *vasanas* and evoke the intuition?

ANTHONY: First of all, PB, for instance, would always look up what a word means *now, today*—not what it meant in its roots or its etymology or two hundred years ago, but what it means now, let's say to the collectivity. And he had an ability to use words in their present-day meaning with all the connotations that our present-day culture surrounds those words with. He would be able to pick out those words that would correctly convey what he's talking about. That's a kind of magic, to make you keep reading them even if you don't penetrate into the innermost depths. You still have a feeling of what he's saying.

For instance, he doesn't use a word like "being" the way the Greeks would. When you see the word "being" in his writings, don't interpret it that way. You have to use it in the contemporary sense, that being is the object of the ordinary intellect that people work with—in other words, sensible becoming. That's what people mean by being today.

Now the art—and this is really a difficult art—is to be able to combine the words in such a way—and this is the magic—so that the words will organize those memory traces in you and to some extent evoke or produce an intuition of what PB is saying. That's the magic in his writing.

AS: Plato says somewhere that you can't directly communicate an idea. Plato, or any philosopher, would first have to put it into a vehicle which is the only thing that actually can communicate. Somehow the words have to be manipulated, and then they can evoke a reminiscence within the hearer if the hearer is attentive enough to it.

ANTHONY: It does require this very serious attentive reflection and affection for these things, so that if you have regard for what was said tonight, "the unperceived Perceiver," you won't sleep. But if you have no affection, no true concern, then you'll sleep very soundly. And if I said, for instance, that you cannot have any objective relations with the unperceived Perceiver, you'd get up and you'd start drinking coffee on top of it! Because then you wouldn't *want* to go to sleep.

Yes, PB's a magician. But then again, isn't any great person, any great artist, a magician? Any great sage?

> THIS IS the paradox that *both* the capacity to think deeply and the capacity to withdraw from thinking are needed to attain this goal.
>
> (v13, 20:4.68 and *Perspectives*, p. 263)

ANTHONY: We could also state it a little differently: It is the nature of the Overself to be self-cognizant and also of a reasoning kind.

AS: It accords with its nature to be both still and active.

ANTHONY: Yes.

AS: To have the fullest realization, you need a method that's adequate to what you want to realize. If the essential nature of what you want to realize is of this complementary aspect, then the method must accord with the essential nature.

ANTHONY: Plotinus stated it very simply: The Soul is a double Knower.[1]

> IN THE FIRST stage of progress we learn to stand aside from the world and to still our thoughts about it. This is the mystical stage. Next, we recognize the world as being but a series of ideas within the mind; this is the mentalist-metaphysical stage. Finally, we return to the world's activity without reacting mentally to its suggestions, working disinterestedly, and knowing always that all is One. This is the philosophical stage.
>
> (*Perspectives*, p. 257)

PD: That seems to imply that a sage's mind doesn't function through vehicles or faculties of knowledge.

ANTHONY: When mind knows the world as idea, it also knows the faculty of understanding, which brings about the World-Idea. It knows that to be mind, too. The third point simply clinches the nondual position: With or without ideas, mind remains itself.

DR: So in this way of speaking the world is essentially the idea that you're speaking about.

ANTHONY: Yes. You have to think of this happening to one mind in order to receive the dramatic impact PB's trying to make. Conceive of your mind stripped bare, without any thought, without the World-Idea. Again, conceive of your mind with the ideas present to it; the World-Idea is present to it, and it recognizes the World-Idea as idea. And then in the third phase one and still the same mind recognizes itself or is identical whether it thinks of itself with ideas or without ideas.

> THE THEORY of philosophy is suited and available to everyone who has the intelligence to grasp it, the faith to accept it, the intuition to recognize its supreme pre-eminence. The practice of philosophy is more restricted, being for those

who have been sufficiently prepared by previous inner growth and outer experience to be willing to impose its higher ethical standards, mental training, and emotional discipline upon themselves. To come unprepared for the individual effort demanded, unfit for the intellectual and meditational exertions needed, unready for the teacher or the teaching, is to find bewilderment and to leave disappointed. A premature attempt to enter the school of philosophy will meet with the painful revelation of the dismaying shortcomings within oneself, which must be remedied before the attempt can be successful.

(v13, 20:2.120 and *Perspectives*, p. 259)

AH: What is the theory as distinct from the practice? The prerequisites for the theory are what I have thought of as the prerequisites for the practice.

ANTHONY: To grasp the theoretical aspects of philosophy, you have to have a certain intelligence, faith, and intuition. Fine. There's nothing hard about that. The next step is a little harder. [Rereads second sentence.] Now you have to draw on experiences that you yourself have had in the past. Has there been sufficient experience to encourage you to apply these principles that you've learned—what we refer to as *ripeness*? Are you sufficiently *ripe* to see the need to apply the system of ethics, for instance, that it imposes? Are you willing to apply that?

AH: It's possible, then, to understand the theory of ethics.

ANTHONY: Yes, and be absolutely incapable of applying it. That's the acid test, isn't it? You must fulfill those requirements—all the shortcomings and limitations you're working with have to be corrected. Then you can talk about getting into the school of philosophy.

The person has to make her or himself a fit candidate in order to enter the school of philosophy. You're not automatically fit to be involved with the school of philosophy. You have to develop the powers of concentration and meditation; you have to *apply* ethics, your own system; you have to learn each of the lessons that is being brought home to you by life itself. These are things that *qualify* you as a student of philosophy. Only after they're done can you properly apply to be a student of philosophy.

DB: What is the transition point when one becomes a student, when you know you've passed the tests?

ANTHONY: It seems that you're asking, "When do I know that I am now capable of becoming a student of philosophy?" You'll know. You'll know if you can concentrate and meditate. You'll know through the experiences that life has brought you what your values really are. You'll really know, don't worry. By that time, you will have been put through it. It won't be in your head, either.

THE WORLD-MIND TEACHES YOU

> PHILOSOPHY is faced with the problem of educating each individual seeker who aspires to understand it. There is no such thing as mass education in philosophy.
>
> (v13, 20:2.289 and *Perspectives*, p. 259)

ANTHONY: Isn't that a nice one! Everyone that's interested in philosophy gets very special consideration. You go through a very private course, private experiences. No Ph.D.s are handed out, no ceremonies are necessary. In what way would philosophy see to it that you're getting this very special education that's required?

LR: You're born.

ANTHONY: Very good. That's a beginning. Fine.

VM: You suffer.

ANTHONY: Yes, but you suffer in a very peculiar way.

LC: It's because your own individual soul is the teacher, not some collective situation.

ANTHONY: Wouldn't you say that the World-Idea is the teacher? Isn't the World-Idea teaching you all these things?

LC: Yes, but isn't it true that the specific way that the

individual would learn from the World-Idea is through one's own soul?

ANTHONY: The World-Idea is what's teaching the soul; it's educating the soul. And it does so in a very precise and exact way, by the kinds of experiences that are going to come to you and by the way you're going to respond to those experiences: whether you're going to apply what you've learned or whether you're going to revert to an atavistic procedure. Because it is the World-Mind, the World-Idea—or, if we take ourselves as inhabitants of this planet, then it would be the planetary Overmind and the individual mind together—that we're talking about. The planetary Mind has provided for the individual unique experiences that are no one else's, no matter how similar they may seem to someone else's experiences.

And the instructions that come are very specific. Each person's natal astrological chart shows the specificity and the chronological arrangement of the experiences that that person is going to go through. What you get out of your experiences shows to what extent you are a philosophic student. To the extent that you grasp the meanings that are inherent in the experiences that you are going through and don't have to repeat them, to that extent, of course, you're a student.

Don't you see that very clearly in the specificity of the experiences that you go through? And they are very, very specific. No two people have the same experiences, no matter how it looks on the surface. So it is not a mass type of education. It's a very specific kind of education that each and every one who is aiming to be a philosopher is going to be put through. The teachers you will meet, those people who will influence you—all these things are very carefully arranged. Sometimes when you think back on some of the things that may have happened to you, you see that a split second in timing would have prevented an important meeting. And you see how often a person has certain experiences, and acts according to the personal interpretation of those experiences. The point is not whether you are right or wrong, but that you're acting on your understanding of those experiences, and based on that then the consequences deliver their lesson to you. So it's not a mass education. These are very highly selected, specific kinds of experiences that each and every one who's on the quest goes through.

There are even times when the World-Mind will bring in experiences that are not even destined for you in terms of your karma, but are just brought in *ad hoc*! Just out of curiosity, you know: "Let's see what you're going to do with this one!"

Ultimately you'll see that the World-Mind is teaching you: The willing, feeling, and knowing is a process that's being superimposed on you. You'll learn to think correctly, whether you like it or not. Sooner or later, usually later, you'll learn to feel properly. You'll learn all these things. But it's the World-Mind that's always teaching you, imposing. So if you read the quote you'll see it: You get the greatest education that can be conceived of, and you're not even grateful for it.

RG: Would you go over why it's the World-Idea and not the individual soul that's providing the experiences?

ANTHONY: Where do your experiences come from? Whether you study the minutiæ of biological science, the formation of the embryo, or any of these things, what is it that you are studying? Isn't it the manifestation of an infinite intelligence revealing itself in that manifestation? Who's teaching you? The soul is what's learning, not teaching. If we're speaking about the soul developing the faculty of understanding, then it's the World-Idea that's going to develop that faculty of understanding in the soul. And that means it has to provide it with a cosmos within which this takes place.

RG: But it also seems that if the World-Idea is presenting these experiences, and out of those experiences the soul garners certain lessons or reacts to that presentation in a certain way, then it's also within the individual soul that that reaction is being developed.

ANTHONY: Well, yes, that's true; it wouldn't deny the mutual reciprocity that's taking place. Is that what you're getting at?

RG: Insofar as each individual reacts to experience in a certain way, the higher aspect of soul teaches the lower aspect.

ANTHONY: When you say each individual soul acts in its own way you mean according to its own past, the historical development of its own past. In other words, I react differently than you do because the historicity that went into my being is a little different than yours. But then again, that is provided for you by the experiences you have received in the world context.

I don't think it takes much effort to recognize that the World-Idea or the World-Mind is the source, the origin, so to speak, the mother of all our learning. Even willing, knowing, and feeling are being delivered into the core of our consciousness by the idea of justice which reigns in the master plan of the universe.

EC: When you receive an answer to your prayers, is that the World-Idea's response?

ANTHONY: It's a sympathy which is enkindled within the All, within the World-Idea. That's what magic is based on. Prayer, all these things are based on the fact that sympathy reigns throughout the one organism which we refer to as the World-Idea.

The point that has to be delivered home is to recognize the grandeur of the World-Idea, its almost motherly way of attending to the needs of the soul's development. In its initial integrity—in other words, like in *nirvikalpa samadhi*—the soul is self-cognizant and is not concerned with the external. There you could speak about a kind of self-sufficiency. Now I'm only playing with words, but when we speak about the soul's need to manifest or get manifested through the World-Idea and evolve its faculty of understanding, then the World-Idea, the master plan of the universe, is the absolute prerequisite in which that development is going to take place. It is guided in a very particular and very specific way from incarnation to incarnation, and even within one individual life one can see a guiding hand. If you call it your soul, what distinction would you be making?

RG: In that understanding, all individual souls are contained within the World-Idea.

ANTHONY: Yes, if you put quotation marks around the word "contained." It doesn't mean anything to me.

RG: Well, how would you say it?

ANTHONY: I can't. I'm not criticizing. I'm just saying we really won't find appropriate language to say that the World-Idea contains soul or soul contains the World-Idea or manifests the World-Idea. The point that has to be grasped is that it is only through the World-Idea that the soul comes to self-recognition.

> ALTHOUGH philosophy propounds statements of universal laws and eternal truths, nevertheless each man [*sic*] draws from its study highly personal application and gains from its practices markedly individual fulfilment. Although it is the only Idea which can ever bring men together in harmony and unity, nevertheless it becomes unique for every fresh adherent. And although it transcends all limitations imposed by intellect emotion form and egoism, nevertheless it inspires the poet, teaches the thinker, gives vistas to the artist, guides the executive, and solaces the labourer.
>
> (v13, 20:1.150 and *Perspectives*, p. 258)

LD: It almost seems that philosophy there would be the way you were speaking about the World-Idea.

ANTHONY: Of course. Philosophy almost seems to coincide with the wisdom function of the undivided mind. That would be philosophy, yes. Philosophy is not to be equated with human ideation, human opinions.

LD: In the last two quotes, it seems like the emphasis of philosophy and self-recognition is an emphasis on the *what*, on contents, and not the pure consciousness itself—not the *who*. It's always the *what*, the *what* is philosophy, the *what* is the teacher, but maybe that's an artificial way of looking at it.

ANTHONY: Right now the emphasis seems to be on the *what*, but there will be times when PB emphasizes the *who*. In one quote he says philosophy suppresses neither the subject nor the object but examines or goes into both of them [*Perspectives*, p. 258]. That is the integral approach of philosophy. That's why he regards the scientist as well as the mystic as shortsighted.

After a while you'll begin to see that this conception of philosophy is really quite beautiful. We've mentioned in classes that the firmament itself, the starry heavens themselves, are coeval with the foundation of wisdom. The world that is manifested is the product of wisdom, the master idea, and it's justice which is going to govern that manifestation of the master idea. And it is inconceivable that wisdom should come from anywhere else except from that World-Idea manifesting itself; in other words, the intelligence of the World-Mind revealing itself through that very manifestation. That's why it's so ridiculous for anyone to deny the world or think of it as illusory. To speak about God's intelligence as illusory is one of the biggest jokes I've ever come across.

If that doesn't humble you, when you look up at the starry skies, then nothing is going to do it except the next time a rock falls on your head—probably sent by the starry skies!

I mean this very specifically, because the disrespect with which many scientists, as well as some philosophers, speak of universal manifestation is really frightening.

> IT IS THE BUSINESS of philosophy to cast out error and establish truth. This takes it away from the popular conceptions of religion. Philosophy by its very nature must be unpopular; hence it does not ordinarily go out of its way to spread its ideas in the world. Only at special periods, like our own, when history and evolution have prepared enough individuals to make a modest audience, does philosophy promulgate such of its tenets as are best suited to the mind of that period.
>
> (v13, 20:2.7 and *Perspectives*, p. 259)

LR: What does PB mean when he says philosophy at certain special periods puts forth its tenets?

ANTHONY: There are certain periods in history when it is appropriate that a certain amount of knowledge is released, because there are recipients for it. Or, similarly, the appearance of an *avatar* [*see glossary*] takes place because the conditions of knowledge that have prevailed in the psyche of humanity at that time require that such a precipitation take place.

HS: What characterizes the present times?

ANTHONY: There is a crisis going on that never occurred before.

> THE SPIRITUAL seekers who followed René Guénon and the poets who followed T.S. Eliot fell into the same trap as their leaders. For in protesting, and rightly, against the anarchy of undisciplined and unlimited freedom, both Guénon and Eliot retreated backwards into formal tradition and fixed myth. Both had served their historic purpose and were being left behind. Both men were brilliant intellectuals and naturally attracted a corresponding type of reader. Their influence is understandable. But it is not on the coming wave of the Aquarian Age. New forms will be needed to satisfy the new knowledge, the new outlook, the new feelings. The classical may be respected, even admired; but the creative will be followed.
>
> (v13, 20:2.66 and *Perspectives*, p. 259)

LR: I wonder what constitutes new forms? Are they given as a gift by the World-Idea?

ANTHONY: Yes, but it takes an individual mind or individual minds to manifest them.

LR: But are those forms contained in the World-Idea?

ANTHONY: Yes, they're all included in that superior knowledge. But the individual mind is the burning focus in which the ideas get manifested and which reveals the world given to it. Without that individual mind, it just is not available.

In a general way PB is pointing out that in our times—and his book *The Wisdom of the Overself* is an example of exactly that—there's a need for a re-presentation of these teachings, but in terms of our own understanding and background, and that the need is really an imperative need. How many of us, when we think back to earlier days, imagine ourselves as kneeling monks in front of a church window and in the quiet of a courtyard; and there we were going to get an illumination and everything was peaceful and quiet. And he's saying those days are gone. They're over. There's a whole new civilization coming out, and we're in the throes of its birth. And in that agony and in that turmoil we're going to have to forge a philosophy which is going to be representative of *us* and not of some people who lived five thousand years ago.

I often found it amusing to read some of these people who seemed to say, "Well, let's turn the clock back to the twelfth century and make believe the past eight hundred years never happened." That's wishful thinking. Anyone who's blind to what has gone on, especially for the past eighty years, is just like an ostrich who's got its head in the sand. And these new forms will develop. PB says he's only a pioneer. Others will come, will follow him. And then they will lay out more and more of this ground plan.

> PHILOSOPHY offers the same meditational experience as mysticism, but it carries this experience to a wider and deeper level and at the same time integrates it with moral social and rational elements.
>
> (v13, 20:4.52)

DB: Is philosophic mysticism tied more into the World-Idea than regular mysticism, which is retreating from the whole process?

ANTHONY: Isn't that exactly the whole point? Vivekananda wanted to enjoy *nirvikalpa samadhi* for days without end. He just wanted to sit and bask in it. And Ramakrishna said, "No. There's something better than that." Look what happened. Instead of sitting in *nirvikalpa samadhi* for the next three months, they started the Ramakrishna/Vivekananda Society, which has a very philosophic approach of using the understanding and applying it to the needs of the world. The mystic would be satisfied with sitting in a corner and enjoying a *samadhi*; the philosopher would say, "No, I have to put it to use in the world." It's got to help evolve the World-Idea.

> WHATEVER were the motives which dictated the exclusive reservation of ultimate wisdom in former centuries and the extraordinary precautions which were taken to keep it from the larger world, we must now reckon on the dominant fact that humanity lives today in a cultural environment which has changed tremendously. The old ideas have lost their weight among educated folk—except for individuals here and there—and this general decay has passed by reflex action among the masses, albeit to a lesser extent. Whether in religion or science, politics or society, economics or ethics, the story of prodigious storm which has shaken the thoughts of men to their foundations is the same. The time indeed is transitional. In this momentous period when the ethical fate of mankind is at stake because the religious sanctions of morality have broken down, it is essential that something should arise to take their place. This is the supreme and significant fact which has forced the hands of those who hold this wisdom in their possession, which has compelled them to begin this historically unique disclosure of it, and which illustrates the saying that the night is darkest just before dawn. This is the dangerous situation which broke down an age-old policy and necessitated a new one whose sublime consequences to future generations we can now but dimly envisage.
>
> (v13, 20:2.8 and *Perspectives,* p. 260)

DB: When did this breakdown of the religious sanctions of morality occur? Was that after Darwin or during the Inquisition or what?

ANTHONY: It was over a period of hundreds of years. The breakdown of traditional values has been going on for a long time. You can pick on Darwin in the 1850s or you can pick on Ruth Benedict who showed the relativity of all morality in *Patterns of Culture.* The consequence of that kind of thinking is that morality, being relative, is considered untrue. These attacks and jabs that have been going on ever since have destroyed most of our traditional values. It has been a long process, though. It didn't just happen overnight.

DB: I was asking because in the history of Western society, it doesn't seem as if religious sanctions have had much to do with anything, in terms of the way people behave.

ANTHONY: What did you say? Religious sanctions didn't have much to do with anything?

DB: They haven't improved the way people behave toward one another: the Thirty Years War, the Hundred Years War, the Inquisition, the Slave Trade, and so on and so forth.

ANTHONY: Yes, but you still had a traditional society with certain norms with which it operated and which were accepted by the majority in the Western tradition, just like you had in other traditions. However, I think one of the unfortunate things that the Traditionalists don't recognize when they write about "the good old days" is that the World-Idea is changing, bringing about climactic changes. There's no going back any more to what has been. This new situation has made it imperative that humankind not be deprived completely of some sort of standards, some sort of ethical values, some sort of philosophic truths.

The interesting thing, I think, that PB points out here is that the custodians of this wisdom have decided to release more of this knowledge. This indicates, first of all, that there are custodians of wisdom or some hierarchy of intelligences that are guiding the earth and its historical cycle; and secondly, that, whether we like it or not, there's no turning back any more to what might have been a couple of hundred years ago.

A patch here and a patch there has been given out: a misrendition of "The Song of the Self" or a misrendition of the *Mandukya Upanishad* has been translated. But the fact remains that even though these things have been translated—and there have been a great deal of these works translated—the doctrine as an integral doctrine has not been available for a couple of hundred years, even more than that. I think the last time it was integrally transmitted was with Plotinus. Parts of it appeared again with Eckhart and Saint John, but it was under the cloak of the Christian church then, so it wasn't universal. In all the books that he's written and in all these notes, PB is presenting a clear formulation without obscuration; he doesn't use words that have doubtful meanings.

> PHILOSOPHY will show a man how to find his better self, will lead him to cultivate intuition, will guide him to acquire sounder values and stronger will, will train him in right thinking and wise reflection, and, lastly, will give him correct standards of ethical rightness or wrongness. If its theoretical pursuit is so satisfying that it can be an end and a reward in itself, its practical application to current living is immeasurably *useful*, valuable, and helpful.
>
> (v13, 20:1.337)

ANTHONY: The practical application would be the living of your life according to those principles that you understand theoretically as embodied in the World-Idea. Unless one *applies* the theory, one is not living a philosophic life, although theory in itself has its value. They made the same division in ancient Greece—what they called practical and theoretical philosophy. They said theoretical philosophy is required to begin with in order to understand what it is that you're doing. But without the practice and the application of these ideas, you have not verified the theory in your own life. And until it is verified in your own life, it is not yet wisdom. It's still theory.

KD: The way you just described it sounds really different

from what you were describing before as wisdom unfolded in your life.

ANTHONY: The description of wisdom unfolded in your life is made from the point of view of practical application. The statement can't be made unless a person has experienced to some extent the application of this theoretical knowledge, to actually see it in operation and to live it.

KD: I thought that what is so important about the description of philosophy as coeval with the wisdom of the World-Idea is the availability of that wisdom in your own life.

ANTHONY: You can think of it this way: Think of wisdom in the sense that the mind is becoming the universe. Think of wisdom as the recognition of that, and the application of that: Your mind is becoming the universe. Gradually, little by little, it's becoming the universe. And as it's doing so, it's beginning to understand the various laws that govern manifestation. When it begins to understand this, and it applies this to itself, then this is wisdom.

We say that the mind becomes the world that you experience. And in the process of the mind becoming the world, it assimilates a certain wisdom which is inherent in the world that it is going to manifest. In that process of assimilating the World-Idea, the mind is assimilating the wisdom that is inherent in it. The mind, in becoming the world, is also unconsciously incarnating that wisdom.

Now this will leave in the mind traces of that assimilation. The mind assimilates traces of the World-Idea. If we say that the World-Idea is an ordered, intelligent whole which is manifesting according to wisdom principles, and we say that the individual mind makes or transforms or metamorphoses itself into the world image, then in that very process, it is assimilating these reason principles. They are inherent as traces in the mind's functioning. They are deposited in the mind as an inherent wisdom within it. To apply wisdom means to draw on that reserve, which we just said is inherent in or deposited in the mind.

Now "theoretical" and "practical" are only words. It's going on all the time. The mind is actually metamorphosing itself into this idea of the world, which is ordered by intelligence, and at the same time learning from that what the meaning of it is all about, even though it may take a long time to come to that recognition.

Similarly, for instance, at night you have a dream: Let's say in the dream a boa constrictor is wrapped around you, and you're brought into realization of what fear is. So the mind not only has actually metamorphosed itself into this dream and produced the fear, but it also experiences the fear; and the fear is left behind as a trace in the mind of its act, of its metamorphosis into that. This is constantly going on, all the time, consciously or unconsciously.

So if the world is the product of wisdom, and your mind is constantly manifesting the world, then your mind is going to get acquainted with wisdom, and become wisdom, whether it likes it or not. That follows from the premise that the mind is becoming the universe; the mind's assimilation of those wisdom principles is a necessary consequence.

KD: Are you saying that the point of identity between the individual mind and the cosmos is what will leave you with this wisdom?

ANTHONY: Yes, we can say that the individual mind receives the World-Idea, portrays that World-Idea, then inhabits part of the World-Idea and experiences it in a sensible way. It's like when we say your mind is where the cloud is, because the whiteness of the cloud belongs to the mind and is a manifestation of a sensation that belongs to the mind. And obviously your mind is learning how clouds are being formed. That's why they keep telling you: All wisdom is within you. It's within your mind.

KD: This approach is radically different: that the wisdom, the philosophy that we all want, that we think we have to do something to attain, is present immediately, now, in the life we're living. There's often an impatience and even a denial of the life we're living in favor of a concept we have about what philosophy is. And PB's description of philosophy suggests a stance towards life that eliminates concepts, eliminates the workings of the lower intellect.

ANTHONY: As long as we are prisoners of our past, our memories, our thoughts, we will never have a bright, happy, new thought. It will always be a rehashing of the same thing.

KD: But the sage is immediate.

ANTHONY: Yes, but the sage doesn't "think."

KD: My mind is always looking ahead or looking back, saying, "I need this, I've got to have that . . ." There's a denial of the immediacy. But you're talking about an elimination of past and future.

ANTHONY: If you cancel out expectation, anticipation, the past, and the future, then you become a receptacle. There will spontaneously come to you thoughts which aren't yours, which are bright, happy intuitions, and they actually do tell you something *new*. That's what PB represents.

KD: If you could control your mind to eliminate all those thoughts of the future and the past, you could somehow be a receptacle for the World-Idea.

ANTHONY: Yes, but the ego won't give you that opportunity. The ego will always say, "What will we have for dinner tomorrow?" or "What did you forget yesterday?" It will always be preoccupied with past or future.

PB made that very clear. The wrong patterns or habits of thought must be broken if we are to approach this wisdom. You can't really approach this wisdom as long as you are a prisoner or a pensioner of your past.

AH: If this mind is busily about the business of becoming the universe, at some point it's going to be impossible to speak of an individual, egotistical point of view.

ANTHONY: Yes, that's the ultimate aim of the World-Idea.

AH: Is that transition from personal to impersonal a gradual one?

ANTHONY: Yes. It takes a long time.

AH: I don't understand how we could speak at once of the unfolding wisdom and, in the same breath, speak about the petty kinds of personal choices that we have to make.

KD: What we consider petty choices aren't petty at all. That's what's so radical. The importance of the life we're living is there in these so called petty choices.

AH: They're not petty even when they're prompted by egotism?

ANTHONY: That's part of what you have to understand when you make a choice.

HS: Is that how someone understands, by becoming the World-Idea? When someone has become more of the World-Idea, would we say that person understands the World-Idea? Is that how you understand things?

ANTHONY: Yes.

HS: Is it a process always from the personal outward—the faculties develop and become larger and wider and more universal?

ANTHONY: Yes, universalization of your mind is taking place. *You are* that which is getting metamorphosed into the world that you experience. And in that process you imbibe the wisdom that's inherent in the World-Idea. There's no "me," no "I," nothing. *You.* The only you that's there. The only you that I'm speaking to. If there is another, let me know, by letter.

KZ: How do we know when we are acting appropriately for this development to take place?

ANTHONY: You have to wait until that time comes. That's no theoretical question. When the time comes, the question will come up in the specifics that the circumstances of life provide for you. You cannot conceptualize that question. You can't imagine it.

These words are only an expediency. But it's not a concept that's available yet, to say that the individual mind is universalizing itself. Potentially it's becoming universalized, because it's becoming the very World-Idea, and through that process becoming universalized; it is assimilating wisdom. This is not something to talk about. It's something you've got to go home and think about for a long, long time. At any rate, let's have another quote.

> NOT TO ESCAPE life, but to articulate it, is philosophy's practical goal. Not to take the aspirant out of circulation, but to give him something worth doing is philosophy's sensible ideal.
>
> (v13, 20:1.340 and *Perspectives*, p. 261)

ANTHONY: He's said everything when he says that. When life can truly articulate itself, you're a philosopher. In the meantime, you're a dodo bird!

> THE LOGICAL movement of intellect must come to a dead stop before the threshold of reality. But we are not to bring about this pause deliberately or in response to the bidding of some man or some doctrine. It must come of its own accord as the final maturation of long and precise reasoning and as the culmination of the intellectual and personal *discovery* that the apprehension of mind as essence will come only when we let go of the idea-forms it takes and direct our attention to it.
>
> (v13, 20:4.67 and *Perspectives*, p. 262)

ANTHONY: It's a process, that once started, is irreversible and must work itself out to a conclusion. The World-Idea is working out its own understanding *in you.* Until that process reaches a culmination, it doesn't stop; it keeps on going.

The intellect is a tool, a tool for biological survival and adaptation. The intellect is concerned with registering, classifying, naming, recording all the events that a person experiences. We began to see that it is the very nature of the intellect not to be able to deal with the kind of formless thinking that the Overself works with. If left to its own devices, the intellect would not be able to think its way out; it will always be in a cul-de-sac; it will always be caught in that realm. Something has to come in and start guiding the intellect, in the sense of manipulating thoughts to produce certain concepts which further your understanding. This is a process that keeps going on, and there will be many obstacles because there will be all kinds of interferences on the part of the ego. But what the Overself has to do—which is the World-Mind working its understanding of itself out *in* you—is to guide those intellectual processes until there's a fulfillment, until there are no more questions. When the questions stop—and PB says this has to happen naturally, not because someone tells you or the doctrine insists—when the questioning has been fulfilled, all the doubts answered, there comes a cessation of the thinking process itself, because now the experience of that reality must be grasped, and that means that the intellect must stay in abeyance.

So what PB is talking about here is that when the World-Idea or World-Mind is working out the solution for you—and of course you understand I'm saying this is the Overself working out the solution for you[2]—it will guide you through the labyrinth, the cave, until all the basic formulations necessary for you to find your way out of the cave are given to you. That could take a lifetime. It varies with different people.

PB told me, and told some others, too, that when he was writing *The Wisdom of the Overself* what he did was to go through his notes, and there was a very careful selection of paragraphs, one following upon the other. Now, what was guiding him was a superior understanding, picking out this paragraph, and then the next paragraph, and then the next. It wasn't just a haphazard flip of a coin, "I'll take this one, leave this one out." But there was this kind of guidance that was prevailing behind the choice of the various paragraphs as he was reading through his notes. I'm only giving this as a kind of analogy.

In a similar way, when you're working out the meaning of the doctrine in all its implications, and you're trying to make it explicit, you'll find that you can't do it under your own power. It's only when this higher power within you, the Overself, starts taking a hand in the game, that you start finding the material you need to answer certain questions, and you find other material to provoke you into asking certain questions, and so this mysterious process keeps going on. When a person is under that kind of surveillance by the higher Power, you can almost say the *Logos*[3] is working its meaning out in that person, and the person will become conscious of that. *Everything* else is secondary. That's the process that happens.

RC: Looking within, hoping your understanding will be guided—that's a very different perspective than what we ordinarily call the activity of the intellect.

ANTHONY: Yes. But if you have honestly made an attempt with your intellect to try to understand these things, you come up against a blank wall, because the intellect can take any position, even contradictory positions, and follow them through. It can agree and disagree about anything. Something higher has to come in to guide it through that. But you do have to initiate the process; you do have to start it. You do have to seek it out. And it comes into play after a while.

KD: Is that process what PB is calling reasoning?

ANTHONY: That, too, would be involved. The process of reasoning follows upon whatever intellectual activity you do. All these things are mixed up. The reasoning becomes more and more firm, and the intellect as we spoke of it becomes less and less prominent. But the interesting thing is that the World-Idea is working itself out and becoming self-conscious in you. That's the amazing thing. And anyone who has experienced that doesn't go around saying "*my* ideas."

AH: But the process must remain uniquely connected with an individual entity.

ANTHONY: Well, let's use the word "intimate." It's very intimate. And even if two people have similar experiences in the process of reasoning that's unfolding the doctrine, it will be very novel for both of them; each one will feel as though it's unique and very peculiar and self-satisfying.

RC: I think it is worth inquiring into the phrase "the apprehension of mind as essence." There is a tendency to think this means having some experience which is formless and uncharacterizable. That may be part of it, but I think he means that in all places and at all times—whatever is appearing, it's mind—whether there's no appearance or there is appearance.

ANTHONY: The apprehension that dawns on one, that mind is the essence, is uncharacterizable. And I think that's what he means there by "apprehension." The understanding that mind is uncharacterizable is not the same as the insight experience.

Apprehension is still in the realm of relativities. Insight is not.

Apprehension is the result of a long, drawn-out process of very precise reasoning, and it isn't something that you can parrot. When a person parrots that the mind is uncharacterizable, unseizable, and so on, it isn't a personal discovery; it isn't the result of a process of reasoning through which he has sweated out this understanding. I think that the term "apprehension" there refers to this fact, this personal discovery. And after this discovery, PB says, you can direct your attention to grasping or seeking an insight into what that mind essence is. That's the way I understand that quote. It is a long, drawn-out affair.

CDA: What did you mean when you said earlier that "you go through a process of reasoning"?

ANTHONY: The reasoning takes place on the data that the intellect is working with. The intellect is working with stored images. The reasoning will have to take from those stored images the implications that are found therein and draw out from those stored images certain concepts, abstract concepts. As that process continues, the person becomes more and more attuned to the abstractions required in order to reach the understanding that mind in itself is uncharacterizable.

There are people who say mind is uncharacterizable, its

essence can't be known; they'll go through a whole routine. But they have not arrived at it through this process.

This process is like an organic process. When you eat food it's got to go through the process of digestion, go all the way through. In a similar way, when this process of reasoning or guidance comes from the Overself and starts working out its meaning in you, it's got to go *all* the way through, right to the very end, and convince you, almost through an organic process, that you cannot get at reality through the intellect. It has to go that way. No amount of memorization is going to convince you at the gut level that mind is uncharacterizable.

RS: This is like Plato's "divided line" [*The Republic,* Book VI]: When we reach the end of intellect and exhaust all the reason, then we are at the threshold of *dianoia.*

ANTHONY: Yes. He starts you off down at the bottom and keeps working you up. Plato specifically worked that way. Start with the level of conjecture, work your way through opinion, then reason, and finally you start getting intuition, or intellectual intuition.

But the marvel of it is, of course, that this is being worked out *in* you by a superior guiding principle, by your own higher Self, naturally.

> WE CANNOT afford to dispense with mysticism merely because we take to philosophy. Both are essential to this quest and both are vital in their respective places. The mystic's power to concentrate attention is needed throughout the study of philosophy. The philosopher's power to reason sharply is needed to give mystical reverie a content of world-understanding. And in the more advanced stages, when thinking has done its work and intellect has come to rest, we cease to be a philosopher and dwell self-absorbed in mystic trance, having taken with us the world-idea without which it would be empty. We can only afford to dispense with both mysticism and philosophy when we have perfectly done the work of both and when, amid the daily

life of constant activity, we can keep unbroken the profound insight and selfless attitude which time and practice have now made natural.

(*Perspectives*, p. 263)

AS: I don't follow the terminology. Why does PB say you cease to be a philosopher? Usually "philosopher" means the final phase. He seems to be using the term differently than usual here.

ANTHONY (*quietly*): When all is said and done, you have to be human.

DB: What does it mean to take the World-Idea with us into trance?

ANTHONY: Do you remember the exercise called the Serpent's Path? What does PB tell you to do there? You transcend the World-Idea by *absorbing* it. You don't transcend the World-Idea by negating or denying it, but by absorbing and understanding it you take it into yourself.[4] Wouldn't that be the same thing here? And if that is so, then your understanding of the mystical states would be adequate. In other words, you would have the necessary background to understand whatever mystical states you may go through.

The philosophic yogi must transcend the World-Idea. How? By understanding it and penetrating it and taking it in, which is the reverse of the ordinary mystic's procedure of negating the World-Idea and residing in the personal self. So, the philosopher who understands the mystical states has achieved not only an understanding of the I AM but also the World-Idea, in which the I AM is always involved. And these two would give the philosopher all that is needed to understand any problem, any situation.

DB: I don't understand this trance state—isn't it normally referred to as *nirvikalpa*?

ANTHONY: No, he didn't say *nirvikalpa*; he said "trance state," didn't he?

DB: There are a lot of trance states, but I thought *nirvikalpa* was one of them.

ANTHONY: Yes, but in *nirvikalpa* there's no thought. There's nothing to understand. Without the fullness of the understanding that comes from having penetrated into the World-Idea—in other words, the full development of the faculty of understanding which comes to a soul through the World-Idea—in the trance state one would be utterly unprepared to understand the mysterious Void.

I'll repeat it. Without the fullness of understanding which the soul acquires or achieves in its penetration into the World-Idea, then when it is in a trance state, and when it penetrates deeply into the nature of its own being, it cannot possibly understand what *is* there.

Or we can put it this way: It will take all the teaching that the World-Mind can bring to bear on the soul, in order for the soul to understand its own origin, its own priors. Now go back to the quote. PB speaks about the person within whom is included the World-Idea, the understanding of the World-Idea; that's what is necessary to become the sort of a philosopher that not only understands the nature of the soul but also something about the prior principles that are, let's say, eternally generating it.

> THE MISTAKE of the mystics is to negate reasoning *prematurely.* Only after reasoning has completed its own task to the uttermost will it be psychologically right and philosophically fruitful to still it in the mystic silence.
>
> (v13, 20:4.69 and *Perspectives,* p. 263)

ANTHONY: The fundamental question is built in: What does life mean? The fundamental question is built into you, and until it gets worked out—until every question is answered—you won't stop.

RC: The best teacher I had in college put a quote on the board from Lao Tzu that said: "Nothing that can be said in words is worth saying." It was a poetry writing course, and the teacher said it's only as you become a poet that you can appreciate how true this statement is. Then he went on to talk about how, for him, the beginning of poetry occurs after reason has been exhausted. You have to think something out as far as you can, and then *rationally* admit that a certain leap of faith has to be made. And when you enter that state then it is possible to actually get some inspiration.

ANTHONY: Would you please repeat that?

RC: He said that he would take an idea and think it out until he couldn't have any more thoughts about it, then he would rationally admit that he had exhausted his own resources and he could actually open himself up to getting an inspiration. It didn't guarantee that there would be one, but it would put him in the proper frame of mind so that he could recognize it if it did come.

ANTHONY: I think I follow what he's saying there. I would probably rephrase it, that once I have gone through the process of reasoning, brought it to maturation, exhausted it, now I am capable of observing. Until then I don't observe, I select.

When a person has thought out or reasoned through what the fundamental meaning of life is, and the reasoning processes have come to a slow halt, so that gradually the person is just not bringing up the questions any more because they've been answered, only then is that person capable of observation. And I think that's what we mean by a poet. Prior to that there's that questioning attitude that the mind works with.

But what you have to try to grasp again is that this fundamental question which is inherent in or built in to the very nature of the individual is a question that goes on asking itself, and it must be answered. It doesn't matter how long it takes—a hundred lives, a thousand lives—but sooner or later it must be answered. You must think of that process of working out the solutions or the answers to most of the questions that arise as very, very natural. Just like a tree grows, and it gets old and dies—you must think of reasoning that way. The soul, by incarnating in so many lives and experiencing the totality of all the thoughts or ideas that made it to be what it is, is now *done* with not only the contemplation of the ideas, but where it could not contemplate the ideas, with the living out of the ideas. Now it is done with all that. Now it can take the position of a poet in the true sense of the word: that the mind can be a mirror in which the universe can be reflected without any distortion.

CDA: In this quote PB says that it is better to wait until this process is completed before entering the mystic silence—but why wouldn't it be all right to get there before?

ANTHONY: You would have to go back and finish up the reasoning process anyway.

CDA: But it doesn't seem like it would be harmful.

ANTHONY: No.

HS: What do you mean when you say that the question is built in?

ANTHONY: I don't think I can make it more available. Everyone who is at all sensitive in any way does have a feeling that there is a secret or a mystery about life.

HS: Is this like wonder?

ANTHONY: Yes, wonder. "Who am I?" "What's it all about?" You're either aware of it or you're not. And most people are aware that there is something of significance in their life—if only they knew what it was.

HS: Does the demand for meaning belong to the World-Idea? Does it belong to you?

ANTHONY: I'd rather it belonged to you personally.

HS: Is that what you were saying about the World-Idea working itself out in you or as you?

ANTHONY: Yes.

LR: To simply *observe* you must have—

ANTHONY: —a quiet mind—

LR: —and contents.

ANTHONY: Yes, true, but it's a mind that has answered all its questions. Otherwise you don't observe, you select, and what you take in is selected by the unanswered questions. You remember there's a quote where PB points out that a Chinese artist tries to get into a state of absolute stillness so that the object is painted on the mind, and until that happens, the artist doesn't paint. The thing first has to be observed by the mind. The mind has to take the form of that thing; now the artist can go ahead and paint it. The mind is in a state of stillness. Remember Wang Yang-ming sitting down, looking at a bamboo for a whole month? A quiet mind is necessary for observation.

KD: What is it that you observe when you are finally capable of observing?

ANTHONY: Well, whatever the situation calls for. Wang Yang-ming, sitting in a forest, observed a bamboo shoot.

KD: In other words, the attention is not tied to the biases, thoughts, and all that.

ANTHONY: Yes. Let me put it this way. Sit down and look at something. Or sometimes when you listen to music, experiment with yourself. As the music is going on, try to notice how often you're interrupted by extraneous thoughts. Are you listening to the music? So when you're looking at a bamboo shoot, are you looking at the bamboo shoot or at every vagrant thought that comes into your mind? Now it can go deeper than that, of course. As you observe just the bamboo shoot, you might be able to see the reason principles that went into making that bamboo shoot. But you first have to see the bamboo shoot.

It's the same with people. You see people, and if your mind is observant, very quiet, your heart's filled, there's no craving, no clinging, no anticipation, no expectation, you'll immediately know the foremost features of that person. Intuitively, immediately. That would be observing the person.

> ORDINARILY the ego is the agent of action. This is apparent. But if an enquiry is set going and its source and nature penetrated successfully, a surprising discovery about the "I" will be made. Its true energy is derived from non-I, pure being.
>
> (v6, 8:1.41)

ANTHONY: Let's try this. Read the first sentence.

> Ordinarily the ego is the agent of action.

ANTHONY: That seems to mean that I will always refer to myself as the agent. I'm the doer.

KD: Right, I'm the doer, the natal chart, the personality.

> . . . This is apparent. But if an enquiry is set going and its source and nature penetrated successfully, a surprising discovery about the "I" will be made.

ANTHONY: The inquiry is into the nature of the ego.

> . . . Its true energy is derived from non-I, pure being.

KD: Maybe the real doer isn't who I think it is.

ANTHONY: So, for example, we can say that the real doer is the transiting planets.[5] That's the real doer. The other one *claims* it's a doer. That might be a way of looking at it. If you set an inquiry into the nature of what this ego is, you realize that it's a puppet, it's more or less manipulated by these forces which are part of the universe, the movement of the universe. This ego goes around saying, "I'm doing this and I'm doing that, I got a great idea," and the person has eighteen conjunctions going on. So the energy doesn't belong to the ego. It belongs to the universe or what we call the undivided mind.

KD: And also the immediacy of this is implied. I have an abundant store of energy immediately available to go do whatever I want to do. I'm going to do this, I'm going to do that. And when he says, "Its true energy is derived from non-I, pure being—"

ANTHONY: Non-I, yes. So, for instance, if you've got Saturn squaring your Mars or Sun squaring your Mars, you say, "Where's my energy?"

It's nice to use astrology as an example because it's so specific. People have certain aspects going on in their chart, and they've got no energy. Then as soon as they start feeling they've got energy, they say, "I'm energetic," but what they really mean is that Jupiter is trine something and they're feeling good. If they've got energy, that's what they mean. But [conventional] language doesn't use that kind of precision.

KD: My question is: What does PB mean by *inquiry* here in this quote? What really hit me after thinking about this was this unseparated thinking activity. It starts all the way up at the level of the World-Mind and then becomes this personality and its world of appearance. To me, that really extends and magnifies the mystery of thought.

ANTHONY: Yes, that's what inquiry means, and that's what we've been doing the past dozen years. We've all been inquiring into the nature of these things. It will set you going and you'll come up with answers that will just boggle your mind. Now I think that PB stopped prematurely for certain very good reasons. He said, "I'm a pioneer. I've got to lay down the basis. Others will come who will give more information." He stopped at a certain place. Where his work told him to stop, that's where he stopped. But what I'm saying is there's more to what he says and it will come out and we've done a *little* of that. The inquiries we've been doing have been concerned with that.

KD: We've spoken about the use of thought that turns upon itself to discover the nature of thinking.

ANTHONY: When thought turns upon itself, of course, then you have a species of *jnana* [deep knowledge]. Once thought turns upon itself you're talking about a different kind of knowledge.

KD: When thought turns upon itself and you have this different kind of knowledge, it reaches a point where thinking stops, I've heard you say. In that experience there is the realization of the distinction between consciousness and thought.

ANTHONY: Yes, a distinction between what thought is and the consciousness of thought.

AH: PB seems to suggest here that when thought turns upon thought, and if it's done in the right way, the conclusion is that the basis of I is non-I.

ANTHONY: Yes, which means the whole of the solar system, the whole universe, *our* universe as far as we're concerned, and that *is* in the nature of a non-I, non-ego.

DB: So the source of the ego's energy is traceable to the non-I, to the entire solar system, the transiting planets. Would it also be true to say that in addition to providing the energy for this ego, this non-I also provides for the ability of this objective part of the World-Idea to take itself as subjective?

ANTHONY: Yes.

DEVELOPMENT AND BALANCE OF KNOWING, WILLING, AND FEELING LEADS TO INSIGHT

PHILOSOPHY must critically absorb the categories of metaphysics, mysticism, and practicality. For it understands that in the quest of truth the co-operation of all three will not only be helpful and profitable to each other but is also necessary to itself. For only after such absorption, only after it has travelled through them all can it attain what is beyond them all. The decisive point of this quest is reached after the co-operation between all three activities attains such a pitch that they become fused into a single all-comprehensive one which itself differs from them in character and qualities. For the whole truth which is then revealed is not merely a composite one. It not only absorbs them all but transcends them all. When water is born out of the union of oxygen and hydrogen, we may say neither that it is the same as the simple sum-total of both nor that it is entirely different from both. It possesses properties which they in themselves do not at all possess. We may only say that it includes and yet transcends them. When philosophic insight is born out of the union of intellectual reasoning, mystical feeling, and altruistic doing, we may say neither that it is only the totalization of these three things nor that it is utterly remote from them. It comprehends them all and yet itself extends far beyond them into a higher order of being. It is not only

> that the philosopher synthesizes these triple functions, that in one and the same instant his intellect understands the world, his heart feels a tender sympathy towards it, and his will is moved to action for the triumph of good, but also that he is continuously conscious of that infinite reality which, in its purity, no thinking, no emotion, and no action can ever touch.
>
> (v13, 20:4.183 and *Perspectives*, p. 254)

ANTHONY: Now I'm interested in what kind of response you have to the notion of willing, feeling, and knowing. Some people might associate that with the World-Mind or the World-Idea. It is the goal of the World-Idea to force our development so that these three faculties are brought to a perfection. We can't do it under our own power. In one lifetime, or a series of lifetimes, you might be forced into the development of the intellectual, or let's say the cognitive, the knowing aspect, and later you will recognize the feeling aspect. But they all have to be brought up, and it seems that they can't all be brought up at the same time. So there are phases in the evolutionary development of the individual when a faculty is being developed.

Now remember, we're speaking about people who have extraordinary development and refinement of each one of these faculties. Then, when these faculties have reached their ultimate perfection—which seems to require that the World-Mind or the World-Idea has this development in store for you—and only when they achieve such a pinnacle, can we start speaking about the three of them being combined or integrated to produce something which is different from them—not utterly different, but different qualitatively—what PB refers to as insight.

The whole doctrine of insight is really quite a revolutionary teaching. We're acquainted with it through our studies of Plotinus, where he keeps urging us to recognize that the soul is a self-knower. Contemporary literature has no conception of what this insight is.

These are very, very profound questions. What is knowing? What is feeling? What is willing? As a matter of fact, in the little work that we did on astrological charts of people in whom the higher knowing was operating, it was not something that the person going through the experience understood.

> SUCH A revolutionary acquisition as insight must necessarily prove to be in a man's life can only be developed by overcoming all the tremendous force of habitual wrong thinking, by neutralizing all the tremendous weight of habitual wrong feeling, and by counteracting all the tremendous strength of habitual wrong-doing. In short, the familiar personal "I" must have the ground cut from under its feet. This is done by the threefold discipline. The combined threefold technique consists of metaphysical reflection, mystical meditation, and constant remembrance in the midst of disinterested active service. The full use and balanced exercise of every function is needful. Although these three elements have here been isolated one by one for the purpose of clearer intellectual study, it must be remembered that in actual life the student should not attempt to isolate them. Such a division is an artificial one. He who takes for his province this whole business of truth-seeking and gains this rounded all-comprehensive view will no longer be so one-sided as to set up a particular path as being the only way to salvation. On the contrary, he will see that salvation is an integral matter. It can no more be attained by mere meditation alone, for example, than by mere impersonal activity alone; it can no more be reached by evading the lessons of everyday external living than by evading the suppression of such externality which meditation requires. Whereas metaphysics seeks to lift us up to the superphysical idea by thinking, whereas meditation seeks to lift us up by intuition, whereas ethics seek to raise us to it by practical goodness, art seeks to do the same by feeling and

appreciating beauty. Philosophy in its wonderful breadth and balance embraces and synthesizes all four and finally adds their coping stone, insight.

(v13, 20:4.178 and *Perspectives*, p. 253)

ANTHONY: He says it's a revolutionary acquisition. Doesn't that entice you?

HS: The road to insight begins with the naughting of the ego. Will you buy that?

ANTHONY: No, I will not! PB is talking about the development of different faculties and you talk about naughting the ego.

HS: He talks about getting the ground cut out from the I.

ANTHONY: You think you're going to go into battle with the ego the way you are now? What would be some of the armaments you would want to bring in? If you want to start battling your ego, what do you want to have with you? A knife? An axe? A battle-axe? A .45? What do you need to kill it?

AH: Philosophic perspective.

ANTHONY: What would that include?

AH: The understanding that to be stuck in one path or one view is to ingratiate the ego rather than confront it.

ANTHONY: To confront the ego, you're saying then, you're going to have to have very highly developed faculties: a very acute, intense, concentrated kind of thinking, which will probably undo all the kinds of thinking you've done before that; the kind of feelings that are probably the reverse of the ones you have now, and to go against that current is going to be an ordeal; and the ability to apply what you understand in a practical way so that you can establish the sovereignty of ethics. These are just preliminaries before you cut the ground out from under the ego. I think it will be very difficult to get rid of the ego. Most of us are aware that the ego will be right there "helping" you!

[*repeat*] . . . the familiar personal "I" must have the

> ground cut from under its feet. This is done by the threefold discipline. . . .

ANTHONY: You notice the word *discipline*? Threefold discipline.

> . . . The combined threefold technique consists of metaphysical reflection, mystical meditation, and constant remembrance in the midst of disinterested active service. . . .

ANTHONY: Let's discuss those three for a moment. First, in metaphysical reflection you have to analyze the nature of experience, try to find out the kind of cosmogony that's interwoven with epistemology, and realize the unreality of the ego—that it's a structure of thought. You have to go through all those things and you have to understand them in a legitimate way. What I mean is you don't just take somebody's word for it. You actually have to go through that reasoning process of understanding. And then he speaks about meditation. Probably the only thing that could reorientate your feelings would be meditation or some kind of glimpse as to the nature of the Self, which brings in different kinds of feelings than the ones we ordinarily have. And then on top of that, while you're busy being of service to the world, constantly remember the higher Self. He says these three things. Of course, you can't isolate them, because life itself can't be cut up into compartments. There's always a mixture of them going on.

Which one seems the hardest depends on the individual. Some people are good people—they live an ethical life—but if you bring up to them the possibility of metaphysical reflection, they get upset. Other people can reflect metaphysically very well, but if you tell them now to start *doing* what they're talking about, they get upset. It depends on the individual. PB says these three things have to be done. You have to go through the discipline of developing them to a very fine point. Then what does he say?

> . . . The full use and balanced exercise of every function is needful. . . .

ANTHONY: So imagine that you've developed your thinking faculty to the extent of Kant, and then you've developed your willing to the extent of Caesar, and you've developed your feeling to the extent of Mother Theresa. When you do develop these to that extent, *then* we start talking about integrating them. You don't integrate them if you've got a retarded mentality when it comes to metaphysical reflection and a superior kind of feeling function when it comes to loving people. You can't integrate unequals: You have to evolve all three of them. So when he's speaking about balance, he's speaking about when these three reach their ultimate or penultimate stage of development. Then you speak about integrating them. That means that while you're going through the development of one of them, we'll allow you some insanity. Genius is allowed a little insanity. But you have to grasp the point PB's making here, that you have to reach the fulfillment of these functions. Prior to that, you're kidding yourself. If you talk about integrating these three functions, and you're at the level of an advanced gorilla, you're not going to get insight.

HS: Would you say that it's possible to have all those three functions developed in one life?

ANTHONY: Well, I don't know that you have to do it all in one life. For example, Kant had a very highly developed rational faculty; I'm almost willing to think that he probably had quite a few lifetimes before he reached that development. Then if we think of the highly developed feelings of a Beethoven or Brahms, it's obvious they must have had quite a few lifetimes doing that. I mean, Mozart wasn't born in one life. It took quite a few lives, I would imagine half a dozen. If you think of it this way, say you were born five hundred times in Asia, five hundred times in Africa, five hundred times in Australia—then you've got a lot of time to develop these faculties. I think you get the point. You practically have to be a genius in each one of these faculties. You're not going to get insight because all of a sudden you read about it. So let's try to define insight very simply.

PB has pointed out that insight includes a combination of these three faculties when they are fully developed, but also that it is qualitatively different than any one of the three or all three of them. Now let's try to be practical: We know that each and every one of us has these faculties of willing, feeling, and thinking, and we know that they're interwoven with each other. And we're speaking about our lives: I'm speaking about my life and you're speaking about your life. And insofar as we are trying to experience the refinement of the feeling function, or experience beauty and appreciate it, or think a problem through to the very end—isn't it in a sense the life trying to understand itself? That might be a meaning of insight.

Don't you think you're trying to understand all the time? And what are the means you use to try to understand this life?

CDA: By feeling, thinking, and the actual experience.

ANTHONY: That part's obvious. But now if these three were integrated, couldn't we say that life understood itself and this is what we mean by insight?

AH: You're speaking of life understanding itself.

ANTHONY: Your life. My life. Individual life.

AH: Can that be so from the perspective of one of those developing functions, or is that statement only so from the perspective of those three functions being integrated?

ANTHONY: Well, we were just discussing the attempt to understand life either through one of these three means or through a combination of them in various ways. But somehow there's a kind of incompleteness about it, isn't there? You never feel fully satisfied that you understand your life. Well, why?

PD: Are you implying that on the one hand you try to think out an idea, understand an idea deeply, and yet there's something incomplete in the grasping of the idea, so then you may try an aesthetic contemplation of a feeling—

ANTHONY: —or let's say of that same idea—

PD: —and in that approach, it's very moving and very deep, yet still there's something incomplete?

ANTHONY: Yes. Now you try to *will* that into your practical life, your daily activity. And that's the way we generally work: one or two or three. But now he's saying all three of them simultaneously functioning or combined will produce that articulation which life itself wants to grasp—what its own meaning is. If you do it with one or two or three or each one of them, but distinct from one another, then there's always that feeling of incompleteness. Life hasn't understood itself. It has fumbled around, formulated a feeling about it or thoughts about it, or has even applied it in terms of will. But to combine all three, to fuse them all together, and instead of having these three different approaches, to just have this insight into life itself—life understanding itself, without dividing itself into three different ways of doing so—then the result would be a different kind of understanding. It wouldn't be an objective understanding; it would be intrinsic to that life which perceives its own ex-pression.

HS: It's living.

ANTHONY: Yes, that's a way of putting it, that it is living. But you see what a roundabout way we used to try to understand what it means to be living? You see, we all use the word "living." How many of us *know* what that means? We don't, do we? But we use the word at least a hundred times a day: "I'm alive. I'm well. I'm living." Yes, so is an amoeba!

Life expresses itself or articulates itself, and that very understanding of its own expression or articulation, without dividing it up into different ways, is what I think PB means by insight. Life understands itself without any medium: willing, feeling, thinking. But it has to go through the development that willing, feeling, and thinking make possible.

SP: So you're saying that it cultivates these faculties and then sort of lives itself in an unbiased way through those cultivated faculties?

ANTHONY: Yes. After they're fully developed, they're combined or they simultaneously function. Now use the example we just used. You think an idea deeply, thoroughly, right to its very conclusion. At the same time, simultaneously, you aesthetically appreciate and feel the idea. And at the same time, again, you apply the idea in your daily activity. Now imagine these three things happening simultaneously. I think this would be life understanding itself. This would be insight.

I'm trying to deal with a term that's impossible, because the very meaning of the term insight deprives you of having something objective. If we say, "life understands itself," there isn't anything objective. It's life itself that understands itself, and that understanding of itself isn't different from itself.

SP: You're talking about an exalted phase, a sage's experience?

ANTHONY: Yes. That's why it's very difficult to understand. But PB does start by saying this is a *revolutionary* concept, a revolutionary acquisition. And it *is* revolutionary. If you grasp what he's saying, then you see it's the only thing that's really worth going after.

RC: You were talking once before in terms of an "in-seeing."

ANTHONY: Yes, that too would be applicable. And you can see that the terms that the Hindus use—*karma, jnana, bhakti yoga*—correspond to those three functions. But a sage doesn't work like that. The sage doesn't say, "Today I'm going to practice *karma yoga*, and tomorrow *jnana yoga*." The sage is an integrated person. All three functions operate simultaneously. It's impossible for the sage to have an idea and not apply the idea and aesthetically appreciate it with real feeling. All these three things are operating simultaneously.

You cannot become a sage by developing mystically alone. Every aspect of your being has to be developed, and they all have to be developed to a very high level. Those three things have to be integrated in order to be a philosophic sage. Keep in mind what he means by a *philosophic* sage: a person who has achieved the highest, who has the knowledge of the truth and can also communicate the truth because the necessary means has been acquired by which to do so. The philosophic sage has achieved that permanent view of what truth is because the sage *is* that truth; the truth and the sage are not distinguishable.

You see that, for instance, when you study Plotinus or Plato. Here you have men who are at the acme of the Hellenic culture. They have at their disposal the understanding of their whole culture, their whole civilization. They're at home in any part of it.

RC: It seems PB is saying in this quote that not only am I to develop these mental faculties to their fullest possible extent; I'm also to realize that fundamentally the real Being that I am is that very Mind from which those functions are operating.

ANTHONY: From which they arise. Usually you develop each one of these as fully as you can, and then when all three are fully developed, they're brought together in a lifetime or a series of lifetimes where they get integrated and they become insight.

We usually try to indicate that with pictures. In the natal chart, for example, Uranus, Neptune, and Pluto represent those three functions in you. As transiting, they represent the functions in themselves. They don't represent insight. Beyond them is insight.

You can see that in many of the personages. We've been studying Atmananda, and if you read his works, you see the man had a flare, a logical genius, a fully developed intellect. It wasn't something that he picked up in that life; it was there. Let's say it's a tendency that he brought over from the past and that he went on developing. So you read one or two of his works and you can see in twenty pages he says what it takes most people two thousand pages to say. The same with his aesthetic appreciation. Remember about the initiation that PB received from Atmananda in the evening, at night, in the moonlight?[6]

But basically I think you'll find—and I have found this to be so—that the sages are generally very wise people, very cultured, very refined. They are not lunatics. They've gone beyond that stage.

JFL: Would we say that for any one of these three functions, what makes it different from philosophic insight is that it necessarily restricts the other two from operating?

ANTHONY: It isn't that it restricts the others; it's that each is partial. When you're thinking, it doesn't necessarily restrict your feeling function. It could still be highly developed. But it is partial; it is incomplete. It doesn't give you the totality of the aspects of the object. You not only want to know your wife, you want to feel for her.

JFL: For the mystic, it's clear that there's an ultimate goal to be attained. That would be *nirvikalpa*. But that would exclude action in the world, because it's a trance state.

ANTHONY: Yes, and no critical reflection can take place. There can't be any feeling either. And there's no application of anything.

JFL: So the insight, in that sense, is partial by that definition.

ANTHONY: No, that's not insight. When the mystic brings that into the everyday world and perceives that the reality that was there is also here, *that's* insight. Now most mystics go into *nirvikalpa* and when they come out there's the world confronting them like a shark. They're frightened by it; they run away: "I don't want anything to do with that."

The philosopher says, "No. What is ultimately real in that world that I perceive through the senses, and that which I experience in *nirvikalpa*—they're the same." The philosopher has to bring that to bear on worldly experience. That's insight. In other words, if I say I'm looking at that object, I know that the innermost being of myself is pure Consciousness. I also know that the innermost being of that object is pure Consciousness. That's insight. That never comes; that never goes; that is permanent. Once a sage has that, it's for good. It can never be lost.

Only when you reach that kind of maturity do you have the sufficient intelligence or understanding or critical ability, the necessary feelings and will, to crucify or to give up the ego mentally. Not before. Because it will outwit you at every step.

AH: Would the sage's insight be a dualistic knowledge, or would you speak of it as nondual knowledge?

ANTHONY: Insight is both. It's dual and nondual. I know you feel uncomfortable with that, but it's both.

RC: This seems to be pointing to a recognition that the dualism arises within a mind which itself is one.

ANTHONY: Which is nondual, yes.

RC: And that the appearance of dualism is not a contradiction of the mind in which it appears.

ANTHONY: That's why I say both: dual and nondual. Because if you say nondual, people automatically think monistically. So I carry on a rear-guard activity by saying it's both.

HS: Is insight a fruition of the perfection of these three functions? Is it a production of these three?

ANTHONY: Well, I could answer by saying both. There is the development, the fruition, of the three functions which brings about their integration or brings about insight. That insight at the same time recognizes that it wasn't something new. It was always there. From the point of view of time, it's something we develop. But from the point of view of achievement, it has always been there. And that's the way I understand the Buddha's smile. He smiled because there it was, all the time. He didn't have to go anywhere. It was always there. It isn't something new; it's something you discover, but it was always there. So from one point of view it looks as though you're going towards it. You're developing these three functions, and you go through a myriad of lives to bring about that integration. Then when you do succeed, you recognize that that was always you. It's self-recognition, self-cognition.

ME: Would you say that a prerequisite to having insight is the ability to enter the thought-free state?

ANTHONY: Oh, yes. That would fall under the discipline of meditation—that you can bring about a quiet state, silence. So you see what's required. You have to be quite good at being able to produce a still state, no thoughts, which acquaints you with feelings which are really quite heavenly. So that's going to reorient the whole feeling nature. When you come out of something like that, you could never accept the feelings that you had before. The conflict is there immediately, and you know you have to start altering the kinds of feelings you had. It's the same way when a person goes through a tremendous effort at critical reflection. Remember what Kant pointed out after he went through these studies: He said it was like a Copernican revolution. That reorients all your thinking and you've completely turned everything inside-out and upside-down. It's just like telling a primitive, "It's not the sun that goes around, but the earth." To us it's nothing, but to a primitive it requires real effort. The same way with the will: to learn to will the Good and not take for granted that it's going to happen.

AH: What is meant by "constant remembrance in the midst of disinterested active service?"

ANTHONY: It's very specific. While you're doing some kind of selfless work—while you're engaged in some kind of activity that is basically altruistic—you have to also keep in mind the higher Self. So when somebody comes over and peppers me with a lot of questions, the first thing I think is, "Help me, PB." Then I try to figure out what's going on.

AH: This is a specific reference to altruistic service rather than our day-to-day lives?

ANTHONY: Everyday life can be altruistic. You have to keep in mind that you have to practice the remembrance exercise in the midst of your activities. This has to constantly go on. You can see what's developing here. PB's definition of philosophy is, as he says somewhere else, life made articulate.

So, these are the disciplines necessary in order to bring about that possibility of self-recognition: "metaphysical reflection, mystical meditation, and constant remembrance in the midst of disinterested active service."

ME: It seems in the first two, the function gets depersonalized.

ANTHONY: Or universalized.

ME: But the last one, developing compassion, seems different.

ANTHONY: That's the hardest part. That's where the most purgation takes place. That, of course, is going to require every ounce of strength you have. I won't say any more.

THE QUEST has three aspects: metaphysical, meditational, and morally active. It is the metaphysician's business to think this thing called life through to its farthest end. It is the mystic's business to intuit the peaceful desireless state of thoughtlessness. But this quest cannot be conducted in compartments; rather must it be conducted as we have to live, that is, integrally. Hence it is the philosopher's business to bring the metaphysician's bloodless conclusions and the mystic's serene intuition into intimate relation with practical human obligations and flesh-and-blood activities. Both ancient mystical-metaphysical wisdom and modern scientific practicality form the two halves of a complete and comprehensive human culture. Both are required by a man who wants to be fully educated; one without the help of the other will be lame. This may well be why wise Emerson confessed, "I have not yet seen a man!" Consequently, he who has passed through all the different disciplines will be a valuable member of society. For meditation will have calmed his temperament and disciplined his character; the metaphysics of truth will have sharpened his intelligence, protected him against error, and balanced his outlook; the philosophic ethos will have purified his motives and promoted his altruism, whilst the philosophic insight will have made him forever aware that he is an inhabitant of the country of the Overself. He will have touched life at its principal points yet will have permitted himself to be cramped and confined by none.

(v13, 20:1.173 and *Perspectives*, p. 256)

ANTHONY: What do you think Emerson was talking about when he said, "I have not yet seen a man"?

AB: The people that he met did not have the full development of all these faculties.

ANTHONY: And he went to Europe twice looking for such a person. How about us? We have seen two of them.

BS: How does reason affect illumination?

ANTHONY: You will find adequate description of that in PB's notes. He keeps pointing out that the extent of the illumination that is available to you depends on how prepared you are for it. To the extent that only the reasoning, or one or two faculties are developed, to that extent when illumination comes, those faculties will get fully illuminated and developed. The others will remain behind. So one has to prepare oneself in all possible ways, balance the psyche in every possible way, evolve, develop and refine each of these things, so that when the illumination comes, you will receive a *full* illumination.

There are quite a few notes on that in PB's writings. They are much more adequate as far as a response to your question is concerned. [See, for example, v13, 20:4.9 in the *Notebooks* series.—ed.] There are many different schools of yoga and philosophy that are devoted to this task of preparing ourselves for the illumination. And the recommendation of course is always to use the philosophic, the highest schools, so that the training that you subject yourself to will be according to the highest teachings which will prepare you in the most complete way for illumination. If you get a glimpse and you have distortions or complexes, those complexes get enormously exaggerated, just as the good parts also get very developed and become very useful and very penetrating.

So, let's try some examples. Imagine a David Hume. He thought a problem all the way through in philosophy. His willing side wasn't developed, and his feeling side wasn't really developed, but he did think and think very hard. Towards the end, do you know what he did? He stayed home and played dominoes! You take any one of these men, like Schopenhauer or J.S. Mill, and you can see that they thought a problem out to a certain extent, but the other two faculties were not involved.

On the other hand, take a person who has very highly developed feelings who doesn't think or will anything. Schubert is a good example, with a very fine aesthetic development but absolutely impractical. He would write his music on restaurant menus.

So if you take examples of each one, you can see that this is certainly not going to be a philosopher. Someone, for instance, who can think something out but then can't apply it and doesn't feel the full consequences or evaluate it properly is not a philosopher. So again, we go back to this point that these three functions have to be integrated in a person before we can speak of having a fully human being. Most of us are pretty deformed—that's obvious. At any rate, I think that that's what Emerson was referring to: the fact that in his journeys, and that included a large area, he never came across a sage. They're pretty rare.

> THE PHILOSOPHER is satisfied with a noble peace and does not run after mystical ecstasies. Whereas other paths often depend upon an emotionalism that perishes with the disappearance of the primal momentum that inspired it, or which dissolves with the dissolution of the first enthusiastic ecstasies themselves, here there is a deeper and more dependable process. What must be emphasized is that most mystical aspirants have an initial or occasional ecstasy, and they are so stirred by the event that they naturally want to enjoy it permanently. This is because they live under the common error that a successful and perfect mystic is one who has succeeded in stabilizing ecstasy. That the mystic is content to rest on the level of feeling alone, without making his feeling self-reflective as well, partly accounts for such an error. It also arises because of incompetent teachers or shallow teaching, leading them to strive to perform what is impracticable and to yearn to attain what is impossible.

Our warning is that this is not possible, and that however long a mystic may enjoy these "spiritual sweets," they will assuredly come to an end one day. The stern logic of facts calls for stress on this point. Too often he believes that this is the goal, and that he has nothing more about which to trouble himself. Indeed, he would regard any further exertions as a sacrilegious denial of the peace, as a degrading descent from the exaltation of this divine union. He longs for nothing more than the good fortune of being undisturbed by the world and of being able to spend the rest of his life in solitary devotion to his inward ecstasy. For the philosophic mystic, however, this is not the terminus but only the starting point of a further path. What philosophy says is that this is only a preliminary mystical state, however remarkable and blissful it be. There is a more matured state—that of gnosis—beyond it. If the student experiences paroxysms of ecstasy at a certain stage of his inner course, he may enjoy them for a time, but let him not look forward to enjoying them for all time. The true goal lies beyond them, and he should not forget that all-important fact. He will not find final salvation in the mystical experience of ecstasy, but he will find an excellent and essential step towards salvation therein. He who would regard rapturous mystical emotion as being the same as absolute transcendental insight is mistaken. Such a mistake is pardonable. So abrupt and striking is the contrast with his ordinary state that he concludes that this condition of hyper-emotional bliss is the condition in which he is able to experience reality. He surrenders himself to the bliss, the emotional joy which he experiences, well satisfied that he has found God or his soul. But his excited feelings about reality are not the same as the serene experience of reality itself. This is what a mystic finds difficult to comprehend. Yet, until he does comprehend it, he will not make any genuine progress beyond this stage.

(v13, 20:4.125 and *Perspectives,* p. 265)

DR: PB says that the feeling state of bliss or exaltation that a mystic experiences is really only preliminary to the full reality. Then, towards the end of the quote, he speaks about a state of serenity that the philosophic mystic achieves. Isn't that also a feeling state and, therefore, not the final truth?

ANTHONY: Feeling, willing, and knowing are all functions of the psyche. And previously PB spoke about these three as having to be fused. In the fusion of these three psychic functions, a new function arises which is different from everything that ever preceded it. And he calls that insight. Now each one of these psychic functions is specified as to how it works. But insight is inconceivable; keep that in mind—it's inconceivable. Don't try to have any ideas as to what it is, except in the language we use now. Insight is life having direct apprehension of itself, whereas feeling would take a certain aspect of life, willing would take another aspect of life, knowing would deal with another aspect of life. When we speak about insight, we're talking about life knowing itself totally and integrally. So if you say that there's a higher type of feeling that is experienced when the philosopher has insight, you're going to get confused. On the one hand we have these psychic functions, and feeling is one of them, and it *can* experience something about reality; and on the other hand we're saying that insight is the direct apprehension of reality.

So PB uses the terms "noble peace" and "serenity" for insight, and this is different from the feeling and knowing and willing. But it is *not* dead or inanimate.

DR: So if we do try to speak of higher feeling, or higher knowing, we are just importing the ways of the psyche into insight.

ANTHONY: Yes, so we have to keep the distinction clear between psychic functions and insight. Insight is knowing knowing, and this goes on whether there *is* an object or there *isn't* an object. Insight is eternal. It has no beginning in time. It always is what it is. And whether the insight is an insight into what the nature of reality is or into what an object is, it is insight and remains insight even if there is no object. So that means that even if there is no feeling, insight remains. Isn't feeling a content? Isn't it something known? But in insight, there is nothing "other" that is being known.

DR: But you say that insight does not change whether there is or is not an object. Logically I'm losing it.

ANTHONY: Let's use an analogy. If you have the lights on, you see the pole. I shut the lights off, you say you see nothing. Seeing goes on in both cases. In one case you saw nothing; in the other case you saw the pole. In the analogy I'm using, seeing itself corresponds to transcendental insight. Reality can't disappear just because appearances disappear. So insight always remains. It's always there.

DR: And for the sage insight does not disappear when there is an apparent world. So clearly the sage can use insight upon an object.

RG: I'm still confused. Doesn't the sage elaborate insight through these functions?

ANTHONY: There's no possibility of elaborating insight. These three modes of cognition are the faculties that, as human souls, we possess. I would suspect that there is some pre-ordained relationship between these functions and insight—that willing, feeling, and knowing can corroborate with insight. But ultimately I would say that they are contingent.

RG: I would agree that they are contingent as functions. But in this quote, for example, insight is spoken of through the idea of peace or serenity, as a kind of higher feeling, and in another quote it's spoken of as gnosis or the true object of knowledge.

ANTHONY: PB tries to avoid the use of "higher feeling," "higher knowing," any of that.

RG: But I get the flavor that the ultimates of those three are somehow fused in insight, and their ultimate realization grants you some experience of them in their purest possible states. You may not call it feeling anymore, but it doesn't seem that you can speak of it as lacking feeling. You may not call it knowing, but you wouldn't call it unknown in the ultimate sense of knowing.

ANTHONY: I think I follow what you're getting at. PB makes the remark that, on the one hand, the balance of these three brings about the possibility of insight, which seems to be a fusion of these three functions. But he also goes on to say that insight is qualitatively different than the three functions. Very different. So I don't think I can answer your question. But I do want to make this one remark: Don't try to conceive insight. It's better to leave your mind blank. And I would make one more remark: It's better, I think, to use the terms he uses for insight, things like "peace," "serenity," and "gnosis," rather than to use any one of the three functions or all three. Because that would be misleading. Insight is not a higher knowing, not a higher feeling, not a higher willing. It's not that. So if we leave ourselves open that way, we're better off; we might get some intuitions about it. But it is totally inconceivable. All right, read another quote.

> WHAT SCIENCE calls the "critical temperature," that is, the temperature when a substance shares both the liquid and gaseous states, is symbolic of what philosophical mysticism calls the "philosophic experience," that is, when a man's consciousness shares both the external world of the five senses and the internal world of the empty soul. The ordinary mystic or yogi is unable to hold the two states simultaneously and, quite often, even unwilling to do so, because of the false opposition he has been taught to set up between them.
>
> (v13, 20:4.122 and *Perspectives*, p. 266)

ANTHONY: Do you think there are two states or one state?

KD: I think it would be one state because that is the critical point at which the world is seen as not other than mind.

DR: That actually does justice to the analogy of critical temperature. At that temperature the substance is in both states and you can't really distinguish them.

ANTHONY: PB says the philosophic experience is like that, that you hold the apparent world and the emptiness of soul together.

KD: And you haven't canceled either one. It's not that there is a thought of the world imposed on consciousness, but that there is no longer any division or separation. There are not two things, consciousness and the world.

ANTHONY: Are you trying to say that the philosophic experience includes the I AM and the World-Idea?

KD: Yes, and that neither one is denied.

JA: How does psychology relate to the World-Idea?

ANTHONY: Your psychology is included in the World-Idea. It didn't go away; it's still there. As soon as you come back you'll find it waiting for you.

RC: What about psychology and the world of the five senses?

ANTHONY: I would say that all that is part of the World-Idea: the ego complex, the five senses, tendencies, thoughts, desires. All that is part of the World-Idea, and then the I AM is the substratum within which is manifested the World-Idea. Philosophic experience is to see both of them together.

RC: In the familiar quote from Chuang Tzu that says, "The mind of a perfect man is like a mirror," is psychology operating there?

ANTHONY: No, there wouldn't be psychology there. But isn't that exactly what is being referred to here as the philosophic experience? It includes both.

TS: So psychology refers to what defines the individuality of the embodied person. The individual's experience is part of the given World-Idea. That is, that which is part of the mind/body complex is experienced as part of the World-Idea, not part of the I AM. So the I AM, which is that genuine individual being, is experienced as empty of any content, but that psychosomatic structure which is its outer actualization is seen as part of the World-Idea. And the consciousness of the philosopher stands poised between both, so that it is neither.

ANTHONY: Not "poised between," but including both; not in between both, but including both.

RG: Do you take the "internal world of the empty soul" to be the experience of the I AM?

ANTHONY: Yes.

RC: Is this the experience of insight? Are we talking about the peak of human development here?

ANTHONY: Well, insight includes recognition of the soul and its manifestation as non-different. Philosophic experience is the same as having insight. Insight is the same as being the double knower. That means that the soul and its manifestation are non-different.

> THE REQUIRED condition of balance as the price of illumination refers also to correcting the lopsidedness of letting the conscious ego direct the whole man while resisting the superconscious spiritual forces. In other words, balance is demanded between the intellect which seeks deliberate control of the psyche and the intuition which must be invited by passivity and allowed to manifest in spontaneity. When a man has trained himself to turn equally from the desire to possess to the aspiration to being possessed, when he can pass from the solely personal attitude to the one beyond it, when the will to manage his being and his life for himself and by himself is compensated by the willingness to let himself and his life be quiescent, then his being and his life are worked upon by higher forces. This also is the kind of balance and completeness which the philosophic discipline must lead to so that the philosophic illumination may give him his second birth.
>
> (v13, 20:3.278 and *Perspectives*, p. 269)

ANTHONY: The World-Idea can present you with a variety of situations and circumstances and the person who is balanced will respond appropriately, sometimes according to the structure of the ego and sometimes by keeping the ego silent and accepting guidance.

The philosophic discipline demands that the whole soul, all

the parts of the soul, are readily available to respond to the variety of situations that can be presented by the World-Idea. That means that at one time the soul insists that the ego do its own thing. Another time the soul insists that the ego keep quiet and listen to what's to be done. At other times, it may be required that the complexity of the whole of the psychic organism be reorganized or be temporarily disowned for the purposes of acting from different presuppositions than the ones it inherits. Isn't this in brief what PB is trying to say?

It's like looking at the two charts together: the natal chart and the transits going on. There are times when you must act from within the center of your own ego; your ego has to decide what to do. There are times when you shouldn't let the ego decide but let the transits or the higher mind tell you what to do. There are times when certain functions have to be negated or denied so that *other* ideas can come to operate. So balance would consist of bringing all of these into some sort of coordination into a philosophic ideal.

KD: Implied in what you're saying is the inner poise of the being, that it's not stuck on any one of those qualities or conditions?

ANTHONY: Well, yes, but that too is required: that the ego sometimes operates and acts from its own needs. That *too* has to be included, because there is need for the ego to evolve along with the World-Idea. The development that it needs also has to be included in the soul's poise, as you call it. Put it this way: it's the ability to apply any of the 360 degrees[7] at any time to any given situation. If you can't, it's because there's something stuck.

So sometimes a particular idea is required in order for me to understand a phenomena or to operate with a phenomena or to act in a situation. And I don't have any planets aspecting the idea that's required. So, I don't habitually operate that way. But that's the idea that's required of me in order for me to respond adequately to a situation. If I lack balance, because of my predisposition to operate only in terms of where the planets are in my chart, I'm going to ignore the ideas that my planets are not sitting on. So what balance means here, I think, is the ability to be able to manipulate any of those ideas, independently of or coordinately *with* the psychic functions.

LDS: What does it mean to do it without the psychic functions? In other words, if you don't have a planet on a degree, how would you have access to that degree?

ANTHONY: Aren't they all included within you? If we say that the World-Idea is given to the Witness I, then all those ideas are within you. But why is it you prefer some over the others? Why do you insist on using the same ones, over and over again? In other words, why do you respond to a situation in a set pattern,[8] where it might not be called for?

LDS: So if I'm going to be able to manipulate any of the 360 degrees, that would entail my ability to take the Witness perspective or point of view?

ANTHONY: Of course. I have no doubt that you are the Witness I. I never think you to be your little toe. And I have no reason to think that you're the body that's presented to me. You *are* that I.

CS: So the sage has risen above the natal chart?

ANTHONY: The sage has risen above the chart and is also in the chart. The sage is the ego and also beyond the ego. The sage uses the ego and at times feels the ego needs a certain development and will develop it. This is balance: the ability to manipulate the entirety of the psychic structure or any of the functions, and also any of the ideas, to respond adequately to any situation that the World-Idea presents you with.

CS: Because all the ideas are within?

ANTHONY: Of course. Where else are they? Do you get a chart with only twelve degrees? Twenty? Twenty-five? You get the 360, or you don't get any.

CS: But they are not all available.

ANTHONY: They *are* all available! Otherwise, how could we communicate with one another?

LR: We don't! [*laughter*]

ANTHONY: When a planet in your chart is sitting on a degree, you respond according to that degree. But you're not sure if your sun or your moon is on degree 23 or 24 and you keep saying to yourself, "It could be this or it could be that. It could be either one. I see both." Right there, there's an indication that all these ideas are within you. They're not foreign to you. Also, these ideas are the very means, the very method, the very medium by which communication takes place. Now if I only had twelve ideas and you only had thirteen—that means twenty-five—we couldn't discuss the other 335. What I'm saying is that the soul includes the ego, which is part of the World-Idea, as part of itself.

The psyche as it is in any one of us is unbalanced. I don't have to tell you that. You look at your chart; you can see that right away. That's what we mean when we say "unbalanced," right? There is a stress here and an underpinning there. So how can you bring it into balance? Well, there are some things you have to do to bring it into balance and there are some things that you don't do but you listen for guidance.

But I find that trying to understanding the problem the way PB stated it is very difficult and complicated. I'm just trying to rephrase it in my own terminology so that I can deal with it more easily. So I'd say that in order for me to be able to respond to the variety of situations or circumstances which arise with the World-Idea, I must operate as a *whole*—not just the ego, but the "I" which includes the ego, intellection, intuition, and all that. But if there are grooves or fixed patterns of operating, *ipso facto* I can't respond adequately or spontaneously to any situation.

So that would be one way of looking at it. Another way would be to look at the fact that the ego, because of certain shortcomings, has to develop itself; this has to be included in the program of bringing balance about.

BUT IT IS of the highest importance to note that the principle of balance cannot be properly established in any man until each of the elements within him has been developed into its completeness. The failure to do so produces the type of man who knows truth intellectually, talks it fluently, and does the wrong in spite of it. A balance of immature and half-developed faculties is transitory by its very nature and never wholly satisfactory, whereas a balance of fully matured ones is necessarily durable and always perfectly gratifying.

(*Perspectives*, p. 269)

SDX: I think PB is saying that any faculty naturally develops to a point of fullness or ripeness, just like a fruit would develop, and if you try to do something with it when it's still in the process of growth it's going to be transitory because it's still developing, still changing.

ANTHONY: Yes, the point is that you can speak about balancing functions that are developed; you can't speak about balancing functions that are *un*developed. Balance isn't possible there.

When PB speaks about balance, he's speaking about people that have highly evolved intellectual abilities, highly differentiated, deep, intense feeling, a daemonic will. Those are the people that have to balance the faculties. We don't have to worry about balancing anything right now. First let me be an extremist and develop the faculties, and then I'll go balance them.

AH: What would it mean to try to balance undeveloped faculties?

ANTHONY: Well, if you think of your thinking as undeveloped and your feelings as undeveloped, and you try to balance these two undeveloped faculties, you're going to find that it's in the very nature of the "balance" you achieve to be quite unstable.

DB: I think I appreciate how balance of the undeveloped faculties is not possible. What I don't understand, though, is how the transitory character of those faculties disappears when they become fully developed.

ANTHONY: The three faculties still remain with you. If you fully develop feeling, and fully develop thinking, and then you have to consider something, you can properly evaluate it in terms of feeling, and you can properly think it out. And it isn't that they're lost; you still have them. The balance that is required is that each function plays the role that is assigned to it, makes the proper consideration. They don't disappear. So a fully developed thinking faculty in the person of the sage doesn't disappear because the sage has insight, nor does the willing or the knowing. They're still at the sage's disposal. But the sage can balance all three. The sage can make a consideration on some subject and all three fully developed faculties can be operative, each playing its role. They'll stay with you.

> THE PROPORTION of development needed by each part of his being will differ with every individual. Only a correct ratio will lead to a correct balance of all the parts.
>
> (v13, 20:3.353)

ANTHONY: The psyche in itself is never integrated, and it's going to take the higher powers of willing, thinking, and feeling to integrate the psychic functions. Basically what corrects the unbalanced functioning of the psyche are the higher faculties, and that very often is independent of the natal chart, the psychic functioning. I mean, you can look at your natal chart and say, "Well, here's a deficiency or an excess of a certain quality." And the soul brings its thinking to bear on that, and its willing to bear on that. But the chart itself would prefer not to have that done.

TS: So you're saying the ratio is not a certain kind of integrity within the ego structure.

ANTHONY: No.

TS: But it is a ratio which is established in spite of the ego structure.

ANTHONY: Yes. You have to depend on the intuitive faculty to point out to me a shortcoming, let's say, in the way my psyche functions, or where it's excessive in regard to something else.

AH: Is it from that point of view of the fully developed perfected functions that the psyche would be in imbalance?

ANTHONY: I don't follow your question. Are you asking if it's from the point of view of insight?

AH: Yes.

ANTHONY: No. That's not a point of view.

AH: But the full perfection or development of the three functions results in insight. Is that so?

ANTHONY: It results in insight or it seems to engender insight, but the three functions remain. They're not canceled out. PB says that willing, feeling, and knowing have to be brought to their highest level of development and then the fusion of these three engenders the faculty of insight; that doesn't deprive the sage of thinking, willing, and feeling. There are still those functions that the sage can work with. But this new faculty which is engendered and becomes operative is not a point of view.

AH: May I pursue this just a minute? Is there a standard that these functions must be brought to that would be uniform or is it peculiar to each person?

ANTHONY: It's individual. And that's why the guidance will have to come from your own intuition.

AH: It says the ratio will differ with each individual but the accomplishment doesn't.

ANTHONY: Yes. True.

AH: The accomplishment is the amalgam of the three functions which . . .

ANTHONY: Well, it's not only the three functions; you have to remember you have some others, too. The Chaldean planets[9] also represent functions; a little different, perhaps, but still they're functions.

But what you say is true. It differs with each person, but the accomplishment is the same for all.

AH: I'm trying to understand the relationship between peak development and engendering something.

ANTHONY: Now you keep changing positions, because before you just wanted to know if there was an objective standard to which the development of a faculty can be referred, right?

AH: Is there or is there not an objective standard?

ANTHONY: Well, there may be an objective standard, but I'm not going to try to answer it unless that's the question.

AH: That's the question. Because I can see what that standard is in regard to the thinking function, but I have no way of understanding what the standard would be with regard to the other functions.

ANTHONY: What would be the standard in terms of the thinking?

AH: It would be the ability for thought to discover its source, the last of the requirements for metaphysical thinking. That would be thought's perfection.

ANTHONY: Well, would you say the same for feeling, that feeling reaches its highest level of development and can properly evaluate whatever situation occurs within the World-Idea?

AH: As feeling?

ANTHONY: Yes, as feeling, as evaluation. And would you say that that would apply to willing, too, in the sense that the person will know what to do and what not to do in accordance, again, with the World-Idea? So that you're saying that the perfection of these functions is basically interrelated with the individual's understanding of, coordination with, and working with the World-Idea. Is that the standard that you're conceiving?

AH: Yes.

ANTHONY: Well, I can't answer, because I don't know. And when I reach that position, I'll let you know.

RC: In the quote we read earlier PB speaks of the person "who knows truth intellectually, talks it fluently, and does the wrong in spite of it." This seems to be a situation in which the thinking or evaluating function knows what needs to be done, but there is imbalance in that the will is not able to put the knowledge into action.

AH: Well, is having a concept of truth—which would be knowing intellectually—the same thing as thought discovering its source?

ANTHONY: To say the person knows what to do is the same as saying that this person knows what is being required—let's say by the World-Idea: circumstances, situations, events, and so on. The person knows what to do, but may not be able to implement that knowledge through the will.

But thought cannot discover its source. Thought cannot know the truth; it cannot discover the truth. By definition, it is barred. It can only know it intellectually.

Feeling, so to speak, can evaluate a situation properly, give it its due recognition as a felt content, and will would have to implement it, or carry out the activity required of it. Now these three things are all still in the domain of relativity. Even if they're perfectly balanced, they're still in the domain of relativity. When they're fused together, and they engender an entirely different faculty, *insight*—THAT is what discovers the source.

AH: I see. I understand now.

JG: Anthony, is there an actual fusing?

ANTHONY: Let's say you're a musician, and you're going to play on the piano. That means the will is going to be employed, right? And you have to know the piece you're playing. There's cognition. And there's an evaluation or a feeling to what you're playing. Now these three things seem to fuse together, and there's a magic that comes out of this: "Wow!" We're talking about fusing in that sense. It's not that they get swallowed up and disappear so you've got no feeling, willing, or knowing.

The three stay; they don't go away in insight. So the fusion engenders, it gives rise to the insight, and then that becomes permanent. Or you try to make it permanent; you keep on trying to repeat it over and over so that the insight becomes a permanent thing.

LR: So then balance seems to be like a posture of the soul acting in an appropriate way at any given moment.

ANTHONY: Yes. That would be a good way of putting it. PB is saying that the entirety of all the different parts of the psyche act in this controlled way. Each knows its place and acts accordingly.

AH: Is that possible without insight?

ANTHONY: Well, I pointed out before that it's a development that takes place through the intuitive faculty. It's your intuition that guides you to do or to develop this, do that and the other thing, whatever's required. This is very individual.

Remember how PB speaks about the Interior Word, the way it guides you and tells you what to do? Well, don't forget those things, because that's all part of the development of the intuition. You actually look inwardly for the guidance about what to do, because you no longer trust the ego. You know it's always up to its own shenanigans.

RC: Anthony, could you say more about what it means to say that the individual faculty is being perfected?

ANTHONY: I don't know if I care for that word, "perfected," because that kind of scares me. Let's say that thinking or willing has to be brought to a level of function where it will adequately serve the soul's development. If it hasn't achieved that level of development, it will always distort whatever intuitions come through and make mayhem of the whole situation. So I'd say that the faculty of thinking or willing or any one of these faculties—and I also include the Chaldean functions—has to be brought to a level where it can adequately respond to the needs of the individual, and it is developed rather than perfected.

I speak of "developed faculties" and not "perfected faculties" because I don't believe in perfection. There's only one thing that's perfect, the One.

LR: In what sense are you speaking of these faculties as serving the purpose of the life? Are you speaking about all the Chaldean faculties as radiations, servants of the sun, to reveal the true purpose of that sun?

ANTHONY: Yes. And further than that, the willing, thinking, and feeling guiding that individual. So you have a kind of hierarchy there. The soul through these three faculties is concerned with the full development of the individual and is required for that, in the sense that the psychical functioning of the Chaldeans may be imbalanced, and the thinking, willing, and feeling are brought into operation—or, if I could, for those three words, use the term "intuition"—to act as a guide as to which of these faculties is underdeveloped, which has to be developed. So it's a question of the whole psyche coming into balance, each function knowing the role it has to play in regard to the whole, in regard to *this* individual whole, not anyone else.

MB: Anthony, when we speak of the full development of the individual doesn't that also include a certain amount of impersonality or detachment from the ego?

ANTHONY: Well, that's absolutely necessary, because if there isn't a certain amount of impersonality in regard to the way the ego functions, one would never know that this rather than that is needed. How can you tell, for instance, that one of your functions is shortchanging you, unless there's a certain impersonality with regard to the way the ego functions?

JFL: The development is being brought on by the individual's higher self, then, not by the circumstances?

ANTHONY: It's a combination. Sometimes circumstances will be in favor of that development; sometimes they'll be against that development and the soul will insist, regardless, that it be carried through. That's why I say you won't find that in the [natal] chart.

Sometimes I look at a person's chart and I say, "No, this person *needs* that. The person has to go through that development. Sure it's an unpropitious beginning, but that's exactly the way it's going to get started. So it's necessary to go through difficulties. It's all right."

RC: Is this condition of balance that PB is speaking of as prerequisite for the birth of insight a potential in every chart, or do you see it as a rare potential?

ANTHONY: No. That's kind of rare.

Those who talk or write truth, but do not live it because they cannot, have glimpsed its meaning but not realized its power. They have not the dynamic balance which follows when the will is raised to the level of the intellect and the feelings. It is this balance which spontaneously ignites mystic forces within us, and produces the state called "born again." This is the second birth, which takes place in our consciousness as our first took place in our flesh.

(v13, 20:3.385 and *Perspectives,* p. 270)

JG: So why is that balance dynamic?

ANTHONY: If we go back to the example we used before about the musician: We said that a moment of magic is created. That's dynamism. And you say to yourself, "Couldn't it be like this all the time?" That's a dynamic state.

PD: The quote also implies that what has happened is not a product of your own activity but is due to these mystical forces, so your willing doesn't create anything, but your *not* willing interferes with something happening.

ANTHONY: Take the example we just used, that you're in a state where your feeling, willing and knowing are being exploited to the utmost, and you will feel yourself to always be a very dynamic person.

PD: But in that quote PB seems to be referring to the release of mystical forces.

ANTHONY: Yes, that's what I'm talking about. Isn't that what happens? Isn't there a release of mystical forces when the willing of the musician, the thinking of the musician, and the feeling of the musician are fused momentarily and you have this magic moment appear and you feel as though you have been reborn in consciousness? But you can't keep it up. Nonetheless it's a good example that if you live like that, there will be many moments in which you experience this dynamic state of being. Or I should say you experience the dynamism that's inherent in being?

The complementarity of these three factors produces the dynamic state. And it is a mystical state. Maybe Bert could give us an example. He plays the piano; he's got to will it; he's got to get down there—you know how hard that is—and then he's got to feel the piece properly and he's got to know everything he's doing. Then he plays and he gets transposed into a dynamic state of being. He feels greater than he's ever been. Then, when that magic moment is over, there's a relapse.

JG: You mean to say that a sage lives like that?

ANTHONY: All the time. The sage is always a dynamic being. That doesn't mean going around lifting up two-hundred-pound weights.

KD: The dynamism occurs as a result of exercising those functions?

ANTHONY: The dynamism is inherent in that state of being. When the three of them are conjointly functioning they produce that magic moment or that state of being.

MB: Anthony, you're saying that this state of balance can be brought about intermittently even when it isn't a fully developed capability?

ANTHONY: Yes. And also I'm making the point that a state of balance is not a state of immobility. When you balance something on a scale and the scale doesn't move any more, that's not the kind of balance I mean. That's stasis. That's inertia.

MB: This quote sounds like it's describing an alchemical process.

ANTHONY: It definitely is.

RC: Balance here seems to be fullness, livingness, clarity, freedom—they all seem to be involved in this.

ANTHONY: Yes. I definitely think so.

HE: If the will is not developed to the level of the intellect and feelings, so that you have a person who knows the good and has a sense of what's to be done but can't do it, how is the person going to overcome that deficiency except by willing?

ANTHONY: You're saying, if the will is insufficient, what can

I do about it? Well, if you wanted to develop the power of memory, how would you go about doing that?

LR: Memorize.

ANTHONY: And if you want to develop the power of will, how would you do it?

JG: You get up each morning and fight.

ANTHONY: Remember what Goethe said: "The battle for freedom is fought anew every day." I hope you don't think it's done once and over.

HE: Are you willing yourself to develop the will?

ANTHONY: No, I'm saying you're exercising the power of the soul to develop the will. Otherwise you'll be running on with wills from here to eternity! If you take the definition of soul the way it was evolved in our studies of Plotinus: Soul has powers. It is present in every one of those powers. It must exercise those powers, or they might just as well not have been.

So if you want to develop the power of memory, you go about memorizing. Every morning you get up and you recite one chapter from the Koran, or you sit down and you memorize it. The next day—you'd be surprised. The power of memory, the faculty of memory actually gets developed. And every day you get up and you do something you dislike or something that you feel that you should do and you can't do; you develop the will to be able to do it.

HE: When PB speaks at the beginning of the quote about "someone who knows the truth but does not live it because they cannot," he doesn't mean *cannot* in any kind of—

ANTHONY: —absolute sense. The person hasn't developed that faculty of the will to bring it up to par with the development of the intellect and the feeling.

HE: And this person may not know that it is possible to develop the will. One just accepts this will as it is: "I just don't have any will. I can't do it."

ANTHONY: Sure. And when you get defeated often enough, you'll suddenly get mad.

BS: So we could make certain efforts to develop. I thought you were saying that these efforts we make . . .

ANTHONY: . . . Count.

BS: Yes, in the sense that they will awaken *in* us the inherent soul power itself. And possibly later you can work directly from that?

ANTHONY: Yes. You awaken a certain soul power when you exercise the faculty of memory, and then you recognize that you *do* have this power to memorize.

BS: I don't mean that the soul power actually awakens.

ANTHONY: Well, they *are* powers of the soul. They are powers. Not every kind of being has those powers. We do. The soul has those powers. Gain it and you'll regain your soul.

AS: I wanted to ask a question relating to the last line in the quote that refers to being born again: "This is the second birth, which takes place in our consciousness as our first took place in our flesh."

ANTHONY: Well, let's try this way. Willing, feeling, and knowing bring us into the body. Willing, feeling, and knowing are going to engender that Witness consciousness in us which *is* the rebirth in consciousness.

AS: Yes, the willing, feeling, and knowing—when they're fully balanced and developed—will be the place of birth of that higher consciousness.

ANTHONY: That consciousness, yes. You become the Witness I.

KD: Through the development of—

ANTHONY: —willing, feeling, and knowing. When they're fully balanced, you find those magic moments that I spoke about. They're magic because at that moment you are the Witness I. It's equivalent to an awareness of awareness.

AS: But not insight?

ANTHONY: No.

LR: Anthony, it seems to me that any one of those three—willing, feeling, or knowing—could bring about that Witness consciousness. Does the Witness consciousness depend upon the fusion of those three the way you speak about insight?

ANTHONY: Yes. The three of them have to be operative. It may not seem so from what you understand of astrology, but the three of them have to be operative in order for the experience of being the Witness to take place. If there's unbalance in them, you will remain the empirical subject.

PC: You mean even a momentary glimpse of that Witness?

ANTHONY: Even a momentary glimpse of being the Witness I requires that these three are, for that moment, in balance. That's why I gave the example of a musician. Those three have to be in operation at the same time. You can see that if one of them is excessive or deficient, that means that some compulsive functioning is going on which would prevent the feeling of being the Witness or the knowledge of being the Witness.

PC: Can it take place in a state where they are quiescent?

ANTHONY: Quiet? Sure.

AH: Is that to say that the only way they're going to be quiet is if they're in balance?

ANTHONY: That's true. You know, will doesn't always have to be some sort of activity. Sometimes will could also be an inhibition. It doesn't always have to operate so that you go run a quarter of a mile. Have you noticed that inhibition is an exercise of the will?

Let's go to another quote on balance. I'm sure to become *un*balanced before the night's over, but let's keep trying!

> THE BALANCE needed by faith is understanding; by peacefulness, energy; by intuition, reason; by feeling, intellect; by aspiration, humility; and by zeal, discretion.
>
> (v13, 20:3.410 and *Perspectives*, p. 271)

ANTHONY: You notice how difficult it is to aspire when you're in a state of arrogance? We can go through that whole list. That's why they're so necessary to know. Develop your faculty of memory: Memorize that. Write them down, because that's the only comment I'm going to make.

> ALL THAT IS needful to a man's happiness must come from *both* these sources—the spiritual and the physical—from the ability to rest in the still centre, in the developed intellectual and aesthetic natures, in the good health and vigour of the body.
>
> (v13, 20:3.272)

ANTHONY: PB is saying, if you want to turn on enthusiasm, you go to the faucet and you open it; enthusiasm comes out. But, in order for that enthusiasm to come out, there have to be two pipes that lead to that faucet. On one side is the ability to be quiet and still in your interior being, and on the other side there are the aesthetic and intellectual capabilities and good health. Then you can turn the faucet on and off whenever you want! Haven't you asked yourself, "Why can't I be enthusiastic all the time? Why does it just come in spurts?" You know, you may have a good meditation and you get up and your knees crumble; there goes that enthusiasm! Or you may be intellectually very perceptive and aesthetically capable and appreciative and your health is in good vigor, but you have no inner quiet; your mind is always agitated. There goes the enthusiasm again. But if you could balance the two of them, then you could turn the faucet on whenever you wanted. You get a little bored with life: Turn the faucet on! And, the strange thing is, the novelty never wears off.

AH: Well, this is obviously a description of a fairly advanced accomplishment.

ANTHONY: Everything is advanced unless you practice it and try it! [*laughter*]

But basically, those ingredients are necessary: the ability to be still, be quiet, identify with that quietness, and also to be able to come out and actively engage in intellectual and aesthetic adventures or just in the sheer act of living. They're both necessary. It's very difficult to imagine how a person could be enthusiastic and happy if this person is spiritually attained but at the same time is suffering, let's say, some very painful disease. So, that's pretty straightforward.

> WHEN A certain balance of forces is achieved, something happens that can only be properly called "the birth of insight."
>
> (v13, 20:4.181 and *Perspectives*, p. 274) [repeat]

ANTHONY: Think of all the functions that life has developed—digestion; breathing; the functioning of the senses; the reproductive faculties; the vegetative, reasoning, and intellective phases of the soul—these are all functions that the power of the soul has evolved. Now think of a moment when all these powers of the soul are harmoniously integrated: At that instant insight is available. Life understands itself without any intermediary. But if there's the least disruption of one of those faculties, then you can't have insight.

I put it a little differently before. I said, "When life articulates itself so clearly that that articulation is understanding, that's the same as insight."

> ONLY A GREAT NATURE can take a great illumination and not become unbalanced by it. That is why the full cultivation, all-around development, and healthy equilibrium of the man is required in Philosophy.
>
> (v13, 20:3.377)

> HE NOT ONLY has to receive this illumination in all the parts of his being rather than any one part, but also to receive it equally. It is the obstruction arising in the undeveloped or unpurified parts which is the further cause of his inability to sustain the illumination.
>
> (v13, 20:3.208)

DB: Are the obstructions and lack of purity found in the three areas of thinking, willing, and feeling?

ANTHONY: Don't restrict it to knowing, willing, and feeling.

DB: What else should we include?

ANTHONY: Any and all parts of the psyche. Any one instinct can come and overwhelm you if it lacks development. So you might get an illumination, and some part of your being—let's say the lower intellect or the erotic nature—can come up and completely overwhelm you and deprive you of retaining that illumination. Or here's one that perhaps many of us are familiar with: We have a good meditation, and we get up and go to the refrigerator and attack it furiously. [*laughter*] And that would be gluttony.

When we speak about the balance of the various faculties of the psyche, we're speaking about the relation between the psyche as embodied and as disembodied.[10]

LD: In the main part, would you equate the ego with the embodied psyche?

ANTHONY: The answer is somewhat complicated. The psycho-somatic organism is a fabrication, an organism built by nature, and therefore it's part of the World-Idea. But then there is the light which is illuminating it, which is the presence of the soul in that psycho-somatic organism. So the ego complex becomes a difficult concept. On the one hand, we speak about it as an organism which has evolved genetically and phylogenetically, but on the other hand, we have to keep in mind that involved in it is this presence of the soul, the immaterial principle that's illuminating its functioning, and that, too, is part of the ego complex. If you take that out you have an organism, but you don't have an ego; there's no one there, even if it's a functioning organism. So it's complex in the sense that these two things are required.

I often interpret what Plotinus calls the living animate in this way. It's a combination of the animal body and the presence of the soul. He calls this the living being or the living animate. That's why it's complex. But for most of us the strength of the animal organism is such that that's primarily the problem.

It's very, very difficult to understand how these mental faculties are present in the physical body. It would require that you go back to the definition of soul the way Plotinus has given it to us, to be able to grasp that the entity or the person is constituted of these two different aspects: soul as unembodied, what we call the I AM, and soul as embodied, what we refer to as the reproductive or embodying soul. And these two things together Plotinus calls the "we." So it's very complicated.

Rather than try to come up with definitions, it's better to try to just simply explain it. Sometimes you can't define something, but you can describe it.

So if you take that point of view—that there's the I AM, the pure soul, and there's a part or a phase of the soul which we call the lower phase of the soul and refer to it as the embodying soul, the reproductive soul, the ability that the soul has to project itself anywhere—and you think of these two, and you call that the "we," you are following Plotinus. Now from the "we" you can factor out the I AM—the eternal, immutable, intellectual being that soul is—and you can factor out that part of the soul which seeks embodiment.

Now that part of the soul which seeks embodiment locates itself in a body which has been fabricated for it by the World-Idea. That body is part of the World-Idea. So on the one hand, it seems that the ego is part of the World-Idea; but on the other hand, the soul which is present in that cannot be part of the World-Idea or, let's say, cannot be part of manifestation. So that makes the ego complex a very difficult thing to pin down, to say it's this or it's that. It's both these things; a combination of these two things.

LRD: What is it that has what PB calls the glimpse? Is it the reproductive soul which has the glimpse?

ANTHONY: Yes. It's the lower phase of the soul that has a glimpse, and not necessarily of the entire. The glimpse would mean self-recognition; it's not something outside.

LRD: In other words, of its source.

ANTHONY: Yes, but it *is* that source.

Let me try it a little differently. The reembodying soul or that lower aspect of the soul—let's call it consciousness—is what gets embodied and is preoccupied with externals. The glimpse that it gets is of its own nature, not of something outside. That's what you mean by a glimpse. It recognizes that its nature is consciousness. Consciousness recognizes itself to be its own principle.

AH: Would it be appropriate to speak of that glimpse as the embodied soul having a glimpse of the unembodied soul?

ANTHONY: Well, again, we pointed out that soul is constituted of these two aspects. One is the I AM, the eternal and immutable, and that's immaterial. The second is the lower phase of the soul, that phase of the soul—let's call it consciousness now—which seeks embodiment and gets embodiment. When that gets a glimpse, what it recognizes is its own nature, its own immaterial essence. Now you can speak about it as unembodied if you want, or you can speak about it as embodied. If you say "I got the glimpse," you're speaking about an embodied soul that got the glimpse. But what it glimpsed was its own immaterial essence, which cannot, so to speak, be understood in any other way except that it is immaterial, and in that sense it can never really be embodied; you can't wrap a body around it.

RC: So when the "lower soul" glimpses its own nature, it doesn't perceive itself as the lower of some higher but as actually in essence being that one soul.

ANTHONY: Yes, because the unity of soul, by definition, is present in its entirety wherever its powers are. Since one of its powers is that it can send forth a projection, it would have to be present there.

AH: Typically we've spoken of soul as two things, and from that point of view we always conceive of the soul as some kind of plurality. But this way of speaking seems to suggest that it's a singular; that it can be no object.

ANTHONY: Plotinus points out that it's a "one and many." It's a unity and it has powers, many powers. But we have to remember that the soul as a unity is present in each and every one of its many powers and in all of them.

Take an example: Mind is present, and totally present—it isn't a piece of the mind that's present—when you're thinking or when you're memorizing or when any mental faculty is being exercised or all of them are being exercised at the same time. The mind as mind remains integrally entire and undivided when you're thinking or when you're memorizing something. Now, the part that remains integrally undivided and totally self-present is what we're calling the higher phase of the soul, the I AM. The powers that it operates with—memory, reasoning, and so on—belong to it, and when you reason, your mind is totally present in the reasoning. When you memorize something, the mind is totally present in that power of memory, in that act of memory.

So it is, in a sense, like speaking about two souls. But if you keep in the back of your mind that it is one soul with *many* powers, and that it is integrally present to each and every one of those powers—either simultaneously or singularly, it doesn't matter—then you begin to see how difficult the concept of soul is that you've got to deal with.

You won't get that in a psychology book, but you will get it from these people—and of course, we get it from Plotinus, where he points out what the definition of soul is. And the definition or description is pretty accurate. If you don't understand it this way, you will always run into difficulty.

BS: If the whole soul is present in each of its powers, would there be a complete unity between the soul and a particular power?

ANTHONY: If you say that, then you've just abolished the distinction you made. The point in saying soul is one and many is precisely to keep apart, or to help you distinguish in your mind, the power of thinking and the undivided mind present to that power of thinking. But if you say that they're a unity—a unity of what? A unity of the soul with the power of thinking? Then you just have unity.

Try an experiment now. Think, and at the same time realize that your mind is present to that thinking. The power is not to be confused with the unity. I do many things—I walk, I talk, I sleep, I yell, I get angry.

Perhaps it would be worthwhile to say it's one substance, many functions.

RG: Anthony, we say one substance, many functions; one soul, many powers. The powers are an unfoldment of that soul. How do we hold the distinction of the powers from the soul? It seems to be a distinction that really isn't a distinction. It's a function, but the essence of the function seems to be the soul or the mind that's inherent in manifesting it. In this view it's hard to understand how those functions are not the mind's inherent nature externalizing itself.

ANTHONY: Well, that is the paradox, isn't it? The mind, as we put it, externalizes itself, and yet remains undivided, remains a unity.

> THE MASTERY of philosophy will produce a supreme self-confidence within him throughout his dealings with life. The man who knows nothing of philosophy will declare that it has nothing to do with practical affairs and that it will not help you to rise in your chosen career, for instance. He is wrong. Philosophy gives its votary a thoroughly scientific and practical outlook whilst it enables him to solve his problems unemotionally and by the clear light of reason. He will, however, be under certain ethical limitations from which other men are exempt, for he takes the game of living as a sacred trust and not as a means for personal aggrandizement at the expense of others.
>
> (v13, 20:1.176 and *Perspectives*, p. 278)

DB: What does PB mean by "the clear light of reason"?

ANTHONY: If you have an overall view of the meaning of

philosophy, implicit in that view would be the fact that the functions that you're working with—knowing, willing, feeling, and the others—are each distinguished from one another. Each has reached a level of development—not perfection, but development—where the proper weight and due for any given situation, event, or circumstances can be examined, and used as the basis of your action.

So if you have that kind of overall bird's eye view of philosophy, it's already presupposed that there's a kind of development of each of the functions. And that means that whenever any situation arises it can be examined in the light of these various functions, each developed, so to speak, according to its own mode. The examination of that situation with a function or combination of functions—but each held distinct from one another—gives you an understanding of the situation and what it is that you can do about it, if anything can be done.

So to act according to the clear light of reason means that you first have to reach the reason that's embedded in a situation; then, when you understand what the reason is that underlies that situation, you'll know what to do. But if you don't understand the reason that underlies a given situation, circumstance, or event, you will not be able to act according to the clear light of reason.

AH: Is that clear light of reason one of those functions?

ANTHONY: No. Those functions help you to get to what the reason is that underlies a situation. If those functions are not distinct—if, for instance, operative in you is a mixture of feeling and willing or any combination of these, and you cannot distinguish one from another—you would have a great deal of difficulty getting to the reason that underlies something, because there would be a confused functioning going on. And if there's a confused functioning that goes on, there's going to be error and illusion. So you first have to get to the underlying reason of a given thing, and that presupposes that your functions are available for that purpose. If they are, then you get to the reason that underlies that thing, and you can act according to the light of reason.

Let's say a person is caught up in a situation—in some sort of relationship—and it's a tangled affair; and the person doesn't know what to do with it. Now, it would be reason that could understand the springs of motivation—let's say, certain neurotic tendencies which are manifesting. It takes reason to be able to single them out and see them as the underlying causes or motivation that is going on. Also, it would take reason to see whether that would fit in with the developmental process you have in mind—in other words, with a certain ideal goal that you're striving for according to what you understand of philosophy. So first it will take reason to understand the situation, single out or factor out those springs of motivation that are of a disturbing character; and then it will take reason to see, according to your philosophic understanding, whether they accord with the goal you have set yourself. And if not, then reason has to show you the correct course of action to follow. We're talking about something very practical here.

If you're investigating into the causes of the behavior that you're exhibiting, it presupposes that you can think, that you can feel, that you can will, and a few other things. If these functions are not clarified—that is, if they're primitive—they have to be developed, because you can't *think* if they're undeveloped. So what is presupposed is that you have to some extent isolated the thinking function from the other functions, and developed it. If the thinking function is caught up with all the other functions, then you can't think, because every time you make an effort, you'll bring everything else up to the surface.

So from a very practical point of view, assuming that a person has these functions somewhat developed, then that person can use them to understand the nature of the neurotic behavior by getting to the causes that underlie it. Now, if you can get to the causes that underlie it, and you can see the appropriate behavior or the proper course of behavior that you're to follow, then you are acting according to the light of reason. This is what we're trying to understand. And I suspect that sometimes when people say "according to the light of reason" they expect a great, booming light to come into their mind and isolate some factor in their behavior. Whereas it's a metaphor: "the light of reason."

DB: It seems like such an elevated form of the word "reason."

ANTHONY: It is. Perhaps it doesn't have the glamour that Hollywood would give to it, but it's a very elevated form of action. As a matter of fact, if you remember, the Buddha insisted that you live according to the light of reason. You don't *have* anything better. Even if you get intuition, it must be explicated by reason, because it's the only guarantee you have about whether this intuition is correct or not. So again you're forced to rely on reason.

AH: In the example you gave, are the functions objective to reason?

ANTHONY: I thought it would be the other way around: that reason would be objective to the functions. In other words, if I examine my behavior very minutely and microscopically, and I see "Ah! Here's a complex hidden, which is manifesting itself in my relationship with others," this has become objective to the functions of thinking, willing, feeling. See all the gold you've got buried in you?

RC: This seems to be drawing out why this balance is so important. If the functions are not balanced, they can't objectify reason without distortion.

ANTHONY: Yes. Remember also that PB pointed out that before we can speak about balancing them they have to be developed. To try to balance undeveloped functions will only give you a very unstable product.

LR: Can this light of reason be contacted through other functions besides the thinking function?

ANTHONY: Yes. When we say a reason principle is objective to these functions, it doesn't necessarily have to be a cognitive thing. For instance, think of your feeling function giving the reasons involved in a situation their proper weight or evaluation in terms of their felt value. Many people *feel* the value of a situation, and if they have a highly developed feeling function, they're usually correct. They've made contact with the substratum reason principles, and given them the proper weight; they know they have to act according to the way revealed by that feeling function.

As a matter of fact, I would go a little further. To understand a reason principle only on a cognitive basis, and ignore the other aspects of willing and feeling, is not to really understand that object. So, for example, consider again that you are a musician who writes a piece of music, and all three functions are distinct within you. You have a cognitive ability—you can think—and you can feel, and you can execute or will. And doing these three things makes you feel like a total person when you're operating. That's why so many people want to play music besides just reading it and feeling. I think it's the experience of most people that they get a different result or a different experience when they also play the piece rather than when listening.

> IT MAY BE SAID that the world's supreme need is exactly what the illumined man has found, therefore his duty is to give it to the world. This is true, but it is equally true that the world is not ready for it any more than he himself was ready for it before he underwent a long course of purification, discipline, and training. Accepting these realities of the situation, he feels no urge to spread his ideas, no impulse to organize a following. However that does not mean that he does nothing at all; it only means that he will help in the ways he deems to be most effective even if they are the least publicized and the least apparent. He is not deaf to the call of duty but he gives it a wider interpretation than those who are ignorant of the state and powers which he enjoys.
>
> (v13, 20:4.264 and *Perspectives*, p. 278)

ANTHONY: Remember the story about the Buddha? Someone

came over and asked, "Why don't you give *nirvana* to everybody?" He said, "Well, nobody wants it!" [*laughs*] "Go out and ask them what they want!" And so the person went around asking, "What do you want?" "Oh, I want another ten acres." "What do you want?" "Oh, I want a daughter." Nobody wanted *nirvana*!

AH: How could I possibly want something that's the undoing of everything I know of myself? What is that motivation? It's certainly not the ego's motivation to want enlightenment. It couldn't want that because it has to get out of the way.

ANTHONY: Yes, but again, this calls into play what you understand in philosophy. If you understand that there is an eternal and immortal soul in the sense that it is what it is—we speak about it as the Intellectual, the Being that we truly are—and if you keep in mind also that lower phase of the soul that we spoke about as the embodying soul and which progressively transmutes the essence of the experiences it goes through until it evolves to a position where it begins to understand the truth, even in this conceptual way, then you can easily understand what it is that seeks enlightenment.

AS: And in that point of view, you can also understand why it takes quite a level of development to *want* the enlightenment.

ANTHONY: Now follow the point here. There is an entity that is progressively accumulating experience and transmuting that experience into some kind of understanding, and this is what you might call a progressive development that's taking place all the time. In the earlier stages, it is not interested in enlightenment. But then it goes through a variety of experiences. You extract the essence of those experiences that you go through in any given lifetime, and that essence is what's building up this entity in progressive stages. Then you reach a point where you cannot turn back any more.

AH: This is the motivation of the soul itself, though, isn't it?

ANTHONY: Well, we could say it's the motivation resulting from the accumulation of the distillation of this experience into understanding. And then it has its own momentum.

AH: The ego thinks it's going to get something out of this in the beginning, and then by the time it finds out that it isn't going to, it's too late to turn back.

ANTHONY: Yes, you got the point. [*laughter*] I try to take advantage of this, when I get a person involved in teaching. Because the ego is involved, you've got to show your superiority to everyone else; so you study, and you understand what you've got to teach, and then you teach it to others. But then there's a subtle influence that starts operating. The very understanding that you've developed through researching and working out the ideas and then presenting them to others starts acting on your ego! And it begins to understand more and more that what it's doing is erecting a technique and a method and an understanding of how to dismantle itself. Then you reach a point where you don't want to teach anybody; you don't even want to teach yourself any more. Now the ego's come in, and it's begun to recognize the *danger* if this goes on.

> WHEN THE masculine and feminine temperaments within us are united, completed, and balanced, when masculine power and feminine passivity are brought together *inside* the person and knowledge and reverence encircle them both, then wisdom begins to dawn in the soul. The ineffable reality and the mentalist universe are then understood to be non-different from one another.
>
> (v16, 25:2.120)

> BY BRINGING into a fusion the masculine and feminine temperaments within himself, he also fuses knowledge and feeling, wisdom and reverence.
>
> (v13, 20:3.414)

TL: If I think in terms of my own masculine and feminine, or the [astrological] Sun and the Moon as the masculine and the feminine, I'd have one particular and one universal.

ANTHONY: No. That's not exactly the way to look at it. Look at the passive aspect as all the Ideas or all the reason principles, and look at the active aspect as the planetary functions or the soul powers which are either embodying those Ideas or manifesting them forth. These are two aspects of our nature, all the time. One is an active power, and we call it masculine, the other is passive and we can call it feminine, but in other traditions they reverse it and say that the active is the feminine and the passive is the masculine. It depends on what tradition you belong to. You can call it Yin-Yang, One and Two, or anything else you want.

TL: If I were to experience my own masculinity . . .

ANTHONY: Tell me what you mean by that.

TL: My Sun nature.

ANTHONY: I just refuse to accept that. The Sun is only one of the many powers which we can refer to as masculinity. Masculinity would refer to the activity, the functioning, of the powers of the soul. If you don't want to use the astrological terminology, that would be the active power in a person.

TL: Can I use feeling and knowing?

ANTHONY: Well, yes. In feeling, when you do get ideas they're primarily *felt* substances. So if you think of the powers of the soul as *active* powers, when they manifest Ideas or a world for an individual it is a feltness that is going to be experienced.

TL: The same for a man or a woman?

ANTHONY: Don't you see that the discussion becomes irrelevant if you bring in a man and woman? Because there are many women who are more masculine than feminine, and there are many men who are more feminine than masculine. The point here is to try to understand that it is the power that you are actively employing and working with that you can call the active or the masculine part.

TL: Let me ask you this question. If I brought to union my feeling and my knowing within myself, would that be the same thing as the feeling and knowing in relation to the Sun and Moon?

ANTHONY: No. It would be the relationship between the planets and the degrees, or the Ideas.

It is *all* the planets and *all* the degrees. These two together represent the active and the passive aspects of our existence. Now, your planets can all be functioning, and they're active, and you call that the masculine principle. And the Ideas can be referred to as the feminine aspect. In the medieval tradition, Sophia, or Divine Wisdom, was always referred to as feminine, and that was the passive aspect, and the masculine aspect was said to seek that and to wish to conjoin with that, and in the union of these two, wisdom is born within the individual. Now, the activity that the active powers engage in, and the passivity—the ideas just lying there waiting to be grasped and manifested—these two can be balanced in a proper way, and then we speak about the union of the masculine and the feminine *within*. When you refer to physiological states—for instance, in the experience of certain spiritual powers, when they reach the head and one feels like there is a conjunction of one's positive and negative aspects—that's the *last effect* of this function. It is a symptom of what I'm talking about. What I'm talking about is primary. These Ideas, or this wisdom, is *within* you, and there's a tremendous variety in that wisdom. This power to grasp the Ideas is also part of your nature. The combination of these two is what they call the Hermetic marriage. When the person combines these powers with these ideas, he or she has achieved the Hermetic union. As soon as you bring in man or woman, you're bringing in a twentieth-century idea.

TL: But we have to come from our own psychology whether we're male or female—

ANTHONY: You have to come from the point of view of reality, not from your psychology. Psychology has got nothing to do with these things. If you're in the realm of psychology you're going to misunderstand. For example, even Jung had to say what he meant, he had to get to the Idea itself and throw out the symbol. The symbol is quite meaningless in itself. Ultimately, what you want is the Idea that is hidden in the symbol. Once you've got the Idea, you throw away the symbol. What need is there for it anymore? So you're dealing with this reality which is within you, the nature of the Divine Wisdom which is within you. That's what PB is talking about here. Active and passive, Yin and Yang—the variety of terms used goes on and on and on. If you have the kernel or the idea that they're talking about, then the words that you use don't matter. Using the Sun and Moon as symbolic of the passive and active aspects of our nature is a misunderstanding which comes from the alchemists—not the true alchemists, the Masters, but the alchemists who don't know what they're talking about. So this is the active and passive aspect, the Yin and the Yang, which after a while you learn to combine properly.

RC: In the process of refining these particular quotes, PB wanted to stress the insideness of it, that things are brought together inside the person. Originally he thought of using the words wisdom and compassion, but then he took "compassion" out and put "reverence" in, to stress the fact that it was *inside* the person.

NOTES

1. See the appendix for a development of this idea. See also pages 133–136 in chapter three.

2. The Overself is here understood as the portion (or allotment) of the universal intelligence of the World-Idea/World-Mind which is operating in and available to a specific embodied person. "Overself is the true inner self . . . reflecting the divine being and attributes. The Overself is an emanation from the ultimate reality but is neither a division nor a detached fragment of it. It is a ray shining forth but not the sun itself." PB, *Perspectives*, p. 296.

3. *Logos* is used here as an alternate term for the World-Idea, intelligence that is both universal and present in the individual.

4. See chapter fourteen of *The Wisdom of the Overself* for a detailed presentation of this very important "ultramystic exercise."

5. Anthony is using astrological symbolism. The planets at the moment of an individual's birth are said to be in their "natal" positions, which represent the ego structure of the individual. In their continuing movement from that moment onward, they are "transiting." See pages 158–163 of *Standing in Your Own Way*, by Anthony Damiani (Larson, 1993), for an explanation and development of this symbolism.

6. Here is the description of this ritual as it appears in PB's *Asiatic Notes* under the title "A Secret Rite with Atmananda":

> In the extreme southwest corner of India where the landscape is bordered by the Ghat Mountains on one side and the Indian Ocean with white and black sands on the other, there is a town with the pleasant sounding name of Trivandrum. Palm trees grow thickly in the area around here with their small bananas and round coconuts. Winding inland lagoons stretch out into the interior country giving, with the sands and fronds, a South Sea-like aspect. Here I came, past the characteristic white wall red-striped temples, to a pre-arranged meeting with Shri Krishna Menon,

otherwise called by his spiritual name of Atmananda. Escaping the sultry afternoon and beginning to feel the exhilaration of a mild breeze from the sea I reached and entered a long, brown compound, fenced with trees, quiet, adjoining a one-storied house. The guru received me in the upper apartment. We creatures dwelling in time, talked of the Timeless.

He allowed me, not at my request but at his invitation, to participate in a rite which was performed only once a year, as a *darshan,* or grace, in which he played the principal role. It was a secret one and none were present save certain disciples. It was a musical, symbolic slow dance where each step was taken as an accompaniment to some mysterious rhythm of his own consciousness, which seemed to be plunged in a half trance. He moved forward in rhythmic steps, then fell back a somewhat lesser distance: Each step, each gesture of the hands, the pose of the head, all movements were made to harmonize in measured rhythm with the handbeats on a small tabla-drum, the shrill accompaniment of a flute, and the twang of a zither. In this way he made a very slow progress in the ceremonial and liturgical dance. Motion and sound seemed to be moving by degrees toward some ultimate emotional event, thus creating a pleasant tension and arousing an exciting expectancy.

The strange gripping emotion of the classical music, the Master's solemn exquisitely rhythmic movements now forwards and now backwards, the intense blackness of the night, the encircling tall palm trees which themselves encircled us, the hushed air of expectancy and gravity which pervaded the little group of disciples—all created an eerie impression at first but a higher one succeeded it. I knew what the participants in the ancient Greek mysteries must have felt.

(See also chapter two, paras 492–495, of *The Orient: Its Legacy to the West,* volume ten in the *Notebooks* series.—ed.)

7. Anthony here begins another astrological analogy: The 360 degrees of the zodiac symbolize/comprise the totality of the mind's possible ideas, and the planets symbolize the various powers the mind has to express and manifest them. These powers are here equated with the individualized functions of the psyche. Having a planet on (or

aspecting) a degree means that the psychic function represented by the planet has access to the idea represented by the degree, and unfolds its meaning in/as the life of the individual.

8. In the astrological analogy, this "set pattern" is represented by the natal chart, i.e., the positions of the planets at the moment of birth. Anthony also calls it "the ego."

9. Anthony represents the "three functions" of knowing, feeling, and willing astrologically as Uranus, Neptune, and Pluto. The seven Chaldean planets are the Sun, Moon, Mercury, Venus, Mars, Jupiter, and Saturn.

10. Anthony used the following diagram to illustrate astrologically the embodied and disembodied/unembodied psyche.

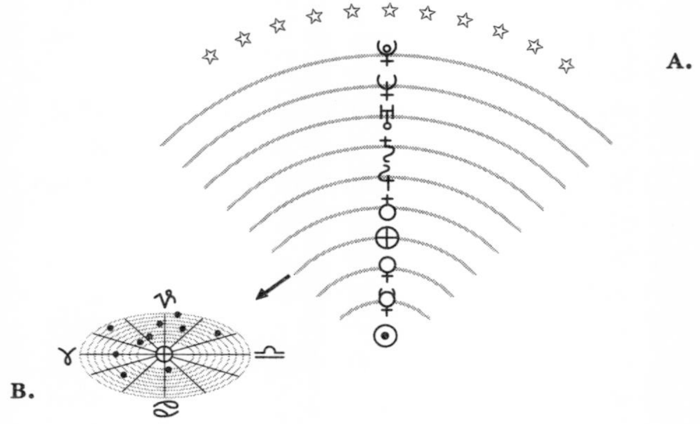

A. The sidereal zodiac and the sun-centered view/experience of the planetary spheres = the unembodied/disembodied psyche.

B. The tropical (geocentric) zodiac and earth-centered view/ experience of the planetary spheres = the embodied psyche.

The light of the soul is fully present in both situations, despite illuminating vastly different conditions.

3

Enlightenment

INSIGHT, INTUITION, AND PSYCHE

> "INTUITION" had come to lose its pristine value for me. I cast about for a better one and found it in "insight." This term I assigned to the highest knowing-faculty of sages and was thus able to treat the term "intuition" as something inferior which was sometimes amazingly correct but not infrequently hopelessly wrong in its guidance, reports, or premonition. I further endeavoured to state what the old Asiatic sages had long ago stated, that it was possible to unfold a faculty of direct insight into the nature of the Overself, into the supreme reality of the universe, that this was the highest kind of intuition possible to man, and that it did not concern itself with lesser revelations, such as giving the name of a horse likely to win tomorrow's race, a revelation which the kind of intuition we hear so much about is sometimes able to do.
>
> (v13, 20:4.152 and *Perspectives,* p. 276)

S: I thought the experience of intuition itself was outside the psyche.

ANTHONY: It's not outside the psyche. It's outside the psycho-somatic organism.

The intellect manipulates the memorized modifications of

bodily functioning. I'm using the language as precisely as I can. If we speak about the intellect as that biological communication that can take place within the psycho-somatic organism, and which has a propensity to retain its experiences, organize and classify them, and so on, that's intellect the way it is used in contemporary language. The intellect can be preoccupied with a problem that you cannot resolve. Then we speak about some intuition arising within the intellect and pointing out to combine things in such-and-such a way, and the discovery is made, or some invention comes forth.

But we can say this much: Intuition deals with and is within the domain of relativities. I think we feel pretty sure about that. It's always *of* something. I get an intuition to do something, or I get an intuition of an idea, or an intuition of a feeling that should be the underlie of a certain experience.

MB: Anthony, would intuition sometimes be false because it is concerned with the realm of manifestation, which is indefinite, in flux, and so forth?

ANTHONY: Yes, it's concerned with the realm of relativity. In the realm of relativity there's a confluence of the forces, you might say, that are operative in the universe: on the one hand Providence and on the other hand Necessity. And intuition is concerned about those two being intermingled.

MB: So even a perfectly developed intuition, if there is such a thing—

ANTHONY: —could be wrong. If you remember, Plotinus pointed out that not even the sage can distinguish sometimes between what is Providential and what is Necessity [see *Ennead* III.3.6]. So that if you look at things from the point of view of Providence, they're predictable to some extent, because it's a flowing out of reason principles in a certain ordered manner. But Necessity very often impinges on that, and the consequence is that there could be some disorder, and so intuition would falter, would be misleading.

Let's go a little further, then. It seems that the intuition has to do with the coordination between the cosmic circuit—the World-Idea—and the individual psyche's response to it. You have the World-Idea—with the entire potential of all circumstances, situations, events, bits and pieces of knowledge that can be brought together or not—and you have a reasoning about that World-Idea on the part of an individual. And intuition very often attempts to coordinate the state of knowledge within the individual and the so-called World-Idea. Whether it is correct or incorrect is something that only reason will be able to demonstrate.

Now notice the distinction. There are two different levels or frameworks being used. On the one hand you have the Cosmic Idea and on the other hand the individual's relationship to that idea and how it is understood. Up to a certain point the intellect is adequate, but then, after that point, intuition has to be brought in to get deeper and deeper into this understanding of the World-Idea. So intuition will always be about relativity—something in the domain of the relative: the coordination of the knowledge that the individual soul or the Witness I has concerning something of the World-Idea.

But insight is not that kind of knowledge, not a knowledge of relativity. Insight would be the soul understanding itself. It's not something outside or external to itself, the World-Idea which is imposed upon it, but soul understanding its own nature. That would be insight. So you can see that they're qualitatively different. Insight is reality understanding itself. And if we say soul is "life," it's axiomatic to say it would understand itself—in a way that's peculiar to itself, and we can't imagine. Being a reality, it would also have to include knowing itself. So that's where I use the phrase "knowing knows itself," and then I restrict it: "knowing knowing." But intuition, as you can see, is like the soul now externalizing, trying to understand something which is not itself: the World-Idea. And the correlation or coordination between these two is where intuition is functioning.

s: Is intuition a faculty found within the ego?

ANTHONY: I think it works both ways. It's a faculty we develop of learning, after we've exhausted all our efforts to understand something, to be able to keep still so that the World-Idea itself can try to influence us or suggest something. For instance, we've studied some astrological charts where we know a person has exhausted every possible resource to understand something, and then tries to give up the problem, and on an auspicious occasion a good aspect shows up and it's as if the universe is trying to inform this person. The planets aspecting each other are trying to inform that person. So you can see that this would be in the domain of relativity, whereas the other is not at all.

In one case, for instance, Einstein had a transit to his Saturn/Mercury, and the intuition came in of relativity. It was as if the World-Idea was trying to inform the soul of something about the way *it* works, and he had a receptivity to receive it and then to work it out with the equipment that his ego had.[1]

S: Insight is the highest form of intuition?

ANTHONY: I don't think it's intuition at all. I think that in our language, in English, the highest form of knowledge was always considered by philosophers to be intution. So even when Plato speaks about intuiting the ideas, you think that he's referring to intuition (as we use the word). But in the seventh Epistle, he speaks very clearly about the spark that bursts into a flame and consumes itself; he's speaking there about insight, not intuition. And he even makes the remark, "I have never written about it, nor will I ever write about it," because insight is a faculty that's almost impossible to understand.

But you see the distinction there? Insight is like reality understanding itself, and when I say reality here, I mean the soul understanding itself. It is a knowing knowing. But then when we speak about intuition we're speaking about how the soul is relating to the World-Idea, trying to understand it. So that there is sense intuition, and then there is intuition of one's own Self, or knowing that I am, the way the Buddhists speak about it. And then they speak about intuitive knowing, which means a direct access, a kind of intuition, is given to the individual to know what the nature of that object is. So, you see, the intuition will always be about the domain of relativity.

And if you go through all the philosophers—Hegel, Aristotle, or whoever—outside of Plotinus and Plato, I don't think you're going to find indications that there is such a thing as the higher form of knowing, insight. Even when Hegel uses "intuition," it's still in the domain of relativity.

> THE FINITE MINDS which are the offspring of the One Mind may not hope to rise in power or understanding to its altitude. Nevertheless, because they are inseparable from it, they may find hints of both these attributes within themselves. The Divine Essence is undiscoverable by human sense and intellect but not by human intuition and insight.
> (v16, 25:1.112)

DB: Would insight be the higher faculty used to understand the Overself unfolding the entirety of the World-Mind and all the powers that it has?

ANTHONY: What you're saying is correct. Insight refers to the faculty of recognizing the substratum, so that with insight you would see that consciousness underlies this object and that object and the third object. So insight is insight into the ultimate Reality that you are searching for.

Intuition is the *reasoning* about the objects. It involves an absolute or, we could say, a highly developed willing, feeling, and knowing. Because any of these three, if they're highly developed, tend to be of the nature of intuition, that is, a stillness, a stopping, a silence. You know something, but not anything in particular.

Insight gives you the understanding or the actual perception, the mystical perception, that water is common to both the ocean and the waves. When we speak about insight, we're speaking about the fact of the recognition of what the perceiver and the perceived have for their substratum consciousness.

That's insight. But intuition is reasoning upon objects to understand the nature of the reason principles. Now PB says that with these two faculties you can find within yourself those attributes which are also reflections from the Intellectual-Principle. In order to understand something about the World-Idea which is within your soul, these two faculties of insight and intuition are necessary.

VM: That union—

ANTHONY: —is with your own higher self. There's no talk about ego here. You couldn't possibly have insight and have ego.

VM: Is it a lapsing of the I AM into its own self-knowing phase?

ANTHONY: I wouldn't say it's a lapsing. That is what you mean by the I AM. How could the I AM lapse? It has two aspects: One is self-knowing and the other is other-knowing. Knowing-knowing and knowing-the-other.

So the two faculties that we need in order to realize the attributes of the World-Mind within us are insight and intuition. Insight is the nature, the perception, of reality. When you attain insight, you know that the underlying reality of that object is consciousness, or Mind, the same way that you know that it is your reality, and there is no distinction between them because there is no relationship here. So to take an analogy, when you recognize—or know—that the waves and the ocean are water, that's nondual. There are no two things. There's only *water.* That's insight.

Now intuition is the *reasoning* employed on any object in manifestation. You employ the reasoning—and you can call it intuition; PB calls it intuition, but I'm trying to expand it because if feeling is developed to the utmost, and willing and knowing, it is intuitive. It doesn't operate like we know it in the separative intellect. Now, with that faculty of intuition, you can intuit what the reason principle is that underlies this particular object, and at the same time you have insight and recognize that consciousness is the substratum of all objects.

If you work with only insight, then there isn't knowing *of* anything. There's *nothing* to know anything about. But that's not the situation. The situation is the same for the sage as for us, in the sense that there's not only a substratum of reality that underlies the appearance, but there's also the appearance which will persist. Now you want to know something about that appearance, so you have to employ the reason.

The soul has these two faculties. When it wants to know or at least understand something about the World-Idea which is within it, then it has to use these two faculties. It *cannot use opinion* [in the Platonic sense, i.e. *doxa,* the doxastic intellect —ed.]. It cannot use the separative intellect, egoistic understanding, any kind of imagery. That's all out.

Insight is the mind perceiving itself. Intuition is always *of* something. One we can refer to as the Higher Knower and the other as the Lower Knower. But they're not really meant as a hierarchy. I think it's better to think of them as two aspects of the soul.

LC: Is the higher knower the essence of soul?

ANTHONY: Essence of Soul is Soul. We come up with this definition of Soul—what makes it to be what it is—that's its essence.

S: How would you describe the insight of a sage?

ANTHONY: When the sage operates with insight, when the I AM has insight, it means that the ultimate reality, the substratum of the apparent world, is recognized to be Mind, consciousness, whatever word you want to use. This insight is in two directions: on the one hand, to its prior, the Intellectual-Principle from which it descends and where it has its source, and, on the other hand, into its content. That's what insight is. It works both ways. Insight is the recognition that Mind is the ultimate reality whether you face up to the transcendent source of your being or face down and look at the substratum of the manifested world within you. Either way, you will see that Mind is the substratum. That's insight. There is *no variation.*

Intuition can be applied to the lower phase. You can intuit, in the manifestations that are taking place within this I AM, the reason principles that constituted that object and made it to be what it is. Intuition into the higher realm doesn't work. But intuition will be necessary to formulate what insight is. You would have to use an intuitive approach to language to formulate the sentences in a certain way to give a person an understanding.

JFL: What is meant by insight into the World-Idea?

ANTHONY: Insight, as we said, is seeing into the substratum of the World-Idea. When the commentators say that the sage sees only Brahman, that's not true. The sage also sees the world. What they mean when they say that the sage sees Brahman is that the sage has insight; the sage recognizes that Mind or consciousness is the substratum. To say that if you are a sage, you don't eat your food, is absurd. The sage *also* sees the food, and eats it.

So these two faculties are necessary in order for the soul to understand itself.

VM: Can we talk about the "finite minds" in the quote?

ANTHONY: In terms of a comparison to the Intellectual, they're finite. I think PB is being drastic, but nonetheless to the point, so that no one would dare make the comparison that the finite mind could become identical with the Infinite Mind. He makes the gap uncrossable; finite mind and Infinite Mind—you can't jump that. There's no way you're going to get over the hurdle.

INSIGHT AND MANIFESTATION

> THE REAL is wholly nothing to the five senses and wholly unthinkable to the human intellect. Therefore and to this extent only it is also called the Unknowable. But there is a faculty latent in man which is subtler than the senses, more penetrative than the intellect. If he succeeds in evoking it, the Real, the unknowable, will then come within the range of his perception, knowledge, and experience.
>
> (v16, 25:1.114)

ANTHONY: When you have insight it doesn't stop the senses from functioning or the mind from thinking, the intellect having thoughts. But you very clearly see that the substratum of both of these is the Real. It isn't a manifestation in the sense of an efflux of the Real: You wouldn't see that. But you can see very clearly that the intellect cannot think this Reality and the senses cannot perceive this Reality, even while your insight perceives it. The word "perception" here is misleading, because it's not a triple relationship; the Mind perceiving itself as the substratum of Reality is not a triple relationship. But that doesn't stop the intellect and senses from operating.

S: In what sense would you say that it's not a manifestation or an efflux?

ANTHONY: That you don't *see.*

You don't see the appearance arising out of consciousness. You're going to have to work that out through hard dialectic and reasoning and understanding. It's not a perceptible fact, even when you have insight going on. When the faculty of insight is developed or functioning, you recognize that consciousness is the Reality, the substratum. In that act, there isn't the realization or the perception of the appearance arising out of consciousness. They're both simultaneous. With the senses and with the intellect you see the apparent-world, and with the faculty of insight you see that consciousness is the substratum. But you don't see it arise out of that. The literature leads you to think that that's what happens—that you have the ocean and a mist arising out of it, and the mist is the apparent world. That's not the way insight operates. Insight is, as we said, an intrinsic self-awareness.

S: PB says that every thought that arises is none other than Mind, none other than Reality.

ANTHONY: Very clearly. I remember that, and that's what I'm referring to. In other words, he says that you have to understand that thoughts arise from the mind; you have to bring the intellect and the intuition to operate on that—that all this arises from the mind, comes from the mind. You're not going to see it.

S: Then how is the philosopher's insight different from the mystic's?

ANTHONY: The philosopher has brought to bear all personal understanding and reasoning and intuition on the fact that the world appearance arises from consciousness. It's a process that you come to, reason out, and understand.

S: Doesn't that reasoning transform the experience?

ANTHONY: Yes, that too. Isn't something similar happening here, or with us—that through our reasoning we recognize that the process of manifestation involves all these steps and that the ultimate thing is consciousness from which all this is manifesting? You don't see the process. It's not supposed to end in just reasoning about it, but it has a transformative value if it's insistently concentrated on. But remember, when all is said and done, you've got to apply it. I'm trying to stop you from evoking fairy tales: "It's going to happen." You're going to *make* it happen.

S: If there had been no philosophic preparation, you would see consciousness as the substratum of everything, but you would not understand how the appearance was connected with it?

ANTHONY: If you're unprepared, of course. Do you think you were born with a golden spoon in your mouth? Why do you think we've gone through all this work, because we have nothing better to do? If that experience brought complete understanding, then why all these schools, why all these teachers, why this use of breath? All you would need is the enlightening experience, and all the understanding would be there too!

S: What is the difference between the mystic and the philosopher?

ANTHONY: The philosopher has prepared the personal self for this, made preparations to understand it; the mystic hasn't, so the mystic goes around saying everything is consciousness. Everything is not consciousness, because the tiger will still bite you.

S: Just because it bites you doesn't mean it's not consciousness.

ANTHONY: You'll feel pain. It's a sure enough negation of consciousness, or—let me be more accurate—it's a sure negation of Self. But the point we want to get here is that with that experience does not necessarily come the understanding. You don't get a certificate saying, "Now you understand the doctrine of mentalism." Do you think they went to all this trouble to develop the brain so that you could put it aside?

So we can reword this sentence a little bit differently. We can say that when insight is operative, the person recognizes that consciousness is the substratum of the world. This person also will recognize that one cannot see that, and one cannot think it. There's insight, there's consciousness. That's all there is in front of you, all right? But your eyes go on seeing the table, and you see that your thoughts can't *think* that Reality.

SS: Is insight an aspect of your own higher self?

ANTHONY: When you reach the higher self, it's the same as reaching insight. You can see both ways: You can become aware of the source of Reality or the substratum that underlies your own being, which would be the Void Mind, and you can also see the reality that is the substratum for the world that you perceive.

AH: Is that awareness positive knowledge of the way things are ultimately, or is it established by default?

ANTHONY: I think the most that the mystics can say is that "It is." It's not knowledge by default; it is the most authentic kind of knowledge one can have. As a matter of fact, it's often referred to as "*pure knowledge*."

AH: Is it anything like the knowledge that we usually have?

ANTHONY: No. In absolutely pure knowledge in the One itself even the logical distinction that exists in the Intellectual-Principle between the Object and the Idea is abolished. We'd be wasting our breath to come back and try to explain that kind of knowledge. Plotinus attempts it and, in certain cases, I think more than anyone else I know of, succeeds in portraying that.

RC: There the fundamental difficulty is that you're not even Soul. Yet it can be spoken about as a knowing state, and what the knowing state is knowing is—

ANTHONY: —Itself; and its knowing is not distinct from Itself. That's what they mean by pure knowledge. Even in the Intellectual there *is* some residue between the Object-in-the-Intelligible and the Object. But in the One itself even that distinction is completely abolished. If the soul has the experience of that, the soul has to be left behind.

> NEITHER THE senses nor the intellect can tell us anything about the intrinsic nature of this Infinite Mind. Nevertheless we are not left in total ignorance about it. From its manifestation, the cosmos, we may catch a hint of its Intelligence. From its emanation, the soul, we may catch more than a hint of its Beneficence. "More than," I say, because the emanation may be felt within us as our very being whereas the manifestation is outside us and is apart.
>
> (v16, 28:2.97 and *Perspectives*, p. 383)

S: What does it mean that we have hints about the World-Mind in manifestation?

ANTHONY: The scientists are giving us an idea of the scope and the depth, the immeasurable aspects of this Intelligence. We haven't even scratched the surface. But it's enough to show that there's this immense wisdom that's overwhelming, that human intelligence is incapable of grasping. But still the universe is a manifestation of that Intelligence, even if it's only a partial manifestation.

S: Would you say something about how we get to know the World-Idea?

ANTHONY: You need both intuition and insight. We've spoken of the intuition as being basically the three modes of absolute willing, feeling, and knowing. We can call all three of them intuition, because they all operate silently. When you have a real intuition, when you have a real knowing about something, or a real aesthetic appreciation about something, it will be silent; it will be absolutely calm. And even when the utmost exertion of will is going to take place, the first apprehension of it is going to be an absolute calmness. And all three can be referred to as intuition. So they're going to be needed as well as insight.

S: What does PB mean by "the emanation may be felt within us"?

ANTHONY: One of the feelings that arises when insight occurs is an utmost friendliness. PB uses the word beneficence. It's like all of a sudden you're in your mother's arms. Here all the time you thought it was something out there.

If there is an act of insight, even if it's momentary, there's a radiation from it of absolute beneficence—that you've always been in the care of this; you've never left. Whereas the development of the feeling function is quite different. It doesn't necessarily have to bring you the feeling of kindness; it could bring a lot of other kinds of feelings. But this friendliness is always there. You're at home. In fact, they call it home.

> INSIGHT IS the function of the entire psyche and not of any single part of it.
>
> (v13, 20:4.184 and *Perspectives*, p. 276)

ANTHONY: Insight is the function of life entire.

S: We've spoken of insight becoming available only after the psyche's functions have been developed.

ANTHONY: But do you think life will have to wait until all the functions of the psyche are developed for it to understand itself? Do you think that life—and we're not speaking about parts of life; we're speaking about life in its entirety—has to wait for the psychic functions to get developed for it to know what it is doing? If you stay with the quote, PB says it's a function of life entire or the psyche entire.

S: By entire you mean—

ANTHONY: —undivided.

S: By "part" does he mean my life?

ANTHONY: My life or any functions of the life as parts. The undivided life, which is the same as universal being, understands or perceives or knows what it is doing. The knowing here is not something external to what it is doing.

It's there all the time. It's not a product of a process. Do you think life has to figure out what the next step in the evolution of a person's growth is and lay out a plan of attack and see to it that these things happen? Do you think that life entire works in the fashion of deliberation or discursive reasoning?

He says that insight is the function of the entire psyche or the entirety of life. If you follow up the thread that life is undivided, an entirety—and we say that it knows what it is doing, intrinsically—then what kind of knowing could that possibly be?

S: Well, it's not going to be the kind of understanding we have here. Would it be a knowing by identity?

ANTHONY: Yes, it would be a knowing by identity.

S: When PB says "the function of the entire psyche," that's harder to understand than when you say "the function of life."

ANTHONY: When we say "life" instead of saying "psyche," then it immediately takes on the characteristics that belong to it, such as universality. Life is universal, universal being, and life understands itself without the use or the need of any intermediaries. It doesn't need eyes, nose, doesn't need reason, doesn't need any of these accessories.

Now the kind of understanding life has of itself is what he's calling insight, and this is the function of life *per se.*

S: Are you saying the World-Idea is self-cognitive?

ANTHONY: I'm not saying the World-Idea is self-cognitive. I'm saying *life* is self-cognitive.

S: Could you explain the relationship between psyche and life?

ANTHONY: I'm using them synonymously. Psyche and life mean the same thing.

S: But my psyche isn't universal.

ANTHONY: I didn't say your psyche is universal. I said your psyche is life. You're speaking about the fact that your psychic functions are not universal.

S: How do I distinguish my psychic functions from my psyche?

ANTHONY: Dissolve them back into their origin.

But what do you mean, your psyche isn't universal? First of all, is it your life? He's not speaking there about my life or your life, your understanding or mine; he's speaking about life in its universality, its entirety. He said that insight is the function of the entire psyche; I just changed one word, "psyche." I used the word "life."

S: Doesn't that imply that I have to universalize my psyche in order to function as insight?

ANTHONY: It doesn't imply anything of the sort. Not that one quote.

S: I thought you were saying that life is already universal.

ANTHONY: Yes, and that life already has intrinsic self-cognition, and that the way life understands itself is through insight.

What does psyche mean?

S: Soul.

ANTHONY: Soul? What does soul mean? Don't you mean life?

S: I think of life as the manifestation.

ANTHONY: No, life isn't the manifestation. What you see is a manifestation of life, but life you can't see. You see its manifestations, but life itself is indivisible in its core. It's an infinite power—you don't *see* that.

Remember those quotes from Plotinus about what soul is, what life is? It is a power infinite to the core; it remains indivisible no matter how often it gets divided; and it has this indivisibility from its prior. We ran through passages from *The Enneads* where I told people, "Memorize these. Write them out on a card, put them over your bed, and when you go to sleep at night, reread them. Keep doing that every night. Fall asleep with that." You think I give you homework for no reason at all?[2]

The individual who has insight is participating in the

knowledge that the soul has of itself. So let's return to the quotation. Life always has insight. Insight is intrinsic to life.

S: Does insight transcend the psyche?

ANTHONY: If you use the word psyche, you're going to get confused. What transcends life? If you use the word life or soul, if you say that soul has a basic insight into its own nature, then it would be more difficult to make this kind of an error of thinking that when you get insight you're going to transcend life or transcend the psyche. The insight is *into* the psyche and *of* the psyche and *by* the psyche. It's life understanding *itself*; not something outside, but itself. So how could it transcend itself? If you use the word "transcend," you'll get confused. You'll think that you're going to go beyond life and understand by looking down at life what the life is about. But the understanding that is being offered by life is in terms of life itself and *is* life itself.

Life is a universal concept, but people have the notion that it's restricted only to what they understand as life: this amoeba crawling around or this grub or this human being walking around. But life is universal in its sweep. It permeates the entire universe and makes the universe possible. It oozes out the universe from within itself. So why speak about transcending it?

S: I was speaking about transcending psychic functioning.

ANTHONY: Oh, okay. That's different, because the psychic functioning is very restricted, isn't it? It's very specialized. Let's say we could even confine it to the instincts that a person has to work with. You say, "Well, life is operating or manifesting itself through the instincts." So in that sense, immediately, the kind of understanding that the life of a person has through the instincts is going to be restricted, confined by that instinctual functioning. But when we speak about life in its entirety understanding itself, it has to transcend all of those restrictive modes or ways of being, in the same way that PB speaks about the fusion of these three: the willing, feeling, and knowing. He points out that knowledge utterly transcends those functions. It is a perception, if I could use this awkward phrase, of life itself, life perceiving itself without the use of any intermediaries at all. But through its own living, life perceives itself. This, of course, transcends all psychic functions and cannot be restricted by any specialized mode of knowing.

S: And even knowing, willing, and feeling are specific and restrictive psychic functions?

ANTHONY: Yes. They're modalizations of its universality. Any modalization of universal life immediately implies a restrictive mode of being. That means it's being singularized or manifested or particularized, and therefore you're speaking about some entity.

S: If you wanted to symbolize the psyche or life, would you say that it extends to the sidereal zodiac?

ANTHONY: Well, from what you understand of life itself, where would you say the origin of life is? If we speak about an origin in our twentieth century contemporary mode, where would you say it came from?

S: The sun.

ANTHONY: I would, too. We speak about the sun as that infinite light and life, and that life has its own mode of understanding which is being referred to here as insight. Eastern philosophy would refer to it as *prajna.* It has its own understanding, intrinsic to itself.

> HE WHO possesses insight does not have to use arguments and reach conclusions. The truth is there, self-evident, inside himself as himself, for his inner being has become one with it.
>
> (v13, 20:4.170 and *Perspectives,* p. 276)

ANTHONY: The question is, how does the inner being become one with insight. What do we mean by "inner being"? What does PB mean when he says "inner being"?

S: Is that inner being the same as the principle of consciousness?

ANTHONY: The question is precisely that: How do I become that principle, considering the way I am?

S: You can't become it.

ANTHONY: Why not?

S: Because you already are it.

ANTHONY: No. I don't feel that I am it and I don't know it either. If I am not the truth, and don't feel that I am and I don't know that I am the truth, what can I do about it? Evidently, the inner being the way it is now is not one with the truth. So what do I do about it in order to become one with that truth?

S: I would say try to get deeper into that inner being.

ANTHONY: Try to get deeper into that inner being? That guy who's full of lies, fairy tales, illusions? Get rid of it! Get rid of that inner being, and you'll be one with the truth.

S: It's not that easy! You start out with little bits at a time.

ANTHONY: Yes, that's the process that is involved. You disidentify or dismiss that inner being that you think you are so that you can be one with what you really are.

PB always uses words in the sense of their meaning today, not the sense that they might mean in any specialized jargon. When you say your "inner being," what do you think you're going to think of? You're going to think of that congeries of feelings, thoughts, memories—all these things that pass through your mind. This is what you refer to as your inner being.

S: PB means that, rather than the evolving power of understanding?

ANTHONY: Yes, I think he means that inner being, all this stuff that's like a seething cauldron. If I think about myself as that inner being, how *do* I make myself one with the truth?

S: By recognizing that the truth is within you and that you aren't all those other things that you're identified with.

ANTHONY: So what's involved?

S: Purifying yourself of those things in order to recognize the truth within you.

ANTHONY: What do you mean when you say "purifying"?

S: Recognizing your identification with . . .

ANTHONY: That's not purifying. If I recognize my soul, that's not purification of my inner being.

s: Changing your habits.

ANTHONY: Yes, and even more precisely, wouldn't you say that by dismissing all those notions about your inner being you'll become one with your soul?

s: But it seems that you're saying the inner being can never become one with the soul.

ANTHONY: You're catching on!

s: Any experience endowed with the personal self-form is not the truth, and it has to be removed from the field of consciousness.

ANTHONY: And then that leaves you with your real inner being, your true inner "I." In other words, you have to dismiss all these vagaries, fantasies, thoughts, memories, selections from your past, anticipations of your future, expectations—you want me to go down the list? You have to remove all that in order to identify with it. Or, in other words, you stop thinking. Now I'm sure after this you'll think much more!

When there is no more thinking, concept forming, which is concerned with creating an artificial object—whether your inner self or your outer self doesn't matter—then the inwardness or the principle that you are, which is illuminating or shining in you, is what you really are. That is, so to speak, always there. But you're not aware of it because you're preoccupied with the images, not with the light which is illuminating those images. If you could temporarily stop those images, then there would be just a light shining, and you would know that "this is what I am." Then the images resume. Now it is possible for the images to go on and to still hold an identity with the light which illuminates the images, and then one could say, "I'm identified with that light and not with the images."

But the point is that the concept-making mind, always producing these concepts and images, is in a sense reifying an object constantly, and that prevents identification with what you really are. Now, the sage does not think, and that's why the sage is in identity with the light. And when you sleep you're not thinking, and you're very happy, but you don't know it.

S: The sage doesn't think, but knows by being?

ANTHONY: Why not both? The sage can think, when necessary. The sage is enlightened because the sage's being and knowing are, so to speak, identical. But suppose the sage has to think and knows, "Well, now I'm thinking. I'm using concepts. Can I say I'm enlightened, that this is what they mean when they say I'm enlightened?" Could the sage formulate that? Sure. Why not?

S: The sage could formulate something from the perspective of thought that would refer to this enlightenment, but—

ANTHONY: The sage wouldn't confuse them.

S: What principle confuses itself with the inner being the way you define it?

ANTHONY: If we speak about this life and light which is imparted by the soul to the psycho-somatic organism and then identifies with that psycho-somatic organism and uses a reasoning which is based on sense perception, which belongs to the organism itself, then of course confusion and misidentification will take place, and the "I" will think of itself as being these images, memories, and so on.

The most direct way to get to this "I," or this life and light imparted to the psycho-somatic organism, is by a process of disidentifying from the images. And this process of disidentification from the images results eventually in isolating the light from the psycho-somatic organism and then recognizing that this is what it is, that this is the "I" that I'm referring to.

When you say "I," the "I-ness" is referring to a plane that's other than that of the psycho-somatic organism but confounded with that plane of the psycho-somatic organism. So what is required, the way it was put, is to purify our inner being. Purification here means to dismiss the thoughts, and all their cousins and nephews and everything that comes with them, to dismiss them. And this is a long process; you don't disidentify from your thinking overnight. It's a long process that takes many years. It's gradual. But eventually there is a reduction in the amount of thinking that takes place, and the possibility of that life understanding itself to be that light which illuminates all these images becomes more available.

When you throw the sense functioning out of gear so that there's only this life, even temporarily, for a moment, you recognize that life to be "I." "That's me." The recognition here is through identity. It's not a discursive kind. When that is over, it reidentifies all over again with the psycho-somatic organism. You can see how that purity of what you felt to be your "I" is now lost, and it again is mixed up and confused with the functioning that is going on in the psycho-somatic organism.

S: So the higher self can be present to this I?

ANTHONY: Actually present, yes. So if you could maintain this state of thought-free consciousness, there wouldn't be any doubt as to what you mean when you say "I." Whereas, insofar as there is a continuing stream of contents in your consciousness, there is that confusion. One will always think of those contents, and of course the main content is the body thought.

S: If fundamentally, in the totality of what we say is the soul, you are this life which is always insightful, then how can it be obscured by a light that it projects forth?

ANTHONY: Ah. If you bring these two quotations together, you're going to have difficulty. The previous quotation did not refer to individual life. That quotation said that the function of insight belongs to the psyche entire. Now put brackets around that and stop right there. Life entire. Did PB say your life or my life or anyone's life? He just said life entire. So, in other words, what he's saying is: One of life's functions, one of the ways that this principle of life can be intrinsically recognized—the mark of life as a universal principle—is that it has self-cognition. That's a philosophic statement. That's got nothing to do with your personality, mine, or anyone else's. It's characterizing or trying to pick out the key feature that belongs to a universal.

You're not speaking about this life or that life or a soul; you're speaking about Absolute Soul. When you speak about Absolute Soul, it's not the soul of anything. But as soon as you start speaking about life in the sense that it's in manifestation, then you're speaking about either the soul of the cosmos or the soul of this plant, this animal, whatever. You're speaking about a unit soul. And if you have a unit soul, the World-Idea is inevitably associated with it; it has to be. There isn't an undetermined life anywhere.

s: Is it cut-and-dried that thought and consciousness are distinct?

ANTHONY: Yes. They belong to two different realms of existence.

s: And whatever we symbolize in language is pointing towards that but is certainly not ever that.

ANTHONY: Yes. The bodily senses are perpetually manifesting an appearance. In other words, insofar as they function, appearances are taking place. Appearances are concomitant with what we call the world as we know it. And it is this that you manipulate. In other words, what you are manipulating are these images, whether they're very abstract images or very concrete images. Images of the light are not the light. So any formulation that is made in terms of images will always be an imitation, a semblance of that life, but never that life.

In other words, a symbolific activity that's going on tries to portray what that life is in its original, native state. It can't do so. It can only paint a picture; no one who understands confuses that picture with you.

So when a person speaks about an enlightenment we know that person is formulating in words that which escapes all formulation. But some indication has to be given to us that these things are there.

s: Is reason segregated from that?

ANTHONY: Embodied reason, yes, is segregated. So most of us, when we reason—if we examine very carefully the reasoning process, the words that we are using or the thoughts that we are employing—we'll see that behind it there is an image. It may be a very abstract image, but there's an image there. When even that is gone, then you're reasoning—but no longer the way we usually understand reasoning. That's a trance state, a contemplative state: no images, even the most abstract kind.

It's worth remembering this point, since you're preoccupied with it. We went through the evolution of the genetic mentality that takes place in any living creature, including the innumerable stages in the development of an animal body, and the fact that it had to learn to respond to an environment, and that it developed senses that provide it with indications of what that environment is, and that these memory traces of what the senses have delivered are stored, registered, classified, memorized, and that this is what you use when you try to communicate with someone. So they're really secondhand copies of what is already—*already,* try to understand—of a bodily sense.

S: But that wouldn't be reason.

ANTHONY: No, I didn't say that was reason. You manipulate these images when you reason. Reason manipulates these symbols to a certain end.

S: I thought reason was when you stopped manipulating the traces or the symbols.

ANTHONY: That is reason unembodied.

S: We did make the distinction between the processes of the intellect on the one hand and reason which is the manipulation of all those processes.

ANTHONY: Yes. In order for me to communicate some understanding of what the reasons are that I think something to be such and such, I have to manipulate these symbols or images which my intellect has stored up. And it doesn't deprive me of the use of the intellect, either.

S: When you try to communicate what your reason has brought to you, that's not the same as the reasoning process *per se.*

ANTHONY: The unembodied reason?

S: Yes.

ANTHONY: Well, they're not the same, but you remember there are passages in many of the texts which say that reason experiences itself differently when it gets embodied than when it was unembodied, but it's still the same reason.

S: When the sage formulates a doctrine about truth, are those same vehicles used?

ANTHONY: Yes.

S: The sage is not privy to some special vehicles?

ANTHONY: Well, the sage is also; that, too, is true. To a person who is sensitive enough, the sage can sometimes communicate directly, without the intermediary of these symbols. It depends on the sensitivity of the person. Sometimes a student will see a teacher, and the teacher gives the student a smile, and that's it; the student has got it. The rest of us have to spend twenty years with the teacher. I'd be careful as to what restrictions I'd place on a sage.

S: There seems to be a lot of controversy about what is scripture and what isn't.

ANTHONY: No, there's no controversy. It's only controversial for those people who don't understand. While you're in a stage of still trying to understand, there's a lot of controversy, pros and cons. When a person understands truly, there's no controversy. It's there in black and white. It's even better than black and white.

In a movie, if the light gets very, very intense, the picture is blurred out; then if the light is retracted somewhat you can see the images. So with the sage: When the sage is not thinking, there's just that bright light. There are images there, but the light just overwhelms them. Then the sage has to focus back to see the images again.

S: PB used to do that.

ANTHONY: All the time.

S: It was such an effort for him to start talking and thinking again, and you got the sense that his whole being was in that consciousness and he was using language and thinking very much like a tool. There was nothing automatic about his speech.

ANTHONY: Everything was always new for PB.

S: So when the sage is using words to convey meaning, that would be embodied reason, not intellect.

ANTHONY: Yes. I tend to use the word intellect more for the biological functioning.

S: And the biological functioning really can't reveal a reason principle.

ANTHONY: Well, remember what we pointed out. The intellect keeps thinking about something, trying to figure out something, spends years on it, and then all of a sudden there's an illuminating flash of light. That's the reasoning, putting together what the intellect can't understand. And, of course, the intellect will go on and say, "Well, look at what I've done." But it's basically the intuition coming from the reasoning that joins together certain strains of thought that seem disconnected, and you suddenly get an understanding of what that's about.

S: So when the sage uses words and concepts to convey meaning, it's the reason that's organizing those contents to reveal something, whereas the intellect can't do that.

ANTHONY: Oh yes. I don't think the intellect can be as precise.

> A MYSTIC experience is simply something which comes and goes, whereas philosophic insight, once established in a man, cannot possibly leave him. He understands the Truth and cannot lose this understanding any more than an adult can lose his adulthood and become an infant.
>
> (v13, 20:4.198 and *Perspectives,* p. 275)

ANTHONY: Notice the phrase "once established." Because you can have insight and lose it, and you can have it and lose it, and you can have it and lose it. But to establish it is a whole different ballgame. Basically once it is established there's no coming or going, whether you're awake or asleep or anything.

S: So what is that point where you can say "established"? Is that the final disassociation from identification with the ego?

ANTHONY: Yes. That definitely would be one of the characteristics. You will never regard yourself as body, although you know that you have a body, that you use a body, that it's a means. But you'll never identify with it.

And even if in the following incarnation you will yourself back into embodiment, it's only a short time before the recognition dawns on you who you were or what you really are. In the early years, the childhood years, the soul is basically preoccupied with the building up of what Plotinus called the Animate, the ego complex. Then as it reaches a certain level—I would say puberty—it can turn its attention to other things. But until then it has to be preoccupied with building up the Animate.[3]

s: It seems that in order for that to be established, the kind of balance that we were reading about would have to be attained. But PB also talks about that balance as being required in order for the insight to arise in the first place.

ANTHONY: Yes. You can see that you may have to spend a number of lives evolving your cognitive understanding—thinking, basically—also your feeling, and your will. And then you bring them into balance so that you can bring about their fusion. And the end product of that fusion is that a quality arises which PB calls insight, a quality utterly different from the willing, thinking, and feeling. The arisal of this quality is being conveyed to us as the result of a process in time. But, on the other hand, it is atemporal. Insight *per se* is atemporal and belongs to the universality of life. So when an individual life evolves sufficiently and fuses these three elements and insight arises, insight was always there. Insight isn't something that you created. You create the necessary equilibrium among all the psychic functions so that it can naturally arise within you.

For instance, a person might say, "Well, I had a *satori,* and in that moment I experienced eternity." Now eternity, of course, is an irradiation. In a sense it's right to say, "I experienced eternity," but it was only for that moment.

s: What is the distinction between mystical glimpses and glimpses of insight?

ANTHONY: Insight, as we said, is a very peculiar and unimaginable kind of knowledge—that is, that life has an intrinsic self-cognition. You might have a glimpse of the soul and be filled with rapture. This isn't necessarily knowledge that life has of its own being. In other words, there are a variety of glimpses. For instance, one could be listening to some beautiful music and get a glimpse of music. Again, this is a very modalized kind of understanding in comparision to the insight that life has into its own being.

S: What makes you lose a glimpse of insight?

ANTHONY: There could be many things, but basically we're not in a condition to hold it.

S: Why? Because of habits?

ANTHONY: Habits, attachments, etcetera: All the things that make us what we are. That's why it's necessary to go into a long, protracted philosophic discipline, to try to be independent from a certain way of functioning, to try to be more detailed and more practical.

If you have the experience of true devotion and adoration, you will always be aware of the Overself. But we're not always in that state of mind. We're more often preoccupied with adoring ourselves. So, if you get a glimpse, it doesn't cancel out the fact of this kind of self-love that we always have, and sooner or later it reasserts itself. The question is, how long can you prevent it from asserting itself? You'll find out; it's kind of limited.

S: How are psychic being and insight related to individuality?

ANTHONY: Wouldn't you say that the insight would provide you with the sense of not being separate from other persons, and that the psychic being that you are provides for the distinction from other persons? So, for instance, this is one of the things we try to bring out when we work in astrology class and try to read a person's chart and understand the psychic components that constitute that person. Let's say you do understand something about the way I'm psychically constituted, and I understand something about the way you're psychically constituted. And I try to work in harmony with the way you are, and you try to work in harmony with the way I am. But if either of us had insight, we would see that life is one and the same, that it is a universal life. We would also see that these psychical components of the personality provide the distinctions between us. So a sage acts in harmony with a person—knowing the basic constituents that make this person to be that person and not anyone else and working in harmony with these constituents. A sage can also work against them and confront them if necessary.

Think of the ocean up north where you have a variety of icebergs. Each has its own shape and form, but ultimately they're all nothing but water. So we could say that the psychic being that you are is a precipitation from that life, and each precipitation is a form that's unique. And the person established in insight can see that water underlies the icebergs, regardless of their shape, form, color, and all that. But nonetheless they are what they are in the sense that this is "A" and not "B," that there are differences.

S: The way I'm conceiving of this universal life is as entirely unappropriable, so that it wouldn't be proper to describe the contact with it as one's inner being.

ANTHONY: Well, theoretically, that's correct; but practically and methodically, it's wrong. Think of yourself as that universal life. Now, this is very peculiar, but the Christian Scientists or the New Thought people, they imagine or they conceive of that universal life as their personal property, and they very often unconsciously want something to happen by trying to employ this substratum that's at their disposal. But philosophically they're wrong. It isn't.

S: The language of "inner" and "outer" has to be one step lower than universal life.

ANTHONY: Yes, of course. But I think all of us recognize this much: that below the threshold of consciousness we operate with there is a life that is universal in its understanding. We speak about it as the subconscious, and it takes care of digestion, takes care of breathing, takes care of everything. Some people do employ this to bring about certain effects. Remember the young boys who had leukemia, and they employed mental imagery where the good guys were beating the bad guys, and the employment of this imagery brought about an improvement of their condition? We would refer to that as employing this knowledge; by concentrating on certain images we can bring about certain effects or help to bring them about. So when you consciously employ that imaging—you think of the good cells fighting the bad cells, and winning—you're employing that knowledge to bring about an improved condition in your own physical being.

s: It seems that the employment of the mind you're speaking about there, when applied to these revealed teachings, is the process of bringing one's inner being into alignment with the truth.

ANTHONY: Yes, to gradually bring your inner being to act in conformity with the rules or the laws that govern us. But remember, when we're speaking about the ultimate path, then we're speaking about dismissing even that.

> WHENEVER I have used the term "the centre of his being," I have referred to a state of meditation, to an experience which is felt at a certain stage. The very art of meditation is a drawing inwards and the finer, the more delicate, the subtler this indrawing becomes, the closer it is to this central point of consciousness. But from the point of view of philosophy, meditation and its experiences are not the ultimate goal—although they may help in preparing one for that goal. In that goal there is no kind of centre to be felt nor any circumference either—one is without being localized anywhere with reference to the body, one is both in the body and in the Overself. There is then no contradiction between the two.
>
> (v13, 20:4.136 and *Perspectives*, p. 276)

ANTHONY: When a person sits down to meditate and succeeds in intensifying their attention, it seems as though this concentration is going through their center. Think of all the radii of a circle converging to a point. And PB says this is the experience that comes from meditation. I would say basically what's happening is that the attention is being restricted or contracted to that point which we refer to as that part of the soul which has been projected; in other words, the re-embodying soul. That's one type of experience. There's another type of experience which goes further than that and takes you to the experience of your I AM, which is beyond the re-embodying soul.

So we could say something like this: when you constrict your attention to a point, and you experience the re-embodying soul, it's like a mystical experience, and we can call that consciousness just for the sake of discussion. And then there's something beyond that which we can call the Mind, the individual I AM. If you go beyond that re-embodying soul and reach that individual I AM, there is no reference to any center. You don't experience the gathering of all your forces and a plunging to a central point in your being. The I AM is an experience which is quite different.

Now the combination of these two—the experience of your center of being and the experience as just being—is what Plotinus referred to as the "We." And that's the philosophic experience: the experience of the I AM, which includes that part or power that the I AM has to project forth. So when we say that the I AM projects forth a part of itself or a power from itself, and this is the consciousness which gets embodied—that's one experience. The experience of the I AM, independent of that, is another. The two of them together is the experience of the soul as the "We" which contains both of them, and that's the philosophic experience.

s: Is the philosophic experience another state of meditation?

ANTHONY: That's more than meditation. That's meditation and philosophic understanding.

s: That's the state of a sage?

ANTHONY: Yes.

s: When you said that there's both the I AM alone and the I AM that projects forth the world—

ANTHONY: —the Witness I, if you want to use that term. The I AM, pure Mind, the individual unit Mind, projects forth from itself the Witness I. Now, the experience in meditation takes you into the center of your being; that's the Witness I. The experience of what's beyond it is the I AM. The two of them together is the "We." The experience of the "We" is the philosophic understanding of both, in the sense that on the one hand you can think of yourself as this body, and on the other hand, you can think of yourself as egoless being.

S: So that would be the state PB refers to when he says the attention is on the temporal moment in the foreground and the permanent "I" in the background.

ANTHONY: Yes, you could use that. This should help us to understand what Plotinus means when he says, "And the We? What are We?" Because that's a very difficult phrase in Plotinus, the nature of the "We": the I AM and the Witness I. The Witness I has the experience of the world and the World-Idea; the I AM doesn't. The two of them together give you the full understanding.

The last part of the quote refers to the Overself.

> [*rereads*] . . . In that goal there is no kind of centre to be felt nor any circumference either—one is without being localized anywhere with reference to the body, one is both in the body and in the Overself. There is then no contradiction between the two.

ANTHONY: For the sage there's the simultaneous function of being the Witness I and of also being that undifferentiated consciousness.

S: So the sage doesn't have anything to do with the World-Idea?

ANTHONY: *Per se,* but you have to hold the two of them together to grasp what PB is talking about, that the sage operates in this way. The two are together: the functioning of the Witness I, which can only be in relation to the World-Idea, and the I AM, which is not.

s: Is this a description of insight?

ANTHONY: This is an attempt to speak about philosophic understanding, that it has to include both: Philosophic understanding is understanding of the functioning of insight that the sage operates with, and also the understanding of the Witness I and its role in the world. It is a way of speaking about the soul as being the double knower, containing intrinsic self-cognition and also discursive reasoning and sense perception.

It is the Witness I which has the experience of the World-Idea. In order to have the experience of a world, the soul must project forth from itself a power, which Plotinus refers to as the projective power or the embodying soul. It is that which has the experience of the world.

Now, in order to get to the center of your being, to use PB's term, you sit down and meditate and draw your consciousness within; you inwardize it and deepen it. It is in the very nature of the mystical experience to be a passing thing: It passes, and the World-Idea resumes and comes back. It will keep coming back, and you can't stop it from coming back as long as you consider yourself to be the Witness I and identified with that. So it's paradoxical, but that's a statement of the truth, even for Plotinus. But the experience of the I AM shows it to be an egoless being, a being that, so to speak, is, and can be, without reference to an ego. And it is the combination of these two which will give us a true philosophic perspective and understanding. They're not contradictory, but they may be paradoxical.

s: So the mystic path leads to the Witness position?

ANTHONY: Yes. The mystic has to go further, but most of them stop there. That's why their efforts are frustrated, because you can have a glimpse for an hour, a day, a month. I knew someone to have it for six months, but it went. And then he was forced to recognize that the world was part of that functioning. Again and again PB points out that the only way really to transcend the World-Idea is by absorbing it, and you absorb it through philosophic understanding. But philosophic understanding requires that you understand the soul in this peculiar way: that it is egoless being, and, on the other hand, this egoless being can restrict itself and employ one of its powers to have experience of a world. If you remember all those passages in Plotinus about the "We," if you read them in the light of what I've just said, you'll see that your understanding of them will clear up automatically. [Reference is especially to *Ennead* I.1.7, MacKenna translation, Larson edition—ed.]

> WHERE we speak either metaphysically or meditationally of the experience of pure consciousness, we mean consciousness uncoloured by the ego.
>
> (v13, 20:4.188 and *Perspectives,* p. 278)

ANTHONY: We spoke about the psycho-somatic organism, and we said it was constituted of many different psychic functions, like the communicator, the evaluation function, this, that, and the other thing. One thing that we should also have heavily stressed is that it also has an emotive or emotional content which is very, very powerful. That will override the intellect almost any time. At any rate, in the experience of yourself as pure consciousness, emotion has to be completely removed, or let's say that in no way is the functioning of the emotive elements in the psyche or the psychic functions themselves operative at the time that you experience the glimpse. If they are in any way operative, no matter how slight they are, they will immediately obscure the glimpse to some extent. So if there's an element of emotion involved while you're having the glimpse, you're not going to have it in its purity. It's going to be colored; it's going to be contaminated, polluted, by this emotional element. If you've entered into the glimpse and there is a very strong thought that you are holding at that time, that too might color the glimpse.

S: So PB uses the word "ego" here to include any trace of the psycho-somatic functioning?

ANTHONY: Yes. But don't forget the emotive, because that's really more often the intruder. The emotive is more often an intruder than even the psychic functions. It's much more primitive. To still that, you really have to go down into the depths of the psyche. In comparison it's much easier to still the intellectual functioning.

s: Are devotional feelings absent in a glimpse?

ANTHONY: The higher feelings do not come from that [psychic] realm.

s: When you say "emotive," you're talking about the lower?

ANTHONY: The basic emotivity that's involved in all protoplasmic functioning. We want to keep it right in the psycho-somatic, because that's what emote means. It's dealing with the psycho-somatic, whereas the higher feelings can be functioning without the psycho-somatic.

Very often the higher feelings will even *invade* the psycho-somatic. They'll come down into the psycho-somatic. Then you'll feel like you're exalted above all beings, etcetera, etcetera.

s: Does pure consciousness mean the same thing as the one life we were speaking about previously?

ANTHONY: I don't think so. I think the thrust is in another direction now.

Suppose a person had such-and-such an experience where the person managed to dismiss all thought of every kind and experienced her or himself as consciousness, which would be a kind of self-recognition. Then PB would say, well, you're coming from the point of view of actual meditational experience. Now, let's forget the mystic and say I just explained this to you. I'm coming from the point of view of metaphysics.

So, on the one hand, I've just come out of a deep meditation, and I experienced myself to be pure consciousness. I had dismissed all thought, and in the dismissal of all thought what remains is this immaterial, unobjectifiable consciousness that I am. And I talk to you and tell you about it. Now, I'm coming to you from a direct experience of it, and I'm explaining to you, or trying to explain to you, and you would say, "Well, you got that from meditation."

Then another person comes along and repeats what I have

said. This person knows theoretically about what it should be all about, but hasn't had the experience. That's coming from a metaphysical point of view. In other words, one person is coming from the point of view of a theoretical understanding, and the other person is coming from a practical experience of what it is like. But they should both be accurate in the sense that this is what you really are like, this pure consciousness.

One person is basically coming form the point of view of the practitioner; the other is coming from the point of view of the theoretician. Remember, the Buddha pointed out that the combination of these two is ideal: the individual who understands this and the individual who experiences it.

s: Could that pure consciousness refer to either of the two?

ANTHONY: No, it generally refers to your Witness I. Remember the sentence where PB says there's awareness of awareness, and then there's pure awareness? When you have the experience of the Witness I, you won't be able to distinguish that it's an awareness of awareness. At the same time that you're having it you're going to think that it's just pure consciousness. It's going to take the experience of the I AM to recognize that it wasn't that pure; it was an awareness of awareness. It's only when you're in the I AM that you are just the awareness.

THE DOUBLE KNOWER: PHILOSOPHIC VS. MYSTICAL REALIZATION, PERMANENT ENLIGHTENMENT VS. TEMPORARY STATES

ALTHOUGH the aspirant has now awakened to his witness-self, found his "soul," and thus lifted himself far above the mass of mankind, he has not yet accomplished the full task set him by life. A further effort still awaits his hand. He has yet to realize that the witness-self is only a *part* of the All-self. So his next task is to discover that he is not merely the witness of the rest of existence but essentially of one stuff with it. He has, in short, by further meditations to realize his oneness with the entire universe in its real being. He must now meditate on his witness-self as being in its essence the infinite All. Thus the ultramystic exercises are graded into two stages, the second being more advanced than the first. The banishment of thoughts reveals the inner self whereas the reinstatement of thoughts without losing the newly gained consciousness reveals the All-inclusive universal self. The second feat is the harder.

(v16. 23:6.88 and *Perspectives,* p. 320)

ANTHONY: If you understand this, you're on the road to philosophy.

The quote first says that, as an aspirant, at a certain point of development you realize that you are that consciousness, rather than any content it would have. You find that you are this awareness. Now what in the world could go beyond that? Suppose I find that in principle, in essence, I am pure consciousness. Within that pure consciousness there manifests the world. That means thoughts. What would be the next requirement in order for me to be complete and to become a philosopher? You have the World-Idea being expressed, and the substratum of that World-Idea is your consciousness. He said that the first achievement—not the harder one, but the easier one, according to this quote—is the recognition that in your essence you are consciousness. The more difficult achievement is the reconciliation that this pure essence is the substratum of the manifested universe, and that the two points of view are to be kept simultaneously alongside each other. This will make you a philosopher.

The philosopher is both: the double knower. The philosopher includes both recognizing your own essence to be pure consciousness and realizing that everything in manifestation of that essence still claims its validity as a manifestation. This makes a philosopher. Not one who takes either stance: that you are pure consciousness or that you are only the whatness of what is being manifest. In other words, for PB, the philosopher-sage is one who is poised in both positions, and includes both positions: that of recognizing your essence as pure consciousness, and the entirety of the manifestation of that pure consciousness, which maintains itself as a principle not separate but distinct from the consciousness.

Remember that quote we were reading from the edition of *Ashtavakra Samhita* with PB's notes?[4] You dissolve the world in your understanding. This means that you understand, not that the world disappears.

> I TRIED to make it quite clear in *The Hidden Teaching Beyond Yoga* that just as psychic experiences were not to be sought for their own sake, so even mystical experiences were not the highest goal. It was only when their intermittent nature became obvious, however remarkable and uplifting they may have seemed, that one who experienced them was ready to seek for the higher Truth. This was not only a matter of personal feeling, but also of impersonal intuitive knowledge confirmed by reason and experience.
>
> (v16, 25:2.34)

LD: There's still a duality, in that it's "*I* am experiencing this."

ANTHONY: Mystical experiences are still on a penultimate stage of the imagination. You become aware of that. And no amount of superlatives will take it away from that stage.

AH: No matter how grand or exalted the experience is, eventually it has to be seen as imagination.

ANTHONY: A penultimate stage of the imagination. It's not the gross imagination as we understand it and experience it in ordinary wakeful consciousness.

AH: But is that to say, Anthony, that the penultimate imagination can never be that perceiver, that consciousness? Is that the distinction that has to be made between mysticism and philosophy?

ANTHONY: It's still not reality.

DB: The occasion for the recognition of this fact takes place within the context of standard waking consciousness—normal waking life. One reflects on the experiences that one has had and somehow it occurs to one that that's not the truth. And I'm not sure how that is proved.

ANTHONY: It might be that it wouldn't occur to you or me, but it would occur to someone like PB.

DB: Okay.

ANTHONY: PB wrote *The Hidden Teaching Beyond Yoga* prior to reaching the *jivanmukta* [liberation in life] stage. And the statement he makes there is that through his personal feeling and intuition he had already grasped the fact that the mystical level is not dominated by reality, and is not that reality. But it would only be the person who has disciplined and developed an extreme rational consciousness who would be able to see through the superlative effulgence of the mystic state, and see its shortcomings.

RG: You said before that the mystic doesn't perceive reality. If you accept that the mystic can have *nirvikalpa,* I don't see how you could not say that in that non-experience, in that thought-free experience, the mystic contacts Reality.

ANTHONY: Because Reality has to include thoughts too.

RG: It seems the problem arises when you come out of the *nirvikalpa.*

ANTHONY: There it is, right there. And it confronts you—

RG: —with a dilemma.

ANTHONY: Yes.

RG: The mystic hasn't taken in the world.

ANTHONY: And the nondual would take both in. That was the amazing statement PB made about Plotinus, that he had tremendous powers of concentrating—*with* thought or *without* thought.

And the difficulty that most yogi-mystics have is precisely that when they come out of *nirvikalpa,* the confrontation with the world is an ordeal—they cannot bring them together. And they go back, and they keep going *back* to that state of the superlative, of exuberance, emotionality, subjectivity, and the prodigality of one's awareness. But when they come out again they're faced with the fact that thought is contradicting that. The highest standpoint reconciles the two of them—the *nirvikalpa*/no-thought state, and the thought-state. So that although in the beginning you go around saying you have thoughts, this too is Brahman, and you don't suppress them, you don't banish them. You know that they are Brahman. Whereas the mystic will not do that.

That was PB's doctrine. That does reconcile the two. But only if you go to the highest. Stay just one hairbreadth short of that, and this conflict is like a thorn.

> THAT OF which everyone is immediately conscious is the body, the emotions, and the intellect. When he can include the Overself too without however excluding these three themselves, he shall have attained the properly maturated divine consciousness. If the mystic attains his highest aspiration when the world is lost from his consciousness, the philosopher attains his only when the world is again restored to his consciousness.
>
> (unpublished)

ANTHONY: All right, the first sentence: Everybody's aware of their own body, their own feelings, and their own intellect. So far we agree. Okay? The next part.

> [*rereads*] When he can include the Overself too without however excluding these three themselves, he shall have attained the properly maturated divine consciousness.

ANTHONY: In other words, at the end of evolution. You're right at the finish line.

JG: I never thought that divine consciousness has to maturate.

ANTHONY: No, but we do.

AH: The idea that one may have glimpses of that Overself from time to time is nothing like this maturated divine state?

ANTHONY: No, nothing at all.

JA: Anthony, you said earlier that the sage, and I assume

when he talks about the philosopher he's referring to the sage, transcends both the I AM consciousness and the World-Idea.

ANTHONY: Yes. By that I mean not so much transcending or above, but as including both in oneself. A person like that would know what their role is in the world, and work with the World-Idea. So this person understands something about the nature of the World-Idea and the direction it's heading, and also knows the nature of their own soul. That person we can call a philosopher.

> [*rereads*] If the mystic attains his highest aspiration when the world is lost from his consciousness, the philosopher attains his only when the world is again restored to his consciousness.

ANTHONY: Remember I told you the story about Vivekananda. He told Ramakrishna, "I want to be submerged in *nirvikalpa* for weeks and weeks." And Ramakrishna said, "There's something better than that." That's what he was pointing to.

> TO VIEW the inferior mystical experiences or the ratiocinative metaphysical findings otherwise than as passing phases, to set them up as finally representative of reality in the one case or of truth in the other, is to place them on a level to which they do not properly belong. Those who fall into the second error do so because they ascribe excessive importance to the thinking faculty. The mystic is too attached to one faculty, as the metaphysician is to the other, and neither can conduct a human being beyond the bounds of his enchained ego to that region where Being alone reigns. It is not that the mystic does not enter into contact with the Overself. He does. But his experience of the Overself is limited to glimpses which are partial, because he finds the Overself only within himself, not in the world outside. It is temporary because he has to take it when it comes at its own sweet will or when he can find it in meditation. It is a glimpse because it tells him about his own "I" but not about the "Not-I". On the other hand, the sage finds reality in the

world without as his own self, at all times and not at special occasions, and wholly rather than in glimpses. The mystic's light comes in glimpses, but the sage's is perennial. Whereas the first is like a flickering unsteady and uneven flame, the second is like a lamp that never goes out. Whereas the mystic comes into awareness of the Overself through feeling alone, the sage comes into it through knowledge plus feeling. Hence, the superiority of his realization.

The average mystic is devoid of sufficient critical sense. He delights in preventing his intellect from being active in such a definite direction. He has yet to learn that philosophical discipline has a steadying influence on the vagaries of mystical emotion, opinion, fancy, and experience. He refuses to judge the goal he has set up as to whether it be indeed man's ultimate goal. Consequently he is unable to apply correct standards whereby his own achievements or his own aspirations may be measured. Having shut himself up in a little heaven of his own, he does not attempt to distinguish it from other heavens or to discover if it be heaven indeed. He clings as stubbornly to his self-righteousness as does the religionist whom he criticizes for clinging to his dogma. He does not comprehend that he has transferred to himself that narrowness of outlook which he condemns in the materialistic. His position would be preposterous were it not so perilous.

Mysticism must not rest so smugly satisfied with its own obscurity that it refuses even to make the effort to come out into the light of critical self-examination, clear self-determination, and rational self-understanding. To complain helplessly that it cannot explain itself, to sit admiringly before its own self-proclaimed impalpability, or to stand aristocratically in the rarefied air of its own indefinability—as it usually does—is to fall into a kind of subtle quackery. Magnificent eulogy is no substitute for needed explanation.

(v13, 20:4.23 and *Perspectives*, p. 251)

ANTHONY: Let's all try to work on this. I'll read one part at a time.

> To view the inferior mystical experiences or the ratiocinative metaphysical findings otherwise than as passing phases, to set them up as finally representative of reality in the one case or of truth in the other, is to place them on a level to which they do not properly belong. . . .

RG: So neither thinking nor the experience of the Mind as Void is enough to give you reality permanently.

ANTHONY: Yes, permanently: That's the important thing. They're inferior because they're not an ultimate standpoint. The metaphysician may be able to enunciate and very clearly delineate the whole outline of the philosophy of truth. Later on that individual will look back and say, "How was I able to go through all that dry rot?" And for the mystic, the glimpse of the Overself not only flickers, but it actually goes out; it goes off and on. To consider that as anything but a temporary phase is misleading. So these two cannot be applied to the philosophy of truth. They have no place there.

> . . . Those who fall into the second error do so because they ascribe excessive importance to the thinking faculty. The mystic is too attached to one faculty, as the metaphysician is to the other . . .

ANTHONY: The metaphysician is too attached to the faculty of thinking, and consequently thinks that his is an ultimate viewpoint. The mystic, who is preoccupied with the interiority of the states of feeling, is attached to them, and thinks that that's the ultimate. But PB says neither of these phases can be applied to the ultimate standpoint.

> . . . and neither can conduct a human being beyond the bounds of his enchained ego . . .

ANTHONY: That's really crucial. Neither mystical glimpses nor reflective metaphysical thinking can take you out of the ego permanently. A glimpse might take you out for an hour, but then you're back there and you're rotten for the other twenty-three hours.

> . . . It is not that the mystic does not enter into contact with the Overself. He does. But his experience of the Overself is limited to glimpses which are partial. . . . It is temporary because he has to take it when it comes at its own sweet will or when he can find it in meditation. It is a glimpse because it tells him about his own "I" but not about the "Not-I" . . .

ANTHONY: It doesn't tell the person anything about the world out there, the World-Idea.

> . . . On the other hand, the sage finds reality in the world without as his own self . . .

ANTHONY: Now, what he's saying here is very important. The sage finds that the world without—the externally manifested idea of the world—*is one's own inner self.* That's quite advanced. There are mystics who have an experience, a glimpse, of their own higher self, and they become recluses and hermits; they run away. But there's another kind of experience that some mystics have where they feel the sacredness of everything around them. They become acquainted with the fact that the World-Idea being manifested in them is also of the nature of the "I." It can actually occur that you come out of a trance state like that and bump into a chair and say, "Excuse me"; you actually feel the sacredness of the whole world. This is not common for most mystics. At any rate, PB is pointing out here that these are shortcomings that mystics have. First of all, it's not a continuous light; it flickers; even worse, it goes off and goes on again.

> . . . On the other hand, the sage finds reality in the world without as his own self, at all times and not at special occasions, and wholly rather than in glimpses. The mystic's light

> comes in glimpses . . . a flickering unsteady and uneven flame, the second is like a lamp that never goes out.

ANTHONY: So the insight that the philosopher operates with is continuous, uninterrupted, without any break. The philosopher continuously sees that consciousness underlies the reality of objects. It's *always* there for the philosopher-sage.

> . . . Whereas the mystic comes into awareness of the Overself . . .

ANTHONY: One's soul.

> . . . through feeling alone, the sage comes into it through knowledge plus feeling. Hence, the superiority of his realization.

ANTHONY: Insofar as the sage recognizes what the substratum of the universal idea is which is being experienced continuously and uninterruptedly, that knowledge never leaves. That in combination with the feeling of the inward Self is permanent.

RG: Does the philosopher make the experience of the mystic permanent by the application of knowledge and reason? Or is that experience transformed into a qualitatively different experience? If you say that the mystic does apprehend reality, you wouldn't say that it changes the quality of the experience but only establishes it permanently. But if there are different levels of that experience of the real, then the application of knowledge and reason to make it permanent could also deepen the experience.

ANTHONY: In a tentative way I'm going to try to answer. In one way it seems to alter the experience that the mystic has, because it introduces a greater element of serenity. In other words, the mystic who has this experience of *pure* Spirit is actually in a state of emotional bliss. There's no possibility of equanimity, tranquility; that's out. The mystic is in a very exalted situation. Now, the sage eliminates that, gets rid of that, because emotions pertain to the body. In the case of the sage, that emotional intensity is eliminated and what is substituted for it is the steady and abiding knowledge of this situation. So it is experienced in a state of unruffled peace, serenity, tranquility, and in that sense it's much deeper—although someone would disagree and say, "Oh, no, it sounds like the other is deeper; that's more intense."

The inwardization of the serenity is rare. In the annals of philosophic mysticism you'll find very few people who have this recognition of the three primal hypostases.[5] If you're acquainted with the mystical literature of the world, you'll see that that's a very unusual person, in the sense that this person is being granted much more than the ordinary mystic.

PC: Wouldn't another difference between the philosopher and the mystic be that the philosopher understands the "not-I," the World-Idea?

ANTHONY: Yes. PB has a quote in which he says that the philosopher frees him or herself from the senses and lives in the pure Spirit, but then goes back and lives in the world of the senses; now the philosopher knows what's going on.[6] That's the point of view that the philosopher has to work with.

Philosophy wakes you up out of your dream, and you understand the nature of that dream world. Then it tells you, "Go back into that dream world now and act according to what you know." So when the imaginary tiger comes chasing you, you run up an imaginary tree! You understand the nature of the so-called sense world now. It doesn't stop it from being what it is. But the understanding that follows when one keeps alert to the fact that one is dreaming will be different from that of the person who's identified with being the dream individual—qualitatively quite different.

So when you reach *nirvikalpa samadhi,* that's not enough. You've got to go back into the world with what you know now and apply it, and establish yourself in that knowledge *in* the sense world.

> . . . The average mystic is devoid of sufficient critical sense. He delights in preventing his intellect from being active in

> such a definite direction. He has yet to learn that philosophical discipline has a steadying influence on the vagaries of mystical emotion, opinion, fancy, and experience. He refuses to judge the goal he has set up as to whether it be indeed man's ultimate goal. Consequently he is unable to apply correct standards whereby his own achievements or his own aspirations may be measured. Having shut himself up in a little heaven of his own, he does not attempt to distinguish it from other heavens or to discover if it be heaven indeed. He clings as stubbornly to his self-righteousness as does the religionist whom he criticizes for clinging to his dogma. He does not comprehend that he has transferred to himself that narrowness of outlook that he condemns in the materialistic. His position would be preposterous were it not so perilous. . . .

AB: Before he said the mystic experiences this light but it sputters on and off.

ANTHONY: The mystic doesn't experience this light—the mystic *is* this thing, is this true spirit. We have to keep this in mind. For those who are *not* mystics, it would be quite an achievement to get to be mystics so that they could be criticized like that!

RG: Is this criticism focused on a particular kind of mystic?

ANTHONY: Most of the yoga practitioners would fit in here.

LR: But when PB says "philosopher," these quotes refer to the philosopher sage. His definition of philosophy seems to be the highest attainment of the sage.

ANTHONY: Let me put it this way. His definition of a philosopher is someone who knows truth. Anything short of that, you're not a philosopher. That's the important thing to keep in mind.

AH: PB describes the mystic's position as perilous. He seems to see the greatest danger in a rigidity of opinion. Why is that so? Why does the mystic hold a rigid opinion?

ANTHONY: Remember that famous remark by Burkhardt:

"Power corrupts; absolute power corrupts absolutely." Well, something like that can be applied to the ego. It is corrupt to begin with, but if it gets a mystical experience, now it's an *exalted* corruption! The mystical experience so inflates the ego that it really is impossible to deal with him or her. Instead of a standard size ego now it's a bigger one, magnified. So to have mystical experiences without some kind of preliminary understanding or metaphysical information can be cumbersome.

HE: Can this be true of metaphysicians, too?

ANTHONY: The intellect does the same. The intellect will be just as proud, just as rigid, just as self-opinionated.

DB: It seems that much of what the study of philosophy has to do with is dismantling the ego.

ANTHONY: Well, not dismantling—keeping it within bounds, hopefully more modest.

> MYSTICISM must not rest so smugly satisfied with its own obscurity that it refuses even to make the effort to come out into the light of critical self-examination, clear self-determination, and rational self-understanding. To complain helplessly that it cannot explain itself, to sit admiringly before its own self-proclaimed impalpability, or to stand aristocratically in the rarefied air of its own indefinability—as it usually does—is to fall into a kind of subtle quackery. Magnificent eulogy is no substitute for needed explanation.

ANTHONY: PB is trying to point out to mystics that they should try to be rational, try to understand the nature of what it is that is happening, and not remain content with the feeling and the emotional ecstasy that does take over. Because that's actually what happens: Emotional reactions take over and really prevent the person from exercising any of the critical faculties.

ME: Can you really apply rational faculties to mystical states, like seeing lights, colors?

ANTHONY: If you start seeing colors or hearing sounds, that's psychical.

ME: Would you put under "mystic" only the experience of *nirvikalpa*?

ANTHONY: No, not necessarily *nirvikalpa*, but it is a state of egoless being. The ego isn't there so it must be more than psychical. There is no sensory perception in that state. As a matter of fact, that's the simple price that you have to pay in order to reach a mystical state: to try to trick yourself out of sensory perception. It's worthwhile to be acquainted with these things so that you don't get lòst, because the psychical realm is so vast, so varied. You can go on having lights and sounds and colors and pictures indefinitely; it can go on for years. And spiritually you haven't moved ahead one iota.

EM: So there's really no evolution within the experiences of that psychic state?

ANTHONY: Right, that's television. Some of the experiences are enjoyable, but it's so easy to be deluded into thinking that they're something other than what they are.

AH: Is it that those psychical states or lower mystical states are so unlike our normal consciousness that unless we have some sort of framework to work in . . .

ANTHONY: No, they're not so unlike our normal consciousness. What's the difference when you look at color on television or you look at color in your mind? Let's put it this way: Imagine you're meditating, and you have the psychical experience of smelling the archetypal rose. And you open your eyes and you look around—there are no roses around, but you're absolutely inundated with the smell of rose. What does that have to do with spiritual development?

AH: I wonder why those experiences are frequently . . .

ANTHONY: Well, you get intoxicated. But don't look for those things. Take it as encouragement to go farther, but don't stop there. Don't make that the purpose of your meditation.

Once I was telling PB about this great experience and he turned around and he looked at me with a real frown: "Psychical." [*laughter*]

So we're beginning to see how unlimited and awesome the position of the philosopher is. Louis has a quote that emphasizes this.

> WE NEED to know the truth, the wisdom-knowledge, but it is not enough. We need to have the living mystic experience, the vital feeling of what I am, but it is not enough. For we need to synthesize the two in a full actual intuitive realization, conferred by the Overself. This is Grace. This is to emerge finally—born again!
>
> (v16, 25:2.51)

ANTHONY: Let's do another one.

> TWO THINGS have to be learned in this quest. The first is the art of mind-stilling, of emptying consciousness of every thought and form whatsoever. This is mysticism or Yoga. The disciple's ascent should not stop at the contemplation of anything that has shape or history, name or habitation, however powerfully helpful this may have formerly been to the ascent itself. Only in the mysterious void of Pure Spirit, in the undifferentiated Mind, lies his last goal as a mystic. The second is to grasp the essential nature of the ego and of the universe and to obtain direct perception that both are nothing but a series of ideas which unfold themselves within our minds. This is the metaphysics of Truth. The combination of these two activities brings about the realization of his true Being as the ever beautiful and eternally beneficent Overself. This is philosophy.
>
> (v13, 20:4.134 and *Perspectives*, p. 250)

AH: How is the goal of the first activity different from the direct perception in the second? Are they two separate goals?

ANTHONY: In the first case PB is pointing out that the goal of the mystical practices is to bring you to a realization of *nirvikalpa samadhi,* a realization of the ultimate substratum of the universe you live in. In other words, it brings you into identity with the Mind that you are. Usually that's where most of the schools stop; they consider the ultimate achievement to be *nirvikalpa,* consciousness without thoughts.

But after that is achieved or acquired, the second thing is to try to get a direct perception into the nature of the ego and the World-Idea. These two are necessary in order to have a full understanding of philosophy. On the one hand you must achieve a state of thoughtless consciousness, and on the other hand you must understand the nature of the world and ego.

You have to recognize that the soul has two aspects. The first we refer to as the intrinsic self-knower, the higher knower; and the second is the lower knower in which the soul has the faculty of understanding the nature of the ego and the world that it lives in. The completeness of philosophy depends upon integrating these two realizations. One without the other would be detrimental to the completion that we're speaking about.

Now, to understand that the world is a series of ideas, or that it is mental, you must first have the experience of *nirvikalpa samadhi.* Here the World-Idea temporarily disappears from your consciousness. Then when that World-Idea has returned to consciousness, you see that the World-Idea arises within consciousness and *is* the result of consciousness. If these two are combined, a person has a feeling of philosophy's completeness.

To have *nirvikalpa* without understanding the nature of the World-Idea is to have an incomplete experience. The tendency then is to desert the world, to regard the world as unreal, rather than to confront the world and master it by understanding the nature of that world.

In distinguishing these two aspects of the total truth, it becomes more available to us.

In Plotinus there's an enormous treatment of the need for the soul to understand that it has intrinsic self-cognition and that it also has the faculty of critically understanding its own activity, that is, understanding the world. For Plotinus, these two were required in order to call yourself a philosopher. You couldn't possibly separate them.

The main point we have to make is that the ultimate, *in you*, is Mind. Until this is experienced personally, it would not be possible to reduce the universe to ideas. In other words, one must have the experience that everything is Mind, that the ultimate principle is Mind. Given that experience, then it is possible to say that anything that Mind manifests must of necessity be an idea. It cannot manifest or manufacture something which is out of Mind, outside of the realm of Mind.

Again, let's use the dream example. If you awaken while in the dream state and recognize that everything is of the nature of your mind, then you know that anything that is occurring within the dream is of the nature of an idea. Then you must bring to bear on the manifested dream content your realization that everything is Mind. Now, if you don't have the experience in some form or shape, it remains theoretical. The working out of this understanding would be satisfactory to the reason, and the intellectual grasp of these ideas would satisfy the intellect; but in order for the whole person to fully accept this, there would have to be the experience that the ultimate principle of *all* is Mind.

Once this is realized—and the realization means that the whole of the individual is involved in this experience—then the second step is comparatively easy: to accept that everything that one can experience must be of the nature of an idea.

LR: What's the difference between the realization of the Overself and the realization of the ultimate Mind?

ANTHONY: There's no difference. You must keep in mind the general tenets that PB indicates. Your Overself is the substratum within which your experience can take place, and the experience of the Overself is the experience of Mind. In other words, you have to get into a thought-free state to experience the Overself.

Let's take the part where PB says, "The combination of these two activities brings about the realization of his true Being as the ever beautiful and eternally beneficent Overself." Remember how we tried another way to show this? We referred to the Soul in Plotinus—that would be the Overself—as a One. And the radiation of the World-Idea which occurs in the Overself we referred to as Being or the Ideas. Both of these in combination were necessary in order to understand the Overself in its universality.

Then it follows, as PB says, that "these two activities bring about a realization of his true Being." So your true being is constituted of, on the one hand, unit Soul or individual Overself or individual Mind; and on the other hand, the World-Idea which is being manifested within that. Now, of course, at the level of Being the World-Idea is unmanifest. But nonetheless, it is a combination of these two that constitutes your real Being.

You have to remember that any time we have a discussion where we speak of the unity of the Soul as *distinct* from the unity of the World-Idea which is radiated upon Soul, those are theoretical abstractions that *never* actually take place. You can't have a unit Soul without the World-Idea radiating into it. That would be trying to separate two ends of the same stick.

RS: So the difference between a mystic and a philosopher is that the mystic attains only to the first, achieving the state of *nirvikalpa samadhi*, and the philosopher has both.

ANTHONY: Yes, I'd agree with that. That's why I brought up our tradition as Westerners, because that was certainly the view of Plato and Plotinus. You're not a philosopher until you've grasped these two.

Now of course a mystic, whether East or West, could easily be confused and think that once the Overself is reached that's it, that's all. But the philosopher would insist that you must include the fact that the universality of your being includes the World-Idea which is emanated through it from Brahman or Universal Mind.

(*Quote is reread, then Anthony continues.*)

It's helpful to remember here how PB uses the term "Mind" —for example, when he says "in the undifferentiated Mind." Now, to deep philosophers—I'm referring to these people who have had experience of this—their higher Self, the Overself, is not distinguished or separated from or spoken of as different from what Plotinus refers to as the three primal hypostases. I make that distinction to help us in our understanding.

In other words, consider the three primal hypostases: One, Intellectual Being, Soul. They're going to call this the Absolute, they're going to call this the Void, they're going to call this Mind. And then they say that from the Absolute Soul there emanates an individual soul which we can call our Overself. For that Overself and for that mysterious Void, they're going to use the same word: Mind. That's how *exalted* that notion of the soul, the individual Overself, is.

With this in mind we can understand how both PB and Plotinus can speak in these two different ways. PB speaks about three initiations once a person has reached the Overself: three levels of inwardness or degrees of penetration. (v16, 25:2.109 and *Perspectives,* p. 348, no. 5) PB speaks about these three different degrees in a psychological way. And this correlates with Plotinus' description: the first degree of penetration is at the level of Absolute Soul, then Intellectual-Principle, then the One. Now, how would you ever know of these except through your own higher self, the Overself?

Further, they both speak of *insight* as having these three different degrees that one can penetrate to actually get to know about the mysterious Void—something about it besides that it is.

JL: Do these also correspond to the three realms of mysticism: the initiative, purgative, and unitive?

ANTHONY: I don't think so, because the realms you're speaking of are all within the realm of individual soul.

Mystical literature explains that these three levels which are taking place within mysticism can be correlated in some way or other with the three primal hypostases, but that is a misunderstanding of their own experiences. For that, we have to go to the quotations where PB speaks about the fallacy of divine identity.[7] When the mystics speak about unity or divine identity or divine union, what they're speaking about—if they're not deluded, if they're not referring to a mental or conceptual level—is something that is taking place in their own soul not within the One itself. There could be no union with the highest, with the One itself.

JL: So, the three states of the mystic would really be initiatory, reaching the first state for the philosopher?

ANTHONY: The initiatory phase would be recognition that one has a Soul. The second would be to realize the need to carry out an ascetic and purgative regime. The third would be unitive, where one achieves union with one's own Soul. But for mystical literature to go beyond that is, I think, misleading. The philosopher points out that this is all taking place within one's own Soul, that the identity that is achieved IS with one's own Soul and that that IS one's God.

JL: Then what is PB speaking about when he talks about the ultimate union?

ANTHONY: The ultimate union IS with your own Soul. There is *no* ultimate union with the One.

JL: So the realization of the function of the World-Idea in the Soul is for the philosopher a stage beyond mysticism?

ANTHONY: Oh, yes, because now what has to be brought to bear, most mystics find difficult. All their intellectual and critical faculties have to be brought into play to understand what this is all about. A very good example of this is the eight hypotheses in the *Parmenides* of Plato; he makes demands on the aspiring philosopher to understand in this physical way "What am I talking about?" He has this list of eight hypotheses and the questions they bring out. If the aspiring philosopher can't answer these, then evidently the experience of *nirvikalpa* hasn't occurred; or, if it has, the person hasn't brought about the development of the understanding and isn't going to understand what this is all about. And the fact that many of the Vedantic writers—not all, but many of them—insist that reaching *nirvikalpa* is the highest stage shows that they stopped halfway.

JL: When you were discussing Plotinus' realization of the

Intellectual-Principle, were you comparing that with the philosopher's comprehension of the World-Mind's functioning in the Soul after the experience of *nirvikalpa*?

ANTHONY: I was referring to Plotinus' notion of the two knowers, the higher and the lower. The higher knower is the one with self-cognition and the lower is the one that has the faculty of understanding what its experience is all about.

JL: But the lower is certainly not the Intellectual-Principle?

ANTHONY: You can make this correlation with the quote that we read. In the first case, the higher knower is the one that has intrinsic self-cognition—insight—as experienced in *nirvikalpa samadhi.* In the second, the lower knower is capable of critically reflecting on the meaning of this experience; that means reason has been developed and objectified, and this knower can apply it to this experience and understand the nature of this experience. Then these two are brought together in order to bring about completeness. PB says the same thing here: First you have to achieve the state of *nirvikalpa* or self-cognition, and then, second, you have to understand the nature of the World-Idea, which means you have to bring in your critical faculties.

So, we have the unity of the Soul and we have the fact that the World-Idea is irradiating it. These two are to be held together. When the mystic insists on just achieving the state of *nirvikalpa* and ignoring the World-Idea, that's just like taking only half of yourself. The other half is being ignored. Whereas the philosopher will insist that the nature of the World-Idea and the role that the person has to play *in* that World-Idea must be understood. It's a very natural outcome. Maybe because we're Westerners, it seems kind of artificial to sit down and be rapt and absorbed forever contemplating intrinsic self-cognition.

ME: Are you equating the direct perception of the World-Idea with the development of the intellectual and critical faculties?

ANTHONY: Yes. There are quite a few quotes where PB points out that the development of the reason is God's way of guaranteeing your safe journey.

JA: I still don't understand which knower undertakes the three degrees of penetration.

ANTHONY: Instead of saying "which knower," it would be better put this way: that the inwardization and deepening of self-cognition reveals that there is an inwardness which can reveal the existence of the three primal hypostases.

Again, we have to be careful because this is getting into semantics. When we speak about the double knower, the higher and the lower, we're not *dividing* the knower. We're just speaking about two different aspects of one and the same thing. And the Soul is such an entity that it cannot be understood by simply ascribing to it self-cognition. You also have to point out that the World-Idea is being irradiated upon it, and is part of its being, and that without the development of the critical faculty of understanding, it would be quite meaningless to speak of a World-Idea there. So then, when we speak about the double knower, we're not speaking about two entities. We're speaking about one person, but we're speaking about a particular aspect of that one entity, one Soul.

JA: Maybe I haven't understood your answer but are the three degrees of penetration something that would be included in *nirvikalpa samadhi,* or are they beyond—a deepening of *nirvikalpa samadhi*?

ANTHONY: That's it, exactly. Deepening, because there's no alteration in that kind of knowledge. Speak about it as a deepening or an inwardization, that's the only way that it can be spoken of. There's no possibility of bringing in any kind of critical understanding in that knowledge.

PB pointed out that what is our innermost is Its outermost. That's simply referring to the fact that our innermost—the Overself—is like the peak or the outermost of the three principles. This is available to *some* of the philosophers. I don't know that all philosophers have had that experience, but the great ones certainly have, and they repeat over and over again that there are these different levels of revelation that are given to sages. This is the kind of philosophy you never get in school.

I'll suggest something here which I usually don't advise. Let's read the short quote on *sahaja* and *nirvikalpa.* It's very similar to this quote but comes from a different angle and caps this one here.

> SAHAJA SAMADHI is the awareness of Awareness, whether appearing as thoughts or not, whether accompanied by bodily activities or not. But *nirvikalpa samadhi* is solely the awareness of Awareness.
>
> (v16, 25:2.140)

ANTHONY: If you let your mind speculate, what thoughts would arise in you with that kind of notion: awareness of Awareness? At that level the sensible world doesn't exist. Does any feeling arise in you as to what it might possibly be for your awareness to be aware of itself and nothing else? Could you see that as a completely subjective state, an extreme introversion, where what is self-evident knowing, so to speak, knows only itself and nothing else?

AH: I don't understand, Anthony.

ANTHONY: I'm trying to pick the words very carefully. Try. Let's concentrate. Think of this principle within us, which we refer to as this consciousness, this illuminating principle. Think of the quote that you often refer to that says that this consciousness is immediately available for all perceptual usage but cannot in any way be objectified[8]—do you have a feeling for that, for what that might be?

AH: Any feeling I have for it is beside the point.

ANTHONY: No, I have to work with your feeling here. I don't expect an explicit conceptual understanding—do you have any feeling for it? Your awareness can be solely preoccuppied with itself and nothing else. That would be awareness of Awareness. That would be *nirvikalpa samadhi.* That would be complete subjective introversion. No World-Idea. Nothing else would exist—if I can be outlandish and say this—except *you.* It is the highest kind of solipsism that is available, although actually the truth will be that it itself is placed in reality so it can't be really solipsistic. But in a sense it is the highest solipsism that's available to us. It is, so to speak, being that I AM principle. Where nothing else matters.

Then the next point is that *sahaja* is different than this. You take that principle—the awareness of Awareness—and speak about it in a different way. This second awareness can remain what it is or be transformed into thought. This he calls *sahaja.* Go over it.

JG: In *sahaja* you have both at the same time.

ANTHONY: Yes.

JG: You have, you see the highest consciousness.

ANTHONY: Yes, you're identified with that.

JG: And yet you also see that awareness of thoughts.

ANTHONY: Or non-thoughts. Either way, it doesn't matter. The sage can be aware of the perceptual world, or the world could be abolished and be just a consciousness before it transforms itself into the world.

JG: If you were at the stage of *nirvikalpa,* then the minute the thought would come in, you'd be hurled into the regular world again.

ANTHONY: You'd be thrown out, yes. So in describing that exercise of the Serpent's Path, which is the one that very often you are called upon to use, PB speaks about this dynamic concentration—he says it's an extremely dynamic concentration—when you try to penetrate between two thoughts and your attention has to be sharper than any surgical knife. To get between two thoughts it has to be so attentive that I can't see why he didn't call it *nirvikalpa.* That's the kind of concentration that's going to be required for you to insert your attention between two thoughts, in order for the exercise to succeed. So in that exercise, as a prerequisite, what is required is this dynamically alert attention that can insert itself between two thoughts that the World-Mind is producing.

Do you get a feeling for what we're dealing with? How these two things are held—

RC: When we speak of this awareness this way, are we speaking of what Plotinus would call the most fundamental and intrinsic process of the soul itself, that life that we call the fundamental nature of the soul?

ANTHONY: Yes, I would say that there is agreement here between PB and Plotinus.

RC: So when it's said that the soul is both one and many, can the same be said of this awareness that we speak of, that this awareness is both single and manifold?

ANTHONY: Yes, sure. And that's awfully complicated because to me that has two different references. They speak about the soul as one and many. Remember the quote where PB says the self of the sun is my "I?"

> "THE GOD in the sun is the 'I' in me" —this put tersely is the essence of man's relationship to divinity. A whole book may be needed to explain it, a whole lifetime to get direct experience of its truth as insight.
>
> (v16, 25:1.1.)

Remember? Now if my "I" is the self of the sun, and your "I" is the self of the sun, and this is so for each of us—then we can say that these many souls are also *one* Soul. But we can also say that that one Soul is these *many* souls, and to try to change the language to accommodate us the way we think here, would be a disaster. When Jung says, "It's obvious there's only one soul," I say, "No, that's his interpretation." And when someone says, "It's many souls," that's their interpretation. Leave it the way it is. It is *both one and many.*

RC: Does the recognition of that correspond with these two *samadhis* that we're speaking of? Is *nirvikalpa* a recognition of the Oneness?

ANTHONY: No. In *nirvikalpa,* you're not required to go through the metaphysical discipline. You can meet mystics of extraordinary attainment who've achieved *nirvikalpa* but have no understanding of the cosmology that has been worked out, whether here or in Plotinus, or any of that. Don't make the assumption that because a mystic has achieved *nirvikalpa* that mystic is going to understand what we're saying here.

RC: If, in *nirvikalpa,* I realize something true about the soul, I realize that the soul is single, and that singleness is all-embracing—

ANTHONY: You won't be able to realize that the soul can be many. Not even the World-Idea exists in that situation or that state.

RC: It seems to follow that *sahaja* is the discovery of the truth that the soul is also many, but it seems to be more than that.

ANTHONY: Well, here I would go as far as Plotinus. The soul now can achieve or understand various states of being, and these states of being of course are manifold, whether we speak about just the undivided mind of our solar system or about the various levels of intellectuality that we find in *Mahat,* the great Buddhic reasoning. The whole point of the philosophic development and *sahaja* is not only that discovery of soul. If you're a mystic and you want to find out that you have a soul, fine. But then also we have to understand what these people are telling us: that the soul is being sent to school. And that there are no classes that say, "This is it, now you've graduated, you're finished." In the universe the soul is never finished with learning, because there's *no* possibility of ever fully comprehending the World-Idea, though we get glimpses of what it might mean.

RC: When we speak of the Soul being simultaneously suspended from both the One and the Intellectual-Principle—

ANTHONY: No, I wouldn't put it that way. The context we use to say these things is all-important. We have to avoid this linear kind of progression or definition that we've been taught: if it's not this, then it's that. We have to forget that kind of logic. As Plotinus points out, we have to reason *essentially.* That means that we have to reason according to the dictates of the soul, and not according to the way we understand the world here.

It isn't that I'm disagreeing. When I'm talking I try to use a *contextual* framework to be understood, rather than expecting that a word itself should give my understanding. It can't do it. So I try to give a whole context, and also the particular in that context, to make it available. I don't say I'm succeeding, but that's what I try to do.

So when I try to define the meaning of soul as one and many, I have to use that whole context. I have to use the context that the self of the sun is your soul and it's also my soul. Now in that case I can see that since that self is one, these many souls are one. But then I reverse it. And insofar as each and every one of us is projected forth from that self of the sun, and each one has a historicity that is different from the others, and has intrinsic powers which are developing and which separate it from the others, then soul is a many. In this context, and only by using contextual language, can that be understood. It cannot be understood by saying, "Well, it's one" or "No, it's not, it's many."

RC: The way *sahaja* is spoken of as the goal of philosophic development, it's a state that reflects nonduality more than just either singleness or multiplicity.

ANTHONY: Exactly. It expresses nonduality more than any other. Consciousness of Consciousness or awareness of Awareness regardless of whether that latter Awareness changes into thought or not. That's nondualism. And that is the point I think we were discussing before. That's different from monism, which reduces everything to one homogeneous block.

RC: For soul to discover something of its own nature seems to be quite a step up from ego-consciousness. And then for the soul to discover something of its being grounded in the *Nous* seems to be even more of a complete position.

ANTHONY: Yes, nondualism. Remember the quote I'm fond of using about Atmananda? A certain gentleman was quite capable of going into *nirvikalpa* and Atmananda said, "Now that you've achieved it, the work ahead of you is to become a philosopher, which is to understand the World-Idea." Once you understand that, then you become a philosopher.

This is also, strangely enough, the story of the physicist Heisenberg. If you read about his life, it's really quite extraordinary. I'd like to recommend it. He first developed this tremendous power, this capacity to concentrate, so that he actually achieved *nirvikalpa samadhi.* And after that, he understood something about the nature of the world. He went through the development naturally. Very concentrated introversion, a high degree of introversion to the point where he achieved *nirvikalpa samadhi,* and then that was brought to bear on the problems he was working out in physics. He applied that.

LR: Anthony, in *nirvikalpa* there are no thoughts. In *sahaja* there may or may not be thoughts. So if one were in *sahaja* and did not have thoughts, would you say it wouldn't be the same as being in *nirvikalpa*? In other words, is the state of *sahaja* without thought different from the state of *nirvikalpa*?

ANTHONY: What situation would you have to be in, or what would be required of you, in order to be able to say that's just pure consciousness or that's thought, consciousness transformed into thought? What would your situation have to be?

LR: You'd have to be in a state of pure awareness.

ANTHONY: Yes. You see what I mean by working contextually?

LR: No.

ANTHONY: All right, ask your question. Try again.

LR: It's not just the presence of thought that separates those two states. One is a more complete state. One, perhaps, is able to traverse *prajna* [sleep, or causal] consciousness, dream consciousness, wakeful consciousness. Whereas the other seems to be only in one state.

ANTHONY: Yes.

LR: If one were in *sahaja* even without thoughts appearing, it wouldn't necessarily be the same as being in *nirvikalpa.*

ANTHONY: Yes.

LR: Even though they're both called awareness of Awareness.

ANTHONY: Why would that be so? Can we use the Serpent's Path exercise to point to the difference?

LR: I thought you said if you penetrate between two thought moments, you can arrive at the state of *nirvikalpa.*

ANTHONY: No. No. I said what is required is practically *nirvikalpa* in order to penetrate between those two thought moments. In other words you have to have an attention that is so acute, so steady, so precise, like an acetylene torch. Did you ever see an acetylene torch? A flame comes out and you can cut steel right in half? Your attention has to be that steady. I can't see what the difference is between that kind of attention and *nirvikalpa.*

LR: Is *nirvikalpa* a state of awareness of the soul, excluding the World-Idea?

ANTHONY: Yes, it excludes the World-Idea.

LR: And I believe you said once that if one were able to penetrate between two thought moments—

ANTHONY: —to use that concentrative ability to penetrate between two thought moments—

LR: And where does that get you?

ANTHONY: This gets you to nonduality.

You find out that underlying the World-Idea is the World-Mind. The World-Mind is what projects the World-Idea. Also, your mind, your I AM principle, is a particle *of* that World-Mind. You come to nondualism.

Now *listen.* Your mind, your soul, is what projects forth the universe for you as an individual. Then your soul, getting involved in the fabrication of the World-Idea, wants to know something about the World-Idea. It must penetrate into the World-Idea. This consciousness-principle, this principle of consciousness within you here and now, this self-evidencing principle is available to you.

You're sitting down and meditating. One thought after another follows, and remember, you're way beyond any kind of sensorial experience. You don't have any experience of the world sensually, when this is going on. The world is coming into manifestation as a thought and exploding as what we would call the world. It's between these two thoughts, in between two seed-thoughts, that you get to the substratum of the World-Idea, the World-Mind.

But what is the World-Mind? Didn't we just say that your mind is a particle of the World-Mind? But then what we're saying is, you find out that you're part of the World-Mind, that your soul is part of the World-Mind. Your soul is a particle of the World-Mind. And you come to nondualism. And this is an absolute affirmation. No two ways about it. The other way has got nothing to do with nondualism.

There is a quote where PB says that in this lifetime you might not get beyond a *nirvikalpa samadhi* trance, but you will be required, nature will force you, to come back and complete the trip. You can't leave it halfway. So nature will force you to become a philosopher and achieve *sahaja*.[9] You remember that quote?

AS: So this is what the Mahayana Buddhists mean when they say that you can't end up as a Solitary Realizer. No matter what the Solitary Realizers think in the Hinayana schools, after you've attained the Solitary Realizer state, the World-Idea will force you to go on to the Boddhisattva path.

ANTHONY: The Mahayanists are, I think, absolutely correct there.

AS: I think that's the same thing as saying you'll have to become a philosopher.

ANTHONY: Yes, whether you like it or not. But still there is a great deal of reason for their ordering: first the Solitary Realizer, then the Hearer, and finally the Bodhisattva.

AS: But this puts it into an ordered perspective, as in the quote where he says you have to attain *nirvikalpa* first. "Solitary Realizer" could mean realizing the solitariness of your own soul.

ANTHONY: As a matter of fact, if you read through a history of medieval mysticism, you'll be amazed how many of the mystics used to hide and you'd never see them again. They'd go off into the mountains and they wouldn't come out. Just think of a few—people like Ruysbroeck who was very hesitant about having anything to do with people. They just didn't want to get involved. But they weren't philosophers. They were heading in that direction, but they weren't there yet. Then, if you read the later writings of Ruysbroeck, he starts condemning people who do that, who run away from their work. Are you getting a feeling for the abyss of this doctrine, how vast it is?

EM: I'm getting a little bit of a feeling for what PB really meant when he always said that he was a student.

ANTHONY: [*softly*] That's all we'll ever ever ever be. It's so frightening to realize how ignorant we are.

JFL: I'm trying to figure out what is delivered in *nirvikalpa.*

ANTHONY: The greatest miracle of all is received. The miracle of the subjectivity which has been completely hidden from us in modern times. They speak about the human being as so many dollars worth of chemicals, but the miracle of subjectivity is something that the vastness of a galaxy can't comprehend. That's what's delivered. And I can't possibly communicate that. I don't think anyone can.

AS: PB almost did it in this quote.

> WE MUST withdraw every thing and thought from the mind except this single thought of trying to achieve the absence of what is not the Absolute. This is called Gnana Yoga: "*Neti, Neti*" (It is not this), as Shankara called it. And he must go on with this negative elimination until he reaches the stage where a great Void envelops him. If he can succeed in holding resolutely to this Void in sustained concentration—and he will discover it is one of the hardest things in the world to do so . . .

ANTHONY: *The* hardest thing. What do you mean "*one* of the hardest things?"

> . . . he will abruptly find that it is not a mere mental abstraction but something real, not a dream but the most concrete

thing in his experience. Then and then only can he declare positively, "It is *This*." For he has found the Overself.

(v15, 23:8.118 and *Perspectives*, p. 327)

ANTHONY: There are more passages where he does this. But this whole business, to try to recognize the miracle of our own being, is something that I don't think can be communicated. It might just happen occasionally. I'm not talking about the miracle of our ego. This is a whole different ballgame. But to die to the ego and to realize that you really ARE now—even if it's for a moment, you really ARE now—this is what I mean about the miracle of our own subjectivity, that we are consciousness or mind. What is the breadth and depth of Andromeda or any galaxy in terms of time and space? To know that you are mind is a greater miracle than that. As a matter of fact, the galaxy is like a terrestrial instance in your consciousness next to that. But could God do any less? If God gave you something, wouldn't it be the best and the greatest there could be? [*said quietly with emotion*]

Just sleep on that tonight. Yes?

LR: I was wondering again about this difference between the two states, *sahaja* without thought and *nirvikalpa,* which is always without thought?

ANTHONY: Perhaps you might follow me astrologically? Think of pure awareness, the awareness of Awareness, the *sahaja,* as the Sun-centered consciousness. And then think of the Awareness, the second Awareness, as the functioning of the undivided mind which can be either pure consciousness or particular manifestations.

The *sahaja* awareness is like the Sun-centered awareness. It knows both. It knows the undivided mind functioning as pure consciousness or producing spontaneously. So the Sun can know both. It can know the functioning of the undivided mind, the planetary powers, it can know that as just pure awareness. It can also know the product of that functioning. And it can know them both simultaneously!

TS: Whereas the undivided mind has to cease in its functioning in order to discover that solar consciousness.

ANTHONY: Yes. In both ways, as a matter of fact, it will cease knowing—also, when it gets involved in one of the products, then it has to cease knowing itself. In other words, the undivided mind functioning through me has to stop knowing itself, in order for me to know myself, in order for Tony to say, "This is Tony." If the undivided mind works through me, I'm not going to say, "I'm Tony." So the undivided mind has to forget itself when it comes into manifestation, when it manifests through a body.

TS: And for the undivided mind to manifest through the body and not forget itself, it must be functioning as the awareness of the solar consciousness.

ANTHONY: Yes, now you've got somebody.

> THE HIGHEST contribution which mysticism can make is to afford its votaries glimpses of that grand substratum of the universe which we may call the Overself. These glimpses reveal It in the pure unmanifest non-physical essence that It ultimately is. They detach It from the things, creatures, and thoughts which make up this world of ours, and show It as It is in the beginning, before the world-dream made its appearance. Thus mysticism at its farthest stretch, which is Nirvikalpa samadhi, enables man to bring about the temporary disappearance of the world-dream and come into comprehension of the Mind within which, and from which, the dream emerges. The mystic in very truth conducts the funeral service of the physical world as he has hitherto known it, which includes his own ego. But this is as far as mysticism can take him. It is an illuminative and rare experience, but it is not the end. For the next task which he must undertake if he is to advance is to relate his experience of this world as real with his experience of the Overself as real. And this he can do only by studying the world's own nature, laying bare its mentalistic character and thus bringing

it within the same circle as its source, the Mind. If he succeeds in doing this and in establishing this relation correctly, he will have finished his apprenticeship, ascended to the ultimate truth, and become a philosopher. Thenceforward he will not deny the world but accept it.

The metaphysician may also perform this task and obtain an intellectual understanding of himself, the world, and the Overself. And he has this advantage over the mystic, that his understanding becomes permanent whereas the mystic's rapt absorption must pass. But if he has not passed through the mystical exercises, it will remain as incomplete as a nut without a kernel. For these exercises, when led to their logical and successful issue in Nirvikalpa samadhi, provide the vivifying principle of experience which alone can make metaphysical tenets real.

From all this we may perceive why it is quite correct for the mystic to look undistractedly within for his goal, why he must shut out the distractions and attractions of earthly life in order to penetrate the sacred precinct, and why solitude, asceticism, meditation, trance, and emotion play the most important roles in his particular experience. What he is doing is right and proper at his stage but is not right and proper as the last stage. For in the end he must turn metaphysician, just as the metaphysician must turn mystic and just as both must turn philosopher—who is alone capable of infusing the thoughts of metaphysics and the feelings of mysticism into the actions of everyday practical life.

(v13, 20:4.115 and *Perspectives,* p. 263)

AH: Is the mystic experience of Mind as essence without content?

BS: The World-Idea would have to be in the Overself in its own unique way. How could you deny the World-Idea is in the Overself?

ANTHONY: You're not denying the World-Idea in the Overself. In the mystic glimpse, it's not that the World-Idea is negated; what is negated is the sensible appearance of the World-Idea. The mystic gets a glimpse of the world in the sense of, let's say, formless universal reason principles. Plotinus would say that Intellection is going on. Intellection means, in this sense, perceiving the universal archetypes, the reason principles, that in their totality and combination are going to become the sensible world. So in the mystical experience this is given to you: a glimpse of the world in its archetypal phase. Pure liquid gold.

CDA: This is in one unific whole vision?

ANTHONY: No, it would be an understanding of universal reason principles, and it doesn't necessarily have to be that you have the whole world. In other words, you don't have the all-time, fixed image of the world. That's not what you're grasping. It's not the cosmos in its entirety, from 25,000 B.C. to 25,000 A.D. Intellection of the formless universal reason principles that constitute the world is what you would perceive there. That's what the mystic gets a glimpse of. In other words, the mystic gets a glimpse of the *archetype* of everything that's here. That's what Plotinus called Intellection. The scope, the amplitude, and the intensity of the Intellection vary: You can have a glimpse for an hour or for a day.

Let's go through the quote one part at a time.

> The highest contribution which mysticism can make is to afford its votaries glimpses of that grand substratum of the universe which we may call the Overself. These glimpses reveal It in the pure unmanifest non-physical essence that It ultimately is. They detach It from the things, creatures, and thoughts which make up this world of ours, and show It as It is in the beginning, before the world-dream made its appearance. . . .

ANTHONY: Here [in the Overself] there's no coming, no going, no creatures—none of that.

> . . . Thus mysticism at its farthest stretch, which is *Nirvkalpa samadhi,* enables man to bring about the temporary

> disappearance of the world-dream and come into comprehension of the Mind within which, and from which, the dream emerges. The mystic in very truth conducts the funeral service of the physical world as he has hitherto known it, which includes his own ego. But this is as far as mysticism can take him. . . .

HS: Would you go so far as to say that what is called *nirvikalpa* is the essence of mind?

ANTHONY: *Nirvikalpa* is a thought-free state. There are no thoughts. It doesn't mean that you're blind.

HS: But in that state—what's there?

ANTHONY: A perception of the universe as it exists in its archetypal manner or form, and the mind which is the substratum of that—in other words, the Overself. These two together.

HS: Is it dualistic?

ANTHONY: It's not dualistic, and there are no thoughts there. What I'm referring to is a perception of the archetypal universe or the Intellectual Cosmos. It's not a thought; there is no thinking.

AH: Is it important to understand the notion of archetypal form as not being any kind of content?

ANTHONY: Well, it is a content, but I think what you mean is that there's no subject/object relationship here.

> The highest contribution which mysticism can make is to afford its votaries glimpses of that grand substratum of the universe which we may call the Overself. These glimpses reveal It in the pure unmanifest non-physical essence that It ultimately is. They detach It from the things, creatures, and thoughts which make up this world of ours, and show It as It is in the beginning, before the world-dream made its appearance. Thus mysticism at its farthest stretch, which is Nirvikalpa samadhi, enables man to bring about the temporary disappearance of the world dream and come into comprehension of the Mind within which, and from which, the dream emerges. . . .

AH: Your description seemed to add the notion of an archetypal world, but if it is *nirvikalpa* and—

ANTHONY: *Nirvikalpa* would be the last step, but in the process of inwardizing consciousness, the mystic perception of the intellectual cosmos takes place. Then if you deepen further and inwardize your consciousness, you will reach *nirvikalpa*, where there are no intellections at all.

Now, at the level where the mystic perceives the Intellectual Cosmos, in a sense, of course, it is a content: It's the Overself and the World-Idea. So you can speak of the World-Idea as a content of the Overself or the Overself as manifesting the World-Idea; I don't care which way you speak about it. But what I'm trying to point at is that at that level, although we can speak of a content, we cannot speak of a subject/object relationship, because the consciousness of the mystic that perceives or has intellection at that level is not different from that of which it has intellection. There, being and knowing are identical. So there's no subject/object relationship there.

> . . . The mystic in very truth conducts the funeral service of the physical world as he has hitherto known it, which includes his own ego. But this is as far as mysticism can take him. . . .

TS: Is it the same thing for the individual to have a glimpse of the Overself as the substratum of the universe and to see the death of the physical world and the ego?

ANTHONY: The mystic experiences the inward transformation of the sensible world into an intelligible, immaterial, archetypal universe, and that is the reality of the universe. So the sensible universe, which is a manifestation of that or a pictorialization of that, receives a sort of extreme devaluation—and with it, of course, the ego which is included in that World-Idea is subject to the same treatment.

TS: Is that devaluation of the sensible world and the ego the direct and inevitable consequence of the glimpse of *nirvikalpa*?

ANTHONY: Not the glimpse of *nirvikalpa,* the glimpse of the archetypal world.

TS: So there's a guarantee that a mystic who has had that glimpse will not have a reidentification with the reality of the ego?

ANTHONY: You'll reidentify, don't worry, but it won't be real. You'll *know* that it's not real, but it will still have power.

TS: So when PB talks of a "funeral service" —

ANTHONY: You're not going to bury it right then and there.

It would be wise not to think of a *time* involved, because it would vary. In some people it's immediate; in some, it's years later. But the important thing here is to get the feeling that he's telling you that the mystic glimpse gives you a perception of the heavenly world. If you perceive the heavenly world, this one is no longer going to mean anything. It's completely devaluated. Everything that you thought was so important here loses its value.

BS: Where does *nirvikalpa* come in?

ANTHONY: If you go beyond the Intellection—Intellection here, of course, in Plotinus' sense—if you go beyond that, if you continue inwardizing your consciousness, you get into *nirvikalpa.*

BS: This would be a stage beyond the archetypal world?

ANTHONY: To speak of "beyond that," I don't know what you mean.

BS: Then I don't understand what you mean by "deepening."

ANTHONY: What *you* mean by "beyond." [*laughter*] I didn't use the word "beyond" deliberately. If you inwardize the consciousness, you go through the mentality, you go through witness consciousness, you go through celestial reasoning and Intellection, and then you go into *nirvikalpa.* It doesn't have to happen that way. You could be shot, catapulted right into *nirvikalpa* and miss everything in between.

But as soon as you say "beyond" you get the feeling that the I AM principle is beyond the World-Idea, and it's not. PB points out that the Overself is basically the ray of the soul and the World-Idea together. And he calls the Overself the World-Idea or the World-Mind in you—a ray of the World-Mind.

> . . . It is an illuminative and rare experience, but it is not the end. For the next task which he must undertake if he is to advance is to relate his experience of this world as real with his experience of the Overself as real. And this he can do only by studying the world's own nature, laying bare its mentalistic character and thus bringing it within the same circle as its source, the Mind. If he succeeds in doing this and in establishing this relation correctly, he will have finished his apprenticeship, ascended to the ultimate truth and become a philosopher. Thenceforward he will not deny the world but accept it. . . .

ANTHONY: Randy, would you give us that story from Aurobindo please?

RC: A man experienced *nirvikalpa* and was very excited about it. He came to Aurobindo to notify and celebrate that now he knew that the only reality was the pure consciousness: He had had the experience and now he knew it for sure. And Aurobindo said in essence, I'm paraphrasing: "That was one experience, now you are having another experience. I want the person who's having them both."

ANTHONY: Do you see why Plato in his "divided line" [in the *Republic*] had at one end the sensible world and on the other intellectual intuition? He said, "Now, if I listen to Parmenides, there's only intellectual intuition, and if I listen to Heraclitus, there's only the snapping of dogs. What about the rest of the range of human knowledge?" So he put in the other two pieces of the line, the other two realms of knowledge. And he says this whole thing is the range of human knowledge: the *nirvikalpa samadhi* and the sensible world. They're all included in reality. He won't deny the world any more. He'll accept it.

> . . . The metaphysician may also perform this task and

obtain an intellectual understanding of himself, the world, and the Overself. And he has this advantage over the mystic, that his understanding becomes permanent whereas the mystic's rapt absorption must pass. But if he has not passed through the mystical exercises, it will remain as incomplete as a nut without a kernel. For these exercises, when led to their logical and successful issue in Nirvikalpa samadhi, provide the vivifying principle of experience which alone can make metaphysical tenets real. . . .

DB: Who would be an example of a metaphysician who has the intellectual understanding? Kant?

ANTHONY: Kant would be a good example. He understood very well that the world is an idea, that it's mental, but he never had the experience of the mentalness of the world. He did generate within himself that understanding that is thorough and grounded on reasoning. But he did not have the vivifying experience; he did not have the *felt* experience that the world is an idea. On the other hand, a mystic might have the experience that the world is idea, because he's feeling it as such, but he might not understand it. He can't understand it; he hasn't brought it out in the reasoning process. So I think what PB is saying is that these two are complementary. They have to be brought together in order to produce the philosopher. On the one hand, to have the mystical glimpse, the recognition that Intellection can take place without the sensible concomitant, and, on the other hand, to have an understanding of the sensible world, and reason your way out of it, but without the Intellection—these two things are separate. They have to be brought together. They're complementary. Wouldn't you think so?

BS: Why is the understanding permanent to the metaphysician?

ANTHONY: If you take a person like Kant as an example, he's thought out in his understanding the categories of thought that make knowledge possible. If you asked Kant when he was forty, when he was fifty, when he was sixty, he would still be able to tell you about those categories of thought, wouldn't he? But for the mystic who has the experience when he's twenty years old, if you ask him about it at thirty, it's only a memory, and at forty, it's only a memory. At fifty, it's still only a memory. But the knowledge that Kant had, for example, was permanent. He didn't lose it. It's part and parcel of his being now.

LR: Are you saying it can stay with him without any experience?

ANTHONY: You try thinking it out. It took Kant about twelve years to work out *The Critique.*

Let's go back to what we said before: that the intellect is a tool for survival, for biological adaptation, and that it's restricted in its operation to what is something that it can use. Then we brought in the fact that this man had to reason, and that meant he had to use the intellect. But the reason was guiding the intellect. He worked out the problems of epistemology and metaphysics by manipulating the intellect; that is, the reason manipulated the intellect until it brought forth the correct answers.

Now, as we said, this was a process that took a dozen years. Can you imagine? If we look at it this way, then what we're saying is that this ray of light which penetrates into the psychosomatic organism and is that illuminating principle within the ego, this guiding light, was directing and guiding the intellect until it reached a point where it understood these metaphysical principles, so that it generated in the continuum of its own consciousness this work, this understanding. Now this is permanent for that individual. When he comes back again the next incarnation; he hasn't lost it. He's not going to lose that ability. Now, this can be kept distinct from the case, let's say, of a Jacob Boehme or another mystic who might experience the Overself and yet not understand any of this.

The point that PB's making here is that these two things have to be brought together. One must try to get a glimpse of the higher self, the Overself, to see how Intellection goes on in that realm, and one must also understand at the level of the intellect the way that the sensible and the Intellectual—in other words, the divided line—is not divided. There's no difficulty here. After all, if you work this hard for the understanding, and you're going to lose it, then why bother getting it?

LR: What about all the quotes about reason exhausting itself?

TS: It says "completing its task"; it doesn't say "wiping itself out."

ANTHONY: Yes, there's a difference here. Someone also used the term "cancels itself out." It doesn't cancel itself out; it *fulfills* itself. That's quite different.

Take a good scientist who's capable of tremendous concentration—Heisenberg, for example. He never studied yoga! He got *nirvikalpa* just by concentrating with all the might he had on the problems he had!

LD: So either way you study, if you study the objective or the subjective, you're going to come up with *nirvikalpa.*

ANTHONY: But in his case it was very unusual, wasn't it? He was studying the nature of the World-Idea.

Remember we used the astrological chart of Einstein as an example. When the idea of relativity came in, there was a state of absolute non-cognition. To us it seems like non-cognition—that's *nirvikalpa.* You don't have to have wings.

LD: But content was brought into that.

ANTHONY: No, that came later; that comes later.

JFL: Can we look at it again from the point of view of *nirvikalpa*?

ANTHONY: In other words, that's the thought-free consciousness.

JFL: Thought-free consciousness—the I AM principle. Most mystics who have attained this, have attained it as a shortcut, in the sense that the bodies that were given to them were not really developed, so they couldn't maintain that state and had to go back.

ANTHONY: Well, no one can maintain that state.

JFL: No one can maintain that?

ANTHONY: No, you cannot maintain *nirvikalpa samadhi*, you cannot maintain a consciousness that's thought-free indefinitely. It's only for a period of time.

JFL: But doesn't the mystic have to take that attention or that concentration back to the World-Idea?

ANTHONY: Yes, but *first* the mystic has to achieve that thought-free consciousness, so that it can be used for a higher purpose.

JFL: Used for a higher purpose. Okay, and that is to turn that towards the world—I think that's what that quote is saying.

ANTHONY: Okay, but do you see what you've done? You've established the I AM consciousness as a principle in its own right.

JFL: And this is where PB says most mystics stop and they go back and deny everything else.

ANTHONY: You remember the example: Vivekananda asked Ramakrishna, "Can't I have this for three or four weeks at one stretch?" And Ramakrishna said, "There's something even better than that." I just throw that in as an example that there are those who recognize that *nirvikalpa* is not the ultimate state. All right. So Vivekananda said, "Okay, what do you want me to do?"

JFL: This is very confusing to me because the individual now has to go back, apparently go back.

ANTHONY: Well, you don't have to do anything, you just open your eyes and there's the world.

> . . . by studying the world's own nature, laying bare its mentalistic character . . .

JFL: So you have to go back to the world experience. If something happens, you're supposed to reflect on it. PB says that now you have to penetrate the nature of the world. He's not talking about going back to *nirvikalpa*; he's saying that now you have to penetrate the World-Idea and look for that source, the World-Mind.

ANTHONY: Well, wouldn't you have to start with a body? Isn't it going to be the body that is going to provide you with the various kinds of consciousness that will give you an insight into the World-Idea? You have to become an inhabitant of a body, and get to know about wakeful consciousness; as an inhabitant of the dream life you become aware of *taijasa* consciousness; the deeper laws will take you into the *prajna* consciousness. In other words, it is the World-Idea which provides you with the necessary vehicles by which that Soul which you experience in *nirvikalpa* knows that it can understand the depths or, let's say, the dimensions in the various levels of being that are *in* the World-Idea.

JFL: Yes. But can an individual do this before this state by—

ANTHONY: Well, what need is there for such a hierarchy: before or after? You're not taking a train. You are either a person who's competent—let's say as a scientist—to investigate the nature of the World-Idea, or you're not. You could be a mystic and you're competent as far as psychological introversion is concerned—you could go inwardly and reach levels in which there is no thought at all.

JFL: Will this actually reveal understanding?

ANTHONY: No. It doesn't reveal understanding.

JFL: I thought you were saying that a scientist could go in one direction and the mystic can introvert, and realize—

ANTHONY: As a mystic, you will introvert and find out what the nature of your own soul is, your own essence, your own being. But this does not automatically include an understanding of the nature of the World-Idea. In order to understand that World-Idea you have to go *into* the World-Idea. What does that mean? It means you have to investigate, you have to go into a product of the World-Idea, a *body* that is created by the World-Mind, and through that body acquire experience of the nature of the World-Idea.

JFL: Great!

ANTHONY: No, that's just a start, that's just openers.

JFL: Then PB says you do this "only by studying the world's own nature, laying bare its mentalistic character."

RG: So we're discussing the task of trying to understand the nature of the world.

ANTHONY: Yes—so how would you start?

RG: First you would have to recognize the mentalistic nature of all your thoughts, that it is a manifestation of *your* mind.

ANTHONY: And you would go from there, right?

RG: Yes. I would start with the experience of this world as real and the experience of the Overself as real, which the mystic "can do only by studying the world's own nature, laying bare its mentalistic character." Now the world is mentalistic in two senses. First, it's individually mentalistic—it's an unfoldment of your own mind *or* your Overself.

ANTHONY: Well, wouldn't you say that your mind, your own mind or the Overself or Soul, is manifesting the World-Idea, and that the World-Idea is not *your* World-Idea?

RG: Yes, and that would be the cosmic mentalism level. But on an individual level, you'd have to say that your perception of the world arises from within your own consciousness. Then you can trace the stuff of that idea two ways. One way to trace it back is through your own ideation: The individual mind gives the form and the World-Idea gives the substance. The second way is to see that the World-Idea arises from a source other than the individual Overself. It arises from the Cosmic Soul or World-Mind, which is putting forth—

ANTHONY: But aren't they the same—isn't the Overself a particle of the World-Mind?

RG: Yes, the Overself is a phase of the World-Mind.

ANTHONY: So then the World-Mind is behind both—then you have nondualism.

You begin to get this awesome notion that, on the one hand, there's this absoluteness of your soul as a principle in its own right, and, on the other hand, the World-Idea is manifested, and the soul can investigate into the nature of that World-Idea, and that investigation is endless. But you can get to the main principles, you can see the main principles that are carried on within it.

JB: Why is the body needed to carry out that latter investigation?

ANTHONY: How can you participate in the nature of the sensible world without a body? In a general way, if you want to get some experience into the nature of the sensible world, you have to have a sensible body through which you can participate in that sensible world. So that when you have certain astrological aspects going on and the formation of perception is altered by those aspects, you *know* that you are a participant in that world. And the same thing will happen, for instance, if you wish to participate in the nature of the subtle world—you must have a vehicle, a subtle vehicle, which can participate in the subtle idea of the world. And then you could go even deeper and try to participate in the nature of the absolute idea of the world, and for that you must have a kind of body that Ishvara provides and you can call that the *prajna* consciousness.

JB: As I understand, a being with just a subtle body or just *prajna* consciousness, if you can imagine such a being, would have some attainment of this deeper World-Idea.

ANTHONY: Yes. Now there's a shortcut that PB's recommending: Get to the point, find out that the nature of the World-Idea is mentalistic, and immediately you'll arrive at the notion that behind it all is Mind. And you already have the information that in *nirvikalpa* your authentic being is Mind. These two together are nondual, and you come up with the doctrine of nondualism.

JFL: Also, he implies here that *nirvikalpa* seems to be the necessary prerequisite for the—

ANTHONY: Well, that's a name you know. *Nirvikalpa* is a name. "Thought-free consciousness" is better—we'll understand each other. So let's look again at the exercise PB describes in *The Wisdom of the Overself,* the Serpent's Path. Remember the passage where he says: what is needed in this exercise is a dynamically alert attention, one that won't wander—I'm paraphrasing here—and with this attention you try, you aim, to get in between two thoughts.

Now the two thoughts are the World-Mind's pulsation of the World-Idea. If the World-Mind pulsates, delivers the World-Idea, one thought after the other, and you're basing yourself on the fact that you're a soul, this pure consciousness, then this principle of consciousness is going to be inserted between two ideas that the World-Mind is projecting forth. So then you can see that the ultimate substratum of the World-Idea is World-Mind. And you speak about getting to the Void.

LD: It sounds like thought-free consciousness must be attained first.

ANTHONY: There is a natural hierarchy. Remember what Atmananda told his student when the student came out of the *nirvikalpa* state: "Now use your mind to understand the World-Idea, so that you can become a philosopher."

LD: You're saying that it's a hierarchy?

ANTHONY: It's a natural hierarchy. But let's keep in mind that the achievement of thought-free consciousness is quite extraordinary.

LD: But then it depends on what you've described as "what is the world." If you equate that with the *sahaja* state of consciousness or with the scientific—

ANTHONY: No. *Sahaja* can only be the result of an understanding of the World-Idea *within* the Soul. That's the only way you can have *sahaja.* But the point is, I'm not trying to create a hierarchy; I'm saying it just exists naturally. The person who has achieved *nirvikalpa*—and that's no mean achievement—has gone quite a way. And yet a sage like Atmananda or PB comes along and tells you, "Now you've got to go further and *use* that consciousness, *use* that ability, to understand the nature of the World-Idea." And when you've succeeded, *now* you can go further and become a philosopher. And then you can go even further than that, and become fully human, and forget all the rest. Because philosophy's for your use. You're not here for philosophy, philosophy's here for you.

> THERE ARE three stages on the path of world enquiry. The first yields as its fruit that the world is but an idea, and this stage has been reached from the metaphysical end by thinkers such as Bishop Berkeley, and nearly reached from the scientific end by such a man as Eddington. The second stage involves the study of the three states, waking, dreaming, and deep sleep, and yields as its fruit the truth that ideas are transitory emanations out of their permanent cause, consciousness. The third stage is the most difficult, for it requires analysis of the nature of time, space, and causation, plus successful practice of yoga. It yields as its fruit the sense of Reality as something eternally abiding with one.
>
> (v13, Cat. 19 intro., p. 2)

ANTHONY: Again, one part at a time.

> There are three stages of the path of world enquiry. The first yields as its fruit that the world is but an idea . . .

HS: Is this first stage subsequent to knowing the ego's truth?

ANTHONY: No, this is the first stage in your development of understanding philosophy. Bishop Berkeley insists that you cannot know anything outside of knowing, that you cannot posit the existence of matter. That's the first elementary introduction into mentalism.

HS: That gives you a conceptual understanding that the world is mind.

ANTHONY: Or that the world is within your thought.

AH: It's not the realization of mentalism.

ANTHONY: No, but it's a good beginning. As a matter of fact, if you read Bertrand Russell, in *Problems of Philosophy*, he says [*paraphrase*], "You know, this position is impregnable. You cannot refute it, but we won't pay attention to it." [*laughter*] Yes,

Bertrand Russell. So that's the first thing you have to recognize, that that position is impregnable. Don't say, "Well, I'm going to ignore it and just go on." Understanding mentalism conceptually is a good beginning.

LR: But then what do you do?

ANTHONY: Well, after you do that for a few years, you go on to the next step. But by that time you've read Berkeley, David Hume, Schopenhauer, all these people are going up and down the ladder. Then you read the next series.

> . . . The second stage involves the study of the three states waking, dreaming, and deep sleep, and yields as its fruit the truth that ideas are transitory emanations out of their permanent cause, consciousness. . . .

ANTHONY: I hope you don't think study here is used the way you understand. Study here means that you're willing to try making little experiments now and then, like when you go to sleep, you're going to dream about something, and you work for a couple of months, to try to determine what kind of dream you have, how you want the plot to unfold, and what you expect to get out of this. Or you work to make available to yourself the idea that if nightmares occur, or any images occur, you will instantaneously awaken yourself. What we're talking about here is the willingness to practice and play around a little bit with the different kinds of states of consciousness you have. And sleep and dream are among those states, which usually you simply take for granted.

AH: Anthony, it seems reasonable to talk about understanding waking consciousness from the point of view of waking consciousness. And it is even remotely possible to understand the dream states. But to speak about having access to the sleep state where there are no images and no contents presents me with a problem.

ANTHONY: Yes, now we're speaking about practicing mystics, and not the *reading* kind.

AH: There are images in waking consciousness, we won't deny that, and there are also images in dream consciousness. But what is it that's examined in the sleep state?

ANTHONY: Again, this is a theoretical question, because it requires that you are a working mystic. By a working mystic I mean, precisely, a person who is capable of introverting into her or his consciousness and experiencing in meditation various states of consciousness. Included would be what we call dream consciousness and sleep consciousness. There's no sense trying to discuss these things theoretically.

PB is speaking about three levels or degrees of understanding mentalism. You start with the easiest, whether it's Berkeley in the West, or a text from the East like the *Yoga Vasistha*, then you attempt to get deeper into the study of mentalism by experimenting with your own states of mind. Or you could read—in Christian Science and New Thought and hypnotism and things like that—about the mind's ability to function in a variety of ways; it's enough to stagger the imagination. And then when you're acquainted and understand and are equipped to deal with that in a way that you can manipulate it, then you go into a deeper study of the meaning of space, time, and causality, such as was undertaken by people like Eddington and Jeans or you read commentaries like Guadapada's on the meaning of causality. And if you understand that, your understanding of mentalism has deepened. That's what he's talking about.

LR: You prefaced your explanation of this by saying that what PB means by study here is not what we think of as the intellectual pursuit, that it's an actual practice, an experimentation with the mind. Now I was trying to see these three levels in that context and I was wondering what kind of experimentation was involved in this last analysis of time, space, and causality. PB has quotes that say the Overself can reveal itself through any vehicle, but it has to do so in accordance with karma. Is this experimentation available only to those at the highest level of development?

ANTHONY: No. We are trying to understand, in our own way, the ultimate meaning of things like space, time, and causality, and we worked on that problem over and over again. Just because you can discuss *jnana* doesn't make you a sage. And the fact that you worked through these three levels of mentalism doesn't make you a sage.

I have a quote from PB, where he speaks about how much work you do before you become a sage, and that you're going to die a hundred deaths and suffer a thousand sufferings. So don't worry about being a sage. But we have to understand the ultimate nature of space, time, and causality with the little brain that we have. It'll be adequate, believe me—if it's used!

~

RC: Three questions have come out of our discussions: What's the ego, What do we mean by the world, and What do we mean by consciousness? To start an inquiry into how we distinguish those three, here's one about the world.

> IT IS NOT possible for sincere, scrupulous thinking to admit, and never possible to prove, the existence of a world outside of, and separate from, its consciousness. The faith by which we all conventionally grant such existence is mere superstition.
>
> (v13, 21:2.104 and *Perspectives*, p. 287)

ANTHONY: So the ego and the world are both ideas and consciousness is distinct from them. We have a division here, where, on the one hand we have consciousness, and on the other side the mind, and in the mind we put ego and the world.

Why don't we do this: Why don't we try to trace the ego and the world back to its origin and trace what we're calling consciousness back to its origin? If you or I introvert, intensely, inwardly, we might end up with *nirvikalpa samadhi*. Then there's the other alternative, ending up with *sahaja*. What would be the difference?

VM: I thought *nirvikalpa* is a thought-free state, absolutely thought-free.

ANTHONY: For whom? What's excluded?

VM: Certainly any notion of world and ego.

ANTHONY: World and ego? For who? For mind, right? It's mind that's excluding the world and the ego, and it becomes free of that. But what about *sahaja*, where the person is experiencing the peaceful consciousness despite the existence of the World-Idea?

Now if you tackle it this way you'll be able to grasp better the distinction I'm trying to bring about between what they call the ego-and-the-world, and the consciousness. What would you trace the origin of the ego and the world to?

VM: Well, I would have to trace them back to this principle of mind.

ANTHONY: You'd say the World-Idea and the World-Mind, wouldn't you?

VM: Okay, both of them, you could say, are contained within the unfolding of the World-Idea by the principle of mind.

ANTHONY: And so there's this mind, this Intellectual-Principle that is our being. And this is a principle in itself. It's a consciousness, it's an intellectual authentic. And if we introspect very intensely we can get to that, and appreciate or experience the thought-free peaceful state which we are calling consciousness or mind. On the other hand, this mind manifests the World-Idea, which means the World-Mind too. World-Mind and World-Idea are both being manifested through this reality. And in manifesting the World-Idea, included in it would have to be a body which you're going to assume is yours, and which you're going to work through. So this body is going to be the ego, and when the consciousness illuminates that ego or shines through that body, a world is going to arise. If it withdraws, there's no world and no ego. It enters—both arise concomitantly.

So now if we try to understand these three things—the ego,

the world, and consciousness—we'll have to make this division. It's not a real separation, it's a distinction. And I grant you that if you reach *nirvikalpa samadhi* or *sahaja,* you would be talking about the same reality. But when we speak about *nirvikalpa* or introversion into our own being, it seems to be psychological. Whereas when we speak about entering into, or trying to understand, the nature of the Intellectual-Principle which is supporting the World-Idea, that seems to be more metaphysical. In other words, insofar as this being that I am penetrates and understands the nature of the ego and the world, not conceptually, not in a twofold way, but by experiencing the World-Mind's consciousness, then we can say that that entity, that I AM, is associated with, or is experiencing, the consciousness of the Intellectual-Principle, and is enjoying *sahaja.* In other words, the World-Idea unrolls, but it doesn't disturb that consciousness.

Now when you read the third chapter of *The Hidden Teaching Beyond Yoga,* you begin to understand that PB had achieved *nirvikalpa samadhi,* but was still very unhappy about the whole situation. [*laughter*]

JG: That's where he also says that it is a psychological achievement.

ANTHONY: Yes, it was a great psychological achievement, but he still went around very discontented and people were telling him, "Well, you achieved the best that could be done, why aren't you happy?" And why wasn't he happy?

VM: It was an impermanent state.

ANTHONY: Yes. But what else?

JG: He didn't know what the world meant. It eludes you in that state.

ANTHONY: Yes, the meaning of the world still escaped him. So how do you go about solving that?

JG: He applied reason, didn't he?

ANTHONY: Yes, he applied reason; but what did that lead to? Didn't that lead to the recognition that the World-Idea is spawned by the World-Mind? And that, insofar as his Overself is part of the World-Mind, the reality he was seeking was the reality of his own being? And that he'd have to see both of them in the light that they were *all* part of the World-Mind? We're trying to amplify these meanings so that at the ground level, when we start talking about the ego and the world and the consciousness, we know what we're speaking about, because we can trace them to their ultimate principles.

RC: Did I hear right? Did PB realize that his Overself was part of the World-Mind and that that included the world?

ANTHONY: And that included the world, and his Overself was manifesting the World-Mind.

RC: The Overself includes the world? I'm just trying to follow.

ANTHONY: That's why we have to go slow, a step at a time. We're saying that each individual's Overself is the means by which the World-Idea is being translated, or by which the ego and the world arise together. It's within *your* mind that these two things arise. So, we have our consciousness, our Overself consciousness, our mind, and then we have the World-Mind's Idea, or what PB called the emanation of that mysterious aura which *our* mind transposes or translates into the World-Idea. And when it does that, my body is part of that World-Idea. Not my consciousness, but my *body* is part of that World-Idea. So when the consciousness is associated with that body, that ego is on the one hand part of the World-Idea, and on the other hand the consciousness can withdraw from that body and be independent or, let's say, free of the World-Idea. So we have this paradoxical situation that we're talking about. On the one hand, the soul as self-concerned in *nirvikalpa,* absolutely self-concerned, rejects everything else and stays in its own identity. On the other hand, we know that this isn't the ultimate truth because it excludes the truth of the world. So PB had to come out of that situation, and he kept on wandering around trying to find out what was the truth. Because he refused to accept that *nirvikalpa* was the truth. It wasn't. So what did he do? You said he went through a process of reasoning. What else do you remember about what he did with this reasoning? [*pause*]

He came to certain conclusions. Do you remember what the conclusions were? What would be the consequence of reasoning upon the World-Idea? Assuming that now, having reached *nirvikalpa,* he understood the nature of his own being, what would be further reasoning on that? Now he comes back, he's achieved *nirvikalpa,* looks at the world, and he refuses to accept the fact or the notion that the world is an illusion, or that it doesn't exist. He just refuses—he throws that out, he throws that out with the rope trick. But then what kind of reasoning follows?

LDS: Part of the reasoning that brought PB to mentalism had to do with the fact that in order for there to be any kind of real relationship between a knower and that knower's world, there has to be a common substance between those two. So mentalism had to be established in terms of the very dynamism of the reasoning process.

ANTHONY: Can we substantiate that with a quote or a passage from PB? How about using the Serpent's Path exercise again?

We're saying that on the one hand, the world is a series of thoughts, one thought following upon the other. And that the purpose of that exercise is to *insert* the attention between two thoughts so that you can contact Void Mind, or Mind. Now, WHO is it that inserts attention between two thoughts? Is it the same nature as mind?

My attention is riveted on the flow of thoughts. My attention is equivalent to my consciousness and it's riveted between these two thoughts. We're beyond the realm of sensation. My mind is riveted and it's waiting to break through two thoughts, so that it can reach Mind. What mind can it reach?

TS: Its source as in the World-Mind.

ANTHONY: It would reach the World-Mind, yes, between two thoughts. The World-Mind is producing these thoughts of the world, so World-Mind would be behind that. But what about *my* mind?

If attention is alert, dynamic, stripped of any preoccupation with anything else, so it's almost like pure attention, it would be equivalent to consciousness. And it is THAT which inserts itself between two thoughts and reaches the World-Mind. So what happened there?

You have the World-Mind producing the world—right?—thought after thought. The exercise says now you focus your attention. And this is an extreme kind of attention, alert, dynamic, concentrated. It's really focused, it's trying to get in between two thoughts. Let's say it succeeds—it gets in between two thoughts—what's behind the thought? We said the World-Mind is producing it. And who's trying to get into it?

My mind, my mind—I'm trying to get enlightened. I would assume that if a person could do that, that person has achieved *nirvikalpa* at least.

That is the level of development a person would need to reach such an intense focus point that it could be used to get into the thought that the World-Mind is producing.

AS: So PB went through this process of attaining *nirvikalpa* where, in a sense, he cut off the world and the ego. But now he has to absorb the thought into himself, tracing the reasoning process to the origin of that world. If he traced the origin of his own *consciousness* to the World-Mind, now it seems he has to trace the origin of the *thoughts* to that very same mind to which he traced the origin of his consciousness. And that seems to me not so much cutting off the thoughts as reabsorbing them, tracing them back to their source.

JFL: What do you mean?

ANTHONY: The question that's coming up here is what PB means when he says the philosophic yogi has to *absorb* the World-Idea. The way I understand the absorption of the World-Idea is that when the philosophic yogi penetrates into the World-Mind between two thoughts, at that instant the World-Idea is absorbed. It has become part of the yogi who *knows* that the world IS consciousness transforming itself into Idea. Now you have *sahaja.* Why do you have *sahaja* NOW?

AS: Because no matter what happens, you are always established in Mind.

ANTHONY: You know that *whatever is, is Mind.*

The Serpent's Path exercise is very complex. PB speaks about achieving enlightenment, full enlightenment. And if you assume that a person who's capable of *nirvikalpa* is *not* enlightened, then you see what PB is leading you to. He's saying now this person has to penetrate into the World-Mind in order to become enlightened. You do *not* become enlightened because you achieve *nirvikalpa samadhi.*

Now, in describing this exercise, he speaks about the yogi who has developed the ability to be able to concentrate to a point where it's possible to penetrate in between two ideas, two flashes of the World-Idea, and grasp the innermost World-Mind's consciousness that's producing—or, let's say, is—the substratum of that World-Idea. Now there are *two kinds of consciousness* involved here. On the one hand, you have the consciousness of the individual practitioner, who's going to try the exercise. It is this attention that is being brought to bear within one's own consciousness on the World-Idea. And the practitioner has to penetrate that World-Idea. The mind of the individual, insofar as it produces the world, does so in this fluctuating way, because that's the way the Intellectual-Principle produces the world, instant after instant.

All right, now, you could take the position of the Buddhist and say that the consciousness is always fleeting: that would be looking from the side of World-Idea. Or you could take the position of the Hindu, that consciousness is always self-identical with itself and never changing: that would be looking from the side of the consciousness of the individual. Or you could combine these two positions by understanding this exercise.

The yogi attempts to focus individual consciousness to such a minute point that the flashing World-Idea can be penetrated. With that consciousness the yogi penetrates into the MIND that is producing the World-Idea. At that instant the yogi has *absorbed* the World-Idea. Why has the yogi absorbed the World-Idea? How else could you absorb something? —if you want to absorb a piece of cake, you gotta bring it into yourself. You gotta *eat* it. And if you want to absorb the World-Mind, you have to take it into yourself. In this case, the recognition would be that your Overself, which is a particle of the World-Mind, is part of the World-Mind.

So at one and the same time, you have this dualistic way that you have to approach the exercise, and you also have to see that ultimately you're speaking about the same reality—the reality of the Overself and the reality of the World-Mind which underlies the World-Idea. It's one and the same reality.

So a simple question, like What is the ego, what is the world, and what is consciousness shows immediately how much of these principles of PB you've picked up—or if you picked up any.

The World-Idea arises and descends, moment to moment. The consciousness of the individual, the Overself of the individual, does no such thing. It always is what it is, never alters, never changes, doesn't get projected forth, is not a continuum. That's the soul.

Now this individual soul projects from within itself the World-Idea, which naturally has for its substratum the World-Mind. So you have this paradox: a consciousness which is always what it is, never alters, and then the World-Idea which is being projected out from within itself and which is discontinuous, moment to moment.

Now, to complicate it even more, within that World-Idea, your consciousness has taken residence in a body which belongs to the World-Idea and which is altering moment to moment. The consciousness that you know is the one that's in the body that sees constant change all around: Your cognitive states are momentary states of consciousness. The consciousness that you don't know is the one that's manifesting the World-Idea.[10] [*pause*]

TS: There's this amazing quote he has that summarizes what you've said:

> THE EGO to which he is so attached turns out on enquiry to be none other than the presence of the World-Mind within his own heart. If identification is then shifted by constant practice from one to the other, he has achieved the purpose of life.
>
> (v6, 8:1.127)

ANTHONY: Would you repeat that again? Would you repeat it in red—I mean, say it real loud?

[*quote is repeated*]

ANTHONY: Wouldn't that be the exercise we were just talking about? Instead of paying attention to the thought, there would be a change or a shift in identification. We tend to identify with the World-Idea, because our ego is included as part of that World-Idea. Whereas what is required of us is to assert the attention or insert it in between two ideas, which would mean the negation of the ego.

So we're saying that *nirvikalpa* is just a prerequisite in order to achieve *sahaja* and understand that the nature of the World-Idea is *not an illusion,* but consciousness transforming itself or mind transforming itself. And that has to be understood as an actual experience, and not a conceptual understanding—just as mentalism has to be understood the same way that you understand bodily pain.

AP: Doesn't the person who meditates in the ordinary mystic way, when introverting the consciousness and dropping it into the heart, also come to that point where the pulsating thoughts come in?

ANTHONY: No, you *exclude* that to come to the thought-free state. Consciousness introverting upon itself does not have any room for the World-Idea. By definition. How could it? When you speak of something that does, then you're not talking about consciousness introverting into itself, you're speaking about the *ego* introverting into itself—which is part of the World-Idea. Consciousness, Mind, introverting into itself, has no room for the World-Idea. [*last sentence spoken softly and emphatically*]

It's a whole different ball game, when you want to become a *philosophic* mystic. Then you have to take that consciousness that is capable of introverting into itself, and use it for the Serpent's Path exercise, so that you can achieve the *sahaja* which is the understanding that the World-Idea is MIND MANIFESTING ITSELF and that the appearance and the reality are coterminous or the same thing.

LR: When you're doing the Serpent's Path, you're also disregarding the thoughts.

ANTHONY: Of course you're disregarding the thoughts, because you're trying to get to the World-Mind! Do you see why PB was in such pain and agony in spite of achieving *nirvikalpa*?

The truth is one thing, but personal comfort is something else—our pleasure, the fact that we're comfortable, is something else.

EM: If a person is in a state where they're able to experience *nirvikalpa,* when they come out of *nirvikalpa,* wouldn't they still have this stinky ego, as stinky as ever?

ANTHONY: Well, no, it's not as bad.

EM: Or would it be a very refined ego?

ANTHONY: You're on your way to self-development. The recognition that there are supreme values is not something that you put off lightly.

EM: Would there still be that push to rid oneself of the lower aspect of the ego?

ANTHONY: You begin to recognize the need to burn out the *samskaras,* the *vasanas* [residual tendencies that interfere with pure perception]—to realize that they have to be transformed. And so you take a text like the *Jivanmukti-Viveka* by Vidyaranya, *The Path of Liberation,* where they prescribe a whole course for how to go about reducing those *vasanas* to a minimum. We're not talking about something that gets accomplished in a short time; it's a long-drawn-out affair. In these texts, they say these *vasanas* have to be burnt, scorched. And they say that the only way that they can be scorched is through knowledge. So I assume that that would mean one has to recognize that ultimately these *vasanas* are also of this mental substance. They *also* are part of the World-Idea, and consequently that is the way to go about getting rid of them or overcoming them.

You see, the big issue here, in terms of what we've been doing, is to understand this double nature of the soul and the peculiar infiltration of the World-Idea *in* it, and that there are these two ways of trying to understand it. There are two alternatives; the soul can get into a thought-free state, or it can get into a *sahaja* state. And PB tries to make clear that the *sahaja* state is a superior state because there you reach the point where you recognize that reality and appearance are really only a distinction that the ego makes, not that the insight permits. And your understanding then becomes more accurate.

You know how Arnold [Sir Edwin Arnold, *The Light of Asia*] tried to describe it? He says, "The Dewdrop slips into the shining Sea." Truly, it is the other way around: the ocean is slipping into the dewdrop! And that would be a way of trying to understand how the individual soul absorbs the World-Idea. But these are metaphors—they're all bunk. If you ever get enlightened, you're going to come and shoot me!—for lying.

> *Sahaja* is the final phase and, in striking contrast to the first phase, the Glimpse, lasts as long as corporeal life lasts. In this he brings the light into every day's thought, speech, and behaviour. It is the phase of Application. So, little by little, disjointedly and at intervals, he gets established in a calm awareness of his connection with, and relation to, the Overself.
>
> (v15, 24:3.317)

VM: I find this a little unsettling, because I thought the state of *sahaja samadhi* is the state when you *do* have calm abiding in the Overself and simultaneously the World-Idea is continuously unfolding.

ANTHONY: It's a continuous process.

VM: You grow into it?

ANTHONY: It's always deepening, so that ultimately it's the soul that is living through that ego. The soul is determining and dictating *every* phase of your existence. The ego has nothing to say any more, and that's the establishment of the soul in the corporeal life. And there's no limit to that. Don't think of it as a one-shot thing. The spiritual is never a one-shot.

JG: Does that mean that there is still effort?

ANTHONY: No. No effort. The variety of situations that arise are occasions for the sage to employ, or use, the wisdom of the soul, as to how to live. So we can look at it that way.

HS: I'd like to hear what you said again, because that was really nice.

ANTHONY: Well, there's another quote where PB says that in *sahaja* there's a relationship, so to speak, with the World-Idea—one knows more what the role of the ego is, what the role of the personality is in the world, and that too is established gradually, or more and more firmly. It's in both directions—in relation to one's own soul and in relation to the World-Idea that's being worked out.

JG: So you know what you have to do?

ANTHONY: Yes. Not perfectly all the time, but you know what you have to do.

JG: But you wouldn't know that after *nirvikalpa*?

ANTHONY: Correct.

HS: Wouldn't you say that there's the establishment of a kind of certitude first, of the truth of this self—

ANTHONY: Yes, you're established in that recognition that everything is Mind. But then it's another thing to understand—how do I live in this new situation? That's what PB is talking about—the establishment of *sahaja.* And it's something that takes place over time—at least I think I saw PB getting deeper and deeper and more beneficent and more encompassing as he went along.

KD: Could you say that the ego or the series of thoughts might be the relationship between the soul as life-principle and the *nous* within it? And that *nirvikalpa* would be the penetration into the soul as life-principle, and *sahaja* would be more fully the experience of the whole soul, as soul plus the Intellectual-Principle within it? And that's why we speak always about duality when we talk about the soul, because of this dual nature of the soul as life-principle plus the Intellectual-Principle within it?

ANTHONY: Go ahead.

KD: And the reason *sahaja* is more complete is that the soul doesn't come to self-knowledge without bringing in this gnostic principle, which is the Intellectual-Principle within it. The World-Idea is the emanation from that *nous* within the soul, and that's why that has to be brought into actualization, or that has to be penetrated before there's a full experience of the soul or before it's actualized. Does that make any sense?

ANTHONY: Yes, yes, I think you said it. That's the entire difficulty that we're always confronting, and it's been going on for a long time. We have this dual nature of the soul: We speak of the soul as concerned with itself and introspecting into itself; we also speak about a soul, with the *nous* in it, the soul as inhabiting or presiding over a part of the World-Idea—that is, a particular body which that World-Idea has created. So you have this strange paradox, that for the soul to gain ultimate enlightenment it must do so through a vehicle, or vehicles, which are provided by the Intellectual-Principle within the soul, through which it can reach that Intellectual-Principle. This is what we've been discussing.

KD: So in that quote of PB's, "The ego to which he is so attached turns out on enquiry to be none other than the presence of the World-Mind within his heart," would you say that that body is produced by the World-Mind, and that that is why it's necessary that the soul's contact with the World-Mind is through that body?

ANTHONY: Yes. The association of the soul with a particular body is the entrance into the unlimitedness of the World-Mind. The soul as identified with a body which is part of the Intellectual-Principle can have experience of the unlimited nature of the intellectual idea, and the mind. In other words, the mind conjoined to the World-Idea can experience this unlimitedness or at least become aware of it. The extent of the World-Idea is something we can't grasp, we can't conceive, because it's actually unlimited. And it's through the fact that the soul can associate with part of the World-Idea that this becomes feasible or possible.

CDA: So the body is part of the World-Idea and it's through this association with the body that the soul is able to experience the unlimitedness of the Intellectual-Principle.

ANTHONY: Yes. So you could have a body, for instance, in the celestial realms—and then you could have a body that belongs to one of the higher spheres or stars. But without the body, you're not going to have the experience of the unlimitedness of the World-Mind and the World-Mind's idea. And that's why these things have to be understood. In Islam, they have this notion about Kabir, they speak about the I AM principle as "Kabir," the green one, the verdant one. You ought to read about it.

> THE UNIT of mind is differentiated out and undergoes its long evolution through numerous changes of state, not to merge so utterly in its source again as to be virtually annihilated, but to be consciously harmonized with that source whilst yet retaining its individuality.
>
> (excerpt from v16, 25:2.204 and *Perspectives*, p. 342)

ANTHONY: PB is saying that the Overself sends forth from itself its progeny, and that progeny will eventually learn to be in harmony with the Overself and work with the Overself.

There would be no sense for the transcendent Overself, which is beyond all relationships, to project forth from itself this entity which is part of itself and have it evolve through the whole of the World-Idea just to reabsorb it. This entity which is projected from the Overself has to eventually learn to work in cooperation with this higher self. And, of course, that would mean ultimately with the World-Mind.

Now to understand this, let's back up a step. We speak about the soul as transcendent, abiding in a serene tranquility, an undifferentiated consciousness, the I AM principle. Then we say that this consciousness has the power to project itself anywhere, anywhither, and it does so in the sense that it projects a portion or a *stream* of life. Now if you think about this continuous stream of life from the Overself to this part of itself which is going to traverse all the kingdoms of nature, then you can see a karmic continuity. This unit of life is continuous and consequently you can speak about a karmic continuity. This is what reaches all the way down to the earth and starts out as an amoeba and goes through all the various kingdoms of nature, rising up to the human level. There it enters the reasoning phase. Now these two together, on the one hand the soul or Overself as transcendent, on the other hand the emanant from that transcendent soul, the individual ego, Plotinus refers to as the "We." Keep that in mind, that's important. Those two together are the "We."

AS: Is the description of that emanant or that stream of life evolving up through all these kingdoms based on its association with that developing World-Idea?

ANTHONY: Yes.

AS: That stream of life is what got associated with all these vehicles which are part of the World-Idea or with the developing World-Idea and it evolves with that.

ANTHONY: That point is very important. We think of the Overself as absolutely transcendent, having nothing to do with the World-Idea, abiding and resting in repose in itself. But then we must also keep in mind that the World-Mind is within the soul, just like the soul is within World-Mind. Now, theoretically, we can abstract these things and we can say that if the World-Mind with the World-Idea is present in the soul, then in order for this transcendent being that our soul is to have experience of that world, it emanates a part of itself into that world, which we call the ego. And it goes through all the kingdoms of nature. But in doing so, it is discovering and finding out something about the World-Idea.

So this transcendent being which is our I AM, in order to know something about the World-Idea, has to send this offspring into the World-Idea and it must evolve through that World-Idea. Now the richness, the variety, the incomprehensibility of the World-Idea is something we don't have to discuss. Right? If you take a primitive, you'll get one version of the world. If you take a scientist, you'll get another version of the world. If you take a sage, you'll get a third version of the world. And you can see there's a deepening, an inwardization, a widening comprehension of the World-Idea, as we deal with people of various levels. So you can see that the World-Idea is going to satisfy all of us in one way or another.

AS: And when this emanant, this stream of life, is going through this evolutionary process, it's always conjoined with that transcendent Overself. That is, it's the "We" that's having the experience. When the lower has the experience, in some way the higher is also having the experience or is the real subject behind it all. In other words, this is all happening with that I AM or soul.

ANTHONY: The notion of the "We" has to be always kept in mind, because even here and now, as you are, that Overself is present with you. It never leaves and you can refer to it as the "We." You and I, me and my shadow.

LG: Are these realms of nature that it traverses different from the World-Idea that's inherent in the soul that gets projected out as the world?

AS: No, all those realms of nature would be part of that World-Idea that is within the soul. Paradoxically. It goes in, out. Just as the soul is within the Nous and then there's an image of the Nous within the soul, then that very soul sends a projection of itself to again be within that World-Idea that's within itself. All those realms of nature are part of that World-Idea that's within this I AM or eternal soul. And then that I AM or eternal soul sends a projection or stream of life to be conjoined with the part of that World-Idea that's within itself, and through that projection gets to know it discriminatively.

BS: Would this process account for the unfoldment of individual consciousness?

ANTHONY: Yes, that traversing through the realms of Nature is what's going to develop and unfold that consciousness, bring it out more and more. In other words, the very experience of the world forces the consciousness of an individual to evolve, so the faculties get developed.

The wonder of all of this is that the cosmic circuit, or the purpose of manifestation, becomes much more overwhelming in importance. In other words, when they say that the purpose of manifestation is to guide and instruct the soul—and only the World-Mind can do that, nothing less than that can do it—then this manifestation is for that purpose, and manifestation becomes meaningful.

NOTES

1. Einstein had three significant trans-Saturnian aspects to his natal Mercury/Saturn conjunction at the time he intuited general relativity. Neptune was trine it (120 degrees), Pluto was square it (90 degrees), and Uranus was septile it (72 degrees).

2. Anthony is referring to the following passages from Stephen MacKenna's translation of *The Enneads:* IV.1 (entire), IV.2 (entire), and VI.2.6.

3. See *Ennead* I.1., especially I.1.7, of the MacKenna translation, Larson edition, 1992.

4. Anthony is referring to a copy of the *Ashtavakra Samhita* that contains marginalia PB entered while studying the text under the supervision of V.S. Iyer.

5. Anthony is referring to The One, The Intellectual-Principle (or Divine Mind), and Soul as the three primal "hypostases" or principles in Plotinian philosophy. He soon correlates (p. 181) these with what PB described as three distinct levels of penetration into the Void in contemplation. Most mystics are aware "only" of the first level, Soul—itself a momentous achievement not to be underrated.

6. The quote Anthony is referring to is: "Philosophy takes its votaries on a holy pilgrimage from ordinary life in the physical senses through mystical life in the sense-freed spirit to a divinized life back in the same senses." (v13, 20:4.113 and *Perspectives,* p. 256)

7. See *Notebooks,* v16, 25:55-186.

8. Reference is to a definition of consciousness by the great Vedantic teacher Citsuka: "Self luminosity [is] the capability of being called immediate in empirical usage, while remaining at the same time a non-object of knowledge." *Tattva-pradipika* translated by T.M.P. Mahadevan in *The Philosophy of Advaita,* p. 140, Ganesh & Co., Madras, India, 1969.

9. Reference is most likely to v14, 22:8.24.

10. Anthony is alluding to a quote not included in the flow of the current dialogue:

> There are two kinds of consciousness, one is in ever-passing moments, the other is ever-present. The one is in time, the other out of it. The ordinary person knows only the one; the enlightened sage knows both.
>
> (v13, 19:3.182)

4

What a Philosopher Is

It is out of such a splendid balance of utter humility and noble self-reliance that the philosopher gets his wisdom and strength. He is always kneeling metaphorically before the Divine in self-surrendering renunciation and often actually in self-abasing prayer. Yet side by side with this, he is always seeking to develop and apply his own intellect and intuition, his own will and experience in life. And because they are derived from such a balanced combination, this wisdom and strength are beyond any that religion alone, or metaphysics alone, could give.

(v13, 20:5.16)

ANTHONY: This is what a philosopher is.

The peace to which he has become heir is not self-absorbed rest from old activities that he deserts, but a divine awareness that subsists beneath new ones that he accepts.

(v13, 20:4.225 and *Perspectives,* p. 280)

ANTHONY: That means when you become a sage, you get more work!

The horoscope indicates the future only for ordinary people and can never become a fixed certainty for the spiritually

> awakened. For wherever an individual has come under Divine Grace, he directly or indirectly through a teacher can be rendered independent of his past karma at any moment that the Divine wills it to be so. The will is free because Man is Divine and the Divine Self is free.
>
> (v6, 9:3.459)

ANTHONY: If someone is "spiritually awakened" and under the tutelage or guidance of a sage, it's very possible that the chart will not work for that person. There may be changes.

EC: So PB's saying that grace can descend at any moment if you're spiritually awakened?

ANTHONY: Yes. If you're under the guidance of a sage, the sage can release you from a certain destiny which is indicated in your chart.

Here's a quote that will give you an idea of the magnitude of the spiritual grandeur of what a sage is. I don't think we can properly grasp it.

> DO NOT PRETEND to be other than you are. If you are one of the multitude, do not put upon yourself the proud robes of the Teacher and pretend to be able to imitate him; unless you stick to the Truth, you can never find it. To put yourself upon the pedestal of spiritual prestige before the Master or God has first put you there is to make the first move towards a humiliating and painful fall.
>
> (v16, 25:5.33 and *Perspectives*, p. 16)

ANTHONY: You see the powers that he's given to a Master? The Master can assign you to a certain work or God can assign you to a certain work. A Master can release you from certain compulsions that you feel your destiny allotted to you. The Master can say: We'll let you get away with it this time. You won't have to go through that and you can be released from it.

Now a Master is a person who has realized the I AM, the Overself, and philosophically has brought that realization into the world and understands the nature of the world—that it is basically a manifestation of Consciousness or Reality—that is a Master. I don't know if you've got any idea what work is involved to reach those heights, but in studying these things I began to realize we're speaking about the quintessence of Divinity as far as humanity is concerned. So, for example, when Ramana Maharshi was a boy, he said, "I'm going to lie down and find out what this business about dying is." And he lies down on the floor and he stops breathing.

You try it. See if you can do it. You'll find out the strength of the *vasanas* is unbelievable. They'll say we're going to scream for help and beg and cry for mercy. Everybody speaks about how superior they are to death—when they're not dying. But when they're dying it's a whole different ball game. The *vasanas* take over, the tendencies are powerful enough to take over completely. I can't conceive of any power except the power of a sage or God to release you from that *compulsive* fear. So the word "Master" has a lot of meaning, tremendous depth and profundity to it, and I don't think that we have any idea of what's really involved. I don't think we have any idea. You're speaking about someone who is in touch with the Lord of the Universe, our world.

> He lives in inwardly silent thought-free awareness of whatever is presented to him, whether it be the body in which he must live or the environments in which he finds himself. He enjoys a supernal calm, being indeed "free while living," as the ancient Indian phrase describes the state.
>
> (v16, 25:2.154)

ANTHONY: The sage is continuously self-aware, as pure consciousness. Anything that occurs is a presentation to that pure consciousness, but the sage *knows* her or himself to be this pure awareness. So there's only presentation and the dissolution of what's presented, but that inner stillness is not disturbed in any way. Because that is always the way it is.

DB: So what is given and then passes away is seen within the context of that stillness?

ANTHONY: Yes. The sage is always identified with that stillness or awareness, and that's why the happiness of the sage is not dependent upon the turning of the wheel.[1]

DB: Would knowledge of that which is given, whether it be the body or the environment, be seen as a modification of that stillness?

ANTHONY: No, the sense of materiality is completely gone in the sage.

DB: I'm trying to understand what is presented to the sage. Not that it's material, but it *is* a presentation—

ANTHONY: Listen to what I said. The sense of materiality is completely gone in the sage. So when something is presented, what is it that's presented? It has to be a thought. But since the sage is not identified with any thought, such as we are with our ego-structure, and is always identified with the stillness, thoughts arise and thoughts settle. But they don't disturb that stillness that the sage is identified with or, let's say, is identical with. And there could be good thoughts, there could be bad thoughts, there could be a thought of a disaster in the family, or there could be the thought of inheriting a million dollars, but it's not going to disturb that stillness.

RC: At one time PB said, "The whole trick is simply: Don't let yourself be hypnotized by any thought." We're always looking for something to be fascinated with.

ANTHONY: Let's say that the *ego* is always looking for something to be fascinated with, in its preoccupation with its own glamour. But that stillness isn't.

AH: There's a distinction between thoughts being presented and the fact that there is no thinking, in the case of a sage. Properly speaking, according to the quote, PB didn't think. He didn't think, but he described thoughts as occurring or being presented. Is that to describe the absence of the ego?

ANTHONY: I don't think we should use the word "absent"; let's say that it's been subdued. The sage still has an ego. The body's still there.

AH: So is it ever appropriate to speak about the sage thinking?

RC: PB spoke about trying to find the right words, when he was actually *trying* to produce a thought. He was saying that he was at times having difficulty forming thoughts—then he said, "No, 'forming' isn't the right word—'receiving' isn't the right word either—'*creating*!' I'm having difficulty *creating* the thought." So, it's not that he's not capable of it, but that the introduction of a thought from within his own center seemed to be recognized as a creative activity to which he was responsible.

ANTHONY: But, we would have to add that even in the process of creating the thought or the word that he was seeking for, he was still identifying with the stillness.

LG: Why wouldn't "formulate" be the right word?

ANTHONY: Because "*create*" is the right word. *You're* doing it. "Reasoning is our own," Plotinus says. WE are the ones who reason. Remember that passage from Plotinus?

RC: PB would talk about actually *thinking* things into existence for ourselves, that it's a creative activity, not a passive activity.

AH: Is that creation a cognitive process?

ANTHONY: And non-cognitive. Yes, it's both. It's cognitive, and it's the non-cognitive. It's the willing and the feeling, too, besides the knowing. It's all three ways of knowing that we create and we employ: willing, feeling, knowing. In this case here he was speaking about the knowing function, but he could just as well have spoken about it as willing and feeling.

> WHAT THIS harmony means is that the hidden centre of consciousness within the other person will be alike to the centre within himself.
>
> (v14, 22:3.109)

AH: Is this akin to the description of how a sage works with a student? The sage imagines the student as the higher self?

TS: The sage takes the other person's center into harmony with his or her own—or with the centralized consciousness within the sage.

ANTHONY: Yes. The guidance that the sage gets is from the other person's self, which guides the sage's behavior toward that other person.

LRD: What part of the aspirant's higher self does the sage connect with? When the sage connects with that higher self of the aspirant, is it with the part that's guiding the person's life in the world?

ANTHONY: The sage is guided by the Logos[2] in the other person's soul as to how to relate to that person. That's what guides the sage's behavior, that's the basis of harmony. The sage is not guided by the ego's proclivities. The sage is guided by the soul of that person and that brings about the harmony. And if you talk to a sage, the sage doesn't tell you what you want to hear, the sage tells you what you *need* to hear.

> THE SAGE is only a man, not a God. He is limited in power, being, knowledge. But behind him, even in him—yet not of him—there is unlimited power, being, knowledge. Therefore we revere and worship not the man himself, but what he represents.
>
> (v16, 25:3.15)

LR: Anthony, could you say something about the difference in power of a sage who's living and one who's not?

ANTHONY: There's a little difference, but they can continue working, even if they're not physically here. Before leaving, the sage sets certain things in motion which will go on, regardless.

> THE ILLUMINATE is the conscious embodiment of the Overself, whereas the ordinary man is ignorant of that which his heart enshrines. Hence, the Chinese say that the illuminate is the "Complete Man." He is the rare flower of an age.
>
> (v16, 25:3.14)

ANTHONY: The sage is the flower, the blossoming of intelligence, throughout eons of time.

PB speaks in another quote about the rare occurrence of a

sage. It is the product of nature's striving to try to bring about such blossoms. It takes a long time to become a sage.

The sage represents the actual manifestation, the *actualization* of the human ideal. And it is something that Nature is producing. The world is the womb of the Buddhas; the world is attempting to produce Buddhas.

AH: What is the appropriate attitude to hold in relation to a sage?

ANTHONY: Reverence.

That doesn't mean the sage is not aware of what attitude you actually *do* have. [*laughter*] The sage will read you just like a book. Like a camera, the sage will pick it right up and know just what the attitude is. But still the appropriate attitude for a devotee or a follower or a seeker is always one of reverence.

AH: What exactly is reverence, Anthony?

ANTHONY: You can't explain that. When you feel it, you'll know it.

AH: Is it self-effacing?

ANTHONY: No. *Reverence.* It's quiet, it's very deep, very persistent, and nothing will shake it.

> WHY ARE they so few, these sages, these serene and urbane self-realized ones? Nature works very hard and only attains her aim once in a multitude of throws. In mankind she may well be contented if she creates one sage in a hundred million people.
>
> (v16, 25:3.39)

VM: Right now [1984] the world population is four billion six hundred thousand—that's forty-six sages around at any one time.

ANTHONY: Just about enough to fill a trolley car. [*laughter*]

VM: Somehow I don't think PB meant the numbers literally.

ANTHONY: Well, would you read that again?

[*Quote is repeated.*]

ANTHONY: He doesn't tell us why it's so hard.

AS: When he says it's nature—

ANTHONY: That's the concept of the *Tathagata.* Sometimes after the word "Nature" PB puts in parentheses the word "God." Nature is a reflection of God's activities.

AS: There seems to be always this double view, that the sage is an expression of the soul, of the individual soul, but also the making of a sage requires the whole cosmos. The *Tathagata-gharba* [womb of the Buddhas], that's almost the primary business of the cosmos.

ANTHONY: You have the same thing in alchemy. They keep harping over and over again that unless Nature cooperates the work will not succeed.

> A CHINESE proverb of antiquity says, "A dragon in shallow waters becomes the butt of shrimps." Hence, the illuminate does not advertise his sagehood, make a noise about his wisdom, or shout his power in public, but lets most men believe he is just like them. "The Tathagata (teacher) is the same to all, and yet knowing the requirements of every single being, he does not reveal himself to all alike. He pays attention to the disposition of various beings," said Buddha.
>
> (v16, 25:3.446)

AH: So when you talk to a sage or ask a question or ask for spiritual guidance, the sage is able to express that knowledge of your requirements?

ANTHONY: Well, the sage is very precise in the guidance given. The guidance is *never* general. It is always very specific and it applies to the individual that the sage is talking to, and no one else. And it's a very profound knowledge of the particularity of your being.

> HE IS NOT working for this generation, nor for this country, nor for any millenium, but for an infinite duration of time. Therefore he is, he must be, infinitely patient.
>
> (v16, 25:3.256)

ANTHONY: The sage is working for the World-Idea.

BERGSON was right. His acute French intelligence penetrated like an eagle's sight beneath the world-illusion and saw it for what it is—a cosmic process of continual change which never comes to an end, a universal movement whose first impetus and final exhaustion will never be known, a flux of absolute duration and therefore unimaginable. And for the sage who attains to the knowledge of THAT which forever seems to be changing but forever paradoxically retains its own pure reality, for him as for the ignorant, the flux must go on. But it will go on here on this earth, not in the same mythical heaven or mirage-like hell. He will repeatedly have to take flesh, as all others will have to, so long as duration lasts, that is, forever. For he cannot sit apart like the yogi while his compassion is too profound to waste itself in mere sentiment. It demands the profound expression of sacrificial service in motion. His attitude is that so clearly described by a nineteenth-century agnostic whom religionists once held in horror, Thomas Huxley: "We live in a world which is full of misery and ignorance, and the plain duty of each and all of us is to try to make the little corner he can influence somewhat less miserable and somewhat less ignorant than it was before he entered it." The escape into Nirvana for him is only the escape into the inner realization of the truth whilst alive: it is not to escape from the external cycle of rebirths and deaths. It is a change of attitude. But that bait had to be held out to him at an earlier stage until his will and nerve were strong enough to endure this revelation. There is no escape except inwards. For the sage is too compassionate to withdraw into proud indifferentism and too understanding to rest completely satisfied with his own wonderful attainment. The sounds of sufferings of men, the ignorance that is the root of these sufferings, beat ceaselessly on the tympanum of his ears. What can he do but answer, *and answer with his very life*—which he gives in

> perpetual reincarnation upon the cross of flesh as a vicarious sacrifice for others. It is thus alone that he achieves immortality, not by fleeing forever—as he could if he willed—into the Great Unconsciousness, but by suffering forever the pains and pangs of perpetual rebirth that he may help or guide his own.
>
> (v16, 25:4.17 and *Perspectives*, p. 359)

ANTHONY: I had a vision that PB knew he was going to pass on, and in that knowledge there was a big drop coming out from his eye. It was a real tear, glistening, golden. [*said very quietly*]

He felt very badly because he had to leave us behind.

This is a little bit of an indication of the way these sages feel about leaving, and their willingness to come back and continue helping their students. . . .

AH: Anthony, would you speak about the individual soul of a sage reincarnating endlessly?

ANTHONY: Read the sentence again, please, about the "knowledge of THAT."

> . . . And for the sage who attains to the knowledge of THAT which forever seems to be changing but forever paradoxically retains its own pure reality, for him as for the ignorant, the flux must go on. . . .

ANTHONY: What do you expect? The World-Idea is what it is.

AH: Anthony, would you explain what you said?

ANTHONY: You've acquired a little understanding of ontology, haven't you?

AH: A little.

ANTHONY: A little. Then what do you expect?

AH: I shouldn't expect otherwise than that the World-Idea should be what it is.

ANTHONY: No. You shouldn't expect otherwise than that *you* and the World-Idea are going to go on forever.

AH: I don't understand what's referred to by "you."

ANTHONY: The soul will always be incarnating with the

World-Idea, and be included as part of the World-Idea, and will evolve alongside the World-Idea. So why look for exits?

AH: Individual soul?

ANTHONY: Yes, that's what I'm talking about. Individual soul will evolve in and as part of the World-Idea. And if this Idea goes on evolving endlessly, again, why look for exits?

If you understand a little bit about the World-Idea and the way the soul is evolving the appropriate and necessary vehicles along with the World-Idea, why should you expect anything different? Why should you expect a finis or a side-issue, like absorption here, absorption there? Why not accept what *is*? If the World-Idea is going to go on forever, and you're part of the World-Idea, then you go on forever, too. . . .

There seems to be some truth in Freud's notion of "the instinct for death," that we all insist that somewhere we write the word "finis." Somewhere along the line, we want to be able to write the words, "It's all finished now. It's all ended." And it's very possible that in trying to understand how they're describing soul, this is one of the psychological obstacles that has to be overcome. In other words, this inherent desire to come to a rest, to write "finis," is one of the things that has to go. This idea that there is an end has to go.

> IT IS NECESSARY to give certain terms often but wrongly used interchangeably, and hence confusedly, a sharper definition. The *Saint* has successfully carried out ascetic disciplines and purificatory regimes for devotional purposes. The *Prophet* has listened for God's voice, heard and communicated God's message of prediction, warning, or counsel. The *Mystic* has intimately experienced God's presence while inwardly rapt in contemplation or has seen a vision of God's cosmogony while concentrated in meditation. The *Sage* has attained the same results as all these three, has added a knowledge of infinite and eternal reality thereto, and has brought the whole into balanced union. The *Philosopher*

is a sage who has also engaged in the spiritual education of others.

(v16, 25:3.102)

ANTHONY: A sage has unbroken continuous awareness of the Self as absolute. That's what a sage is, to PB.

Also, the sage is philosophically capable of communicating that, if that sage's role is to be that of a teacher. A philosophic sage can communicate knowledge according to the mores or the forms of the culture within which that sage lives. The sage who is not philosophic does not necessarily have that capacity, but that doesn't mean that sage does not have insight. That's PB's definition.

Now, regardless of how proficient an adept or anyone else might be, if there is not this unbroken continuity of awareness of the self, PB doesn't consider the person a sage. PB has a very strict philosophic definition of what sagehood is.

MB: But will a sage, who does have that unbroken continuity of consciousness, always be someone who tries to teach others or—

ANTHONY: PB says they have a choice. Some will, some won't.

MB: They won't all necessarily mix with humankind and teach.

ANTHONY: Correct.

AH: But if they're not teaching, aren't they helping humankind equally to one who is?

ANTHONY: Assuming that they've decided to do so and not retire. Even in Buddhism, you have the same possibilities, you have the Bodhisattva, the Pratyeka-Buddha, the Sravaka-Buddha. They're different kinds of sages. Some will take on the role of helping the World-Idea, working with it, in an infinite duration of time, and some will retire, to rest in the Void. The choice is something that will come up in due time for the individual. But it can't be predetermined.

AH: The sage's presence in the world helps the world, no matter what the sage is doing, isn't that so?

ANTHONY: Yes, but the point being made here is that there are two types of sages, or people who have an unbroken continuity of self-awareness: the type that has been geared to teaching, and the type that has not. PB is making the distinction here, but they're both sages, insofar that they have an unbroken awareness of the self.

NH: What about Emerson—he wasn't really teaching.

ANTHONY: How do you know that?

NH: I don't know.

ANTHONY: He worked with a group of people and he fostered their spiritual development. You don't have to use those words. Don't make the mistake of thinking that there are labels as to what they're doing. They could be doing the very same identical things and never use one word that we're familiar with.

Let's give an example of how a sage operates. Tim, tell us about the way PB would pick out paragraphs from an essay and make dots at the important parts.

TS: You're referring to this practice PB had of picking up an article and reading the salient points in the article first. That is, he'd only read the important sentences and then afterwards, just for completeness, he'd read the rest of it.

ANTHONY: And say, "Gee, I wasted all that time," right?

TS: Yes, he'd go through and just dot out the key points. Intuitively, or, you could say, with that insight. There would be a direct contact with the salient points in the article, and he'd only read those passages. He wouldn't read up to them and mark them out. He'd just read those passages first.

ANTHONY: You follow that? You see what he does? I give you a ten-page article and I say, without you reading it, "All right, mention the five most important points," and so you turn to the pages and you say, "This one, this one . . ." OK? Then I read it, and I say, "Gee, you're right." You never *thought* about it, you never *read* it or anything. Let's not try to conceive how the sage thinks. [*laughter*] It's hopeless.

RC: It fascinated me that he'd pick up journals in a library in languages he couldn't read and pick out a few things and say, "Would you get that translated? I think it might be interesting." [*laughter*]

ANTHONY: We have magazines of his, in foreign languages, which have parentheses in certain parts. He couldn't read it, and he's got parentheses.

By the way, do you notice the attitude that people were listening to these remarks with?

AH: It's more reverential than the attitudes we had towards the ego.

ANTHONY: Well, you asked what sort of attitude we should have towards the sage. I think you can get a trace of it here. Now these folks in the room can't even talk, and usually they're willing, at the drop of a hat, to put you in a corner.

> HIS GOODWILL to, and sympathy for all men, rather empathy, enables him to experience their very being in his own being. Yet his loyalty towards his higher self enables him to keep his individuality as the inerasable background for this happening.
>
> (v16, 25:4.20 and *Perspectives*, p. 358)

TS: Anthony, do you have a suggestion on that?

ANTHONY: Take the first part alone.

> His goodwill to, and sympathy for all men, rather empathy, enables him to experience their very being in his own being. . . .

ANTHONY: Yes, that part. What's PB saying? That his soul can experience the soul of another? Let's read the next part.

> . . . Yet his loyalty toward his higher self enables him to keep his individuality . . .

ANTHONY: Stop right there. Go over it.

> . . . his loyalty towards his higher self . . .

ANTHONY: Loyalty to PB's own soul.

. . . enables him to keep his individuality . . .

ANTHONY: Enables PB to keep his ego.

. . . as the inerasable background for this happening.

ANTHONY: As the means by which PB can have sympathy for other people. If he doesn't have that ego, he's not going to be able to be sympathetic with other people.

So the first part is the recognition of other beings in terms of real being. PB recognizes their real being because he has real being.

And the second part says that because PB is capable of devotion to his higher soul, that ego is capable of acting as a medium through which that transference and communication can take place. So it's a very difficult thing he's speaking about there.

> THERE IS still a centre of consciousness in him, still a voice which can utter the words or hold the thought "I am I." The ego is lost in an ocean of being, but the ego's link with God, the Overself, still remains.
>
> (v14, 22:6.266)

ANTHONY: Who is it that says, "I am I"? Who would that be? Ego?

AH: "I am I" must refer to the ego.

ANTHONY: Yes. In spite of the fact that the individual mind projects the whole universe and can hold the whole universe to be an idea, within that idea the ego still retains its place and that mind can still use it and communicate to others—"I am I."

> THE SAGE expresses self without selfishness, individuality without individualism.
>
> (v16, 25:3.244)

> THOUGH he has been caught up into something immensely greater than himself, he still remains an individual—albeit a loosely held one.
>
> (v16, 25:2.219)

LD: PB says the sage expresses individuality without individualism. I don't understand the difference. What does he mean by individualism?

ANTHONY: The sage expresses individuality without individualism. Wouldn't it be the same as saying that the sage can express ego without being egotistical? This would be the same as the second quote where PB speaks of holding onto the ego very loosely. The sage doesn't grasp—it's very gingerly held.

LD: What do we mean when we talk about individuality?

ANTHONY: Whenever PB is using the term "individuality" here, it usually refers to the ego. He points out that everyone has an individuality, and it's unique. There are no two that are alike. The reference here can only be to each person's ego, or let's say the body-mind complex with which the person is operating. And you know from your own studies that there are no two identical individuals. The astrological chart would never permit the existence of two individuals that are identical. So he usually refers to individuality that way. He doesn't use it as Plotinus does in referring to that higher individuality as soul.

> THE ILLUMINED men wrote either out of their intellect or their intuition, sometimes for scrupulous academic scholars and sometimes for simple persons. A sage like Lao Tzu wrote for neither the one class or the other, for he put forward the deep paradoxes of life; but another man not less illumined may have provided footnotes on nearly every page.
>
> (v16, 25:3.115)

AH: Can we characterize the impact of Lao Tzu? Would you say it's poetic? Would you say it's inspired?

ANTHONY: He leaves life the way he found it: mysterious.

> IT IS WRITTEN in some ancient Oriental text that among the signs whereby we may detect a person to be an Illumined One, the condition of the eyes is most important and that in such a person they will resemble a baby's.
>
> (v16, 25:3.398)

ANTHONY: When you look at a baby, what do you see in the baby's eyes? Can you see the soul?

S: Yes.

ANTHONY: You see an angel.

S: Beautiful, pure, sweet.

ANTHONY: Why sweet and pure?

LD: No thought.

ANTHONY: There isn't one thought behind them! If you look at a baby, and we're talking about one who's newborn or a few days old, and the baby looks at you, there isn't one cotton-pickin' thought in that baby's mind.

LG: So what's there?

ANTHONY: That's for you to figure out. That's why they compare them to a sage's eyes. What's there when you look behind a sage's eyes? There's nothing there. The sage hasn't got one thought in mind.

LG: Something's there.

ANTHONY: Yes, but it's not a thought.

The symbolism of the baby's eyes is very common in most traditional literature concerning the sage. The sages don't see like you and I see. And they don't have any thoughts because their eyes are seeing. And the rest follows.

EM: Would this mean seeing the higher and the lower at the same time? Would you say the sage is always seeing the Overself as well as seeing at the worldly level?

ANTHONY: Yes. For us, when we say, "I see a chair," there are all sorts of associations with it. Even the concept necessarily follows the percept for us. This would not be so for the sages. There would be a seeing, but there would be no conceptual reconstruction of the seeing. It's the same for a child; there's no conceptual construction of what's there.

> WHEN THE SENSE of this presence is a continuous one, when the knowledge of the mentalness of this world-experience is an abiding one, and when the calm which comes as a result

is an unshakeable one, it may be said that he is established in the Truth and in the Real.

(v16, 25:2.149)

RC: PB spoke of [T.M.P.] Mahadevan as a sage but also as expressing a particular point of view. What would it mean for a sage living in this continuous presence to express a point of view?

ANTHONY: The sage's point of view is the reason principles working.

LR: Would you say that if you come out of the silence you couldn't be the All, there would have to be some limitation on the Absolute in order to speak at all?

ANTHONY: That's what it means to come out of the silence.

RG: How does this relate to the idea that the sage always lives in the silence and is totally free?

ANTHONY: If there is an uninterrupted continuous awareness—whether asleep or dreaming or awake—PB would say the person is a sage.

RC: When the sage comes out of the stillness to express a point of view, is there a reidentification with the ego?

ANTHONY: No, the sage won't *identify* with the ego—that's not possible by definition. But in order to express an idea, the sage has to use the ego; and that has to be partial, that can't be total.

RG: What's partial?

ANTHONY: The expression. You can't say everything all at once, at one time. Even the sage.

Mahadevan has one thing to do; PB has another thing to do. PB had to go through what he had to do because he had to. And Mahadevan had to go through the Hindu doctrine. Their goals were different.

RG: But they're not essential distinctions.

ANTHONY: No, they're not; they're not essential distinctions. From their point of view, they're quite superficial distinctions.

But nonetheless, the goal that PB had to work for, and the goal that Mahadevan had, were different. Another sage might be ruler of a state or might be doing something else entirely different.

AH: The goal makes them different?

ANTHONY: It doesn't make them different. As RG just pointed out, that's not essential, if you're defining a sage.

AH: The distinction between PB and Mahadevan is only a distinction within the realm of—

ANTHONY: —your conventional truth. In the realm of the empirical world they have different work to do. Each has different work to do.

I have a certain historical background and you have a certain historical background, and yours may be a hundred times richer than mine—that wouldn't make us sages. The sages have continued awareness that's unbroken through all the states of consciousness. That makes the sage. Everything else is incidental. Now if you want to bring in the fact that PB had a versatile background, that he travelled and did all these things, and another one stayed put in one place, that's quite secondary.

BY: The sage's expression may have something to do with his or her mission or goal, so that one sage would have a very different training and teaching than PB, but that's not essential to sagehood or to the truth that they lived in. Yet in terms of the world's receiving the teaching, there would be great differences.

ANTHONY: That's the difference, isn't it? PB had to present an integral doctrine to the West, and therefore needed this comprehensive total framework to operate with. Another sage might have no such goal, no such function. But they're both sages. The important thing—that continuous unbroken awareness—is what counts. The other things are all secondary. Until you're there, you don't know. But when you're there you know what the goal is, what it is you're supposed to do. And you do just that, precisely and accurately.

RC: Can we return to the question of sages coming out of the silence?

ANTHONY: Well, what I think he means—and this is an opinion—is that, if you are a sage, as soon as you talk you are out of the silence, in the sense that you have given utterance. Once you give utterance, you have to break that whole integral vision and operate partially.

LR: Plotinus says: "The Sage, then, has gone through a process of reasoning when he expounds his act to others; but in relation to himself he is Vision." [*Ennead* III.8.6]

ANTHONY: Yes. And once you use reason, it has to be partial. Even the best. That's why there is no totally comprehensive statement of the doctrine, and it's taken humankind many thousands of years to produce different traditions—each, so to speak, a partial statement of that doctrine. We know enough now, even from our studies, to see that it would be impossible to ever give a statement of the transcendent unity of religions.

RC: One time PB said: "They all tell me that I *have* to have some point of view, that I have to be a Vedantist or a Buddhist or a particular—

ANTHONY: No. Not a real philosopher, never!

RC: He said, "It would be more appropriate, if I were to go through a list of things, and say I AM an Advaitin, I AM a Dvaitin, I AM a Vashistadvaitin, I AM a Buddhist . . . I could honestly say that I AM all of those things; but if they tried to pin me down to any one of them and say that's *all* that I am, then they wouldn't be seeing what I am."

ANTHONY: That's the point of view that's prevailed here for a long time, too. Any attempt to avoid synthesis by holding a single point of view—I don't care what point of view it is—can only lead to gross exaggeration and vilification of philosophy. So if you say to me you're a Buddhist, I say fine. If you say you're a Vedantist, fine. But I'd like you to add a few *dozen* other points of view to make it a complete statement.

PEOPLE sometimes ask me to what religion I belong or to what school of yoga I adhere. If I answer them, which is not often, I tell them: "To none and to all!" If such a paradox annoys them, I try to soften their wrath by adding that I am a student of philosophy. During my journeys to the heavenly realm of infinite eternal and absolute existence, I did not once discover any labels marked Christian, Hindu, Catholic, Protestant, Zen, Shin, Platonist, Hegelian, and so on, any more than I discovered labels marked Englishman, American, or Hottentot. All such ascriptions would contradict the very nature of the ascriptionless existence. All sectarian differences are merely intellectual ones. They have no place in that level which is deeper than intellectual function. They divide men into hostile groups only because they are pseudo-spiritual. He who has tasted of the pure Spirit's own freedom will be unwilling to submit himself to the restrictions of cult and creed. Therefore I could not conscientiously affix a label to my own outlook or to the teaching about this existence which I have embraced. In my secret heart I separate myself from nobody, just as this teaching itself excludes no other in its perfect comprehension. Because I had to call it by some name as soon as I began to write about it, I called it philosophy because this is too wide and too general a name to become the property of any single sect. In doing so I merely returned to its ancient and noble meaning among the Greeks who, in the Eleusinian Mysteries, designated the spiritual truth learnt at initiation into them as "philosophy" and the initiate himself as "philosopher" or lover of wisdom.

Now genuine wisdom, being in its highest phase the fruit of a transcendental insight, is sublimely dateless and unchangeable. Yet its mode of expression is necessarily dated and may therefore change. Perhaps this pioneering attempt to fill the term "philosophy" with a content which combines ancient tradition with modern innovation will help the few who are sick of intellectual intolerances that masquerade as spiritual insight. Perhaps it may free such broader souls from the need of adopting a separative standpoint with all the frictions, prejudices, egotisms, and hatreds which go with it, and afford them an intellectual basis for practising a profound compassion for all alike. It is as natural for those reared on limited conceptions of life to limit their faith and loyalty to a particular group or a particular area of this planet as it is natural for those reared on philosophic truth to widen their vision and service into world-comprehension and world-fellowship. The philosopher's larger and nobler vision refuses to establish a separate group consciousness for himself and for those who think as he does. Hence he refuses to establish a new cult, a new association, or a new label. To him the oneness of mankind is a fact and not a fable. He is always conscious of the fact that he is a citizen of the world-community. While acknowledging the place and need of lesser loyalties for unphilosophical persons, he cannot outrage truth by confining his own self solely to such loyalties.

Why this eagerness to separate ourselves from the rest of mankind and collect into a sect, to wear a new label that proclaims difference and division? The more we believe in the oneness of life, the less we ought to herd ourselves behind barriers. To add a new cult to the existing list is to multiply the causes of human division and thence of human strife. Let those of us who can do so be done with this seeking of ever-new disunity, this fostering of ever-fresh prejudices, and let those who cannot do so keep it at least as an ideal—however remote and however far-off its attainment may seem—for after all it is ultimate direction and not immediate position that matters most. The democratic abolishment of class status and exclusive groups, which will be a distinctive feature of the coming age, should also show itself in the circles of mystical and philosophic students. If they have any superiority over others, let them display it by a superiority of conduct grounded in a diviner consciousness. Nevertheless, with all the best will in the world to refrain from starting a new group, the distinctive character of their conduct and the unique character of their outlook will, of themselves, mark out the followers of such teaching. Therefore whatever metaphysical unity with others may be perceived and whatever inward willingness to identify interests with them may be felt, some kind of practical indication of its goal and outward particularization of its path will necessarily and inescapably arise of their own accord. And I do not know of any better or broader name with which to mark those who pursue this quest than to say that they are students of philosophy.

(*Perspectives*, p. 248)

NOTES

1. "Turning of the wheel" refers to the Buddhist image of the constant turning of the wheel of life and death.

2. "Logos" is used here to mean that part of the World-Mind actually functioning in and through the soul of that person.

Appendix

SOUL AS DOUBLE KNOWER: INSIGHT AND UNDERSTANDING

Based on the double nature of the Overself, there is a double nature of knowledge, which Anthony Damiani most often describes with the terms "insight" and "understanding."

> Philosophic understanding is understanding of the functioning of insight that the sage operates with, and also the understanding of the witness-I and its role in the world. It is a way of speaking about the soul as being the double knower, containing intrinsic self-cognition and also discursive reasoning and sense perception. (AD, 7/6/83)
>
> In a general way, the description that's given to us about the activity of this I AM is that it's two-fold. . . . When there is that awareness that is knowing, and it knows its own self-hood, then we say "insight." Insight is the recognition that Mind, Consciousness—whatever word you want to use—is the ultimate Reality. When we say that it is not aware of its own selfhood but only knows the external, whether that external is the ideas or the rational processes or perception of the sensible world, then we say that it is "the faculty of understanding" or "the reasoning faculty"

> or "the reasoning soul" which knows what it is manifesting and deals with it. One faculty can be referred to as the higher knower and the other as the lower knower. One is self-knowing and the other is other-knowing. Knowing knowing and knowing other. They are not meant as a hierarchy. It's better to think of them as two aspects of the soul (I AM). (AD, 6/29/83)

Anthony cautions, however, not to think of two distinct knowers:

> When we speak about the double knower, the higher and the lower, we're not dividing the knower. We're just speaking about two different aspects of one and the same thing [soul]. (AD, 12/7/83)
>
> This double nature of knowledge is the basis for the double standpoint, which gives rise to the absolute and relative, or ultimate and conventional, viewpoints of truth.
>
> Insight, one of these two "ways of knowing, is directed not only into the transcendental "void," but also toward the manifested universe:
>
> This insight is in two directions: on the one hand to its prior, the Intellectual-Principle from which it descends or has its source, and also into its content. Whether you face up to the transcendent source of your being or whether you face down and look at the substratum of the manifested world within you, either way you will see that Mind is the substratum. With insight you know that the underlying reality of the object is consciousness or Mind, the same way you know that it is your reality and there is no distinction between them because there is no relationship here. (AD, 7/6/83)

Understanding, also called "intuition" in many contexts, knows the objects' own nature, the reason principles that make each object to be what it is within the manifest universe.

Soul has these two faculties, insight and intuition, with which to understand something about the World-Idea which is within it. Insight gives you the actual recognition, the mystical perception, that the perceiver and what is perceived have for their substratum consciousness. But intuition is reasoning on objects, understanding of the reason principles. With these two faculties you could find within yourself those attributes which are reflections from the Intellectual-Principle [World-Mind]. In order to understand something about the World-Idea which is within your soul, these two faculties are necessary. (AD, 7/6/83)

UNDERSTANDING: DEVELOPMENT OF INTUITIVE FEELING / WILLING / KNOWING

That phase of the soul which seeks embodiment—also spoken of as a power of projection associating with the manifesting World-Idea—is the phase which must develop this understanding. This reembodying soul is a witness of experience, is the Overself as associated with the stages and processes of manifestation. Intuition, reasoning, understanding are being used in the same way by different authors as the faculty of the reasoning soul by which it understands, interacts with the World-Idea (which soul has manifested). At the most basic level, intuition is modalized as absolute Knowing, Willing, and Feeling. They all operate silently. When you have a real intuition, knowing some idea, a real aesthetic perception or appreciation, it will be silent, calm. This is what Plotinus refers to as reasoning about the objects, or the reasoning faculty in the soul, which is an image of the Intellectual-Principle, having the ideas unrolled and separate. Intuition does not apply to Mind itself, but arises in the soul's relation to the World-Idea. (AD, 7/20/83)

Feeling developed to the utmost (or willing or knowing) will become intuitive. It won't then operate as we know it in the discursive intellect. For the sage, there can be direct perception of the substratum reality as well as the operation of the understanding simultaneously, at any of the levels of ideation. In order to know anything about the contents of the World-Idea, or in order to articulate and formulate what insight delivers, the sage too will need to use understanding. So they're [knowing, willing, and feeling] going to be needed as well as insight. (AD, 7/6/83)

Three levels of understanding the World-Idea are referred to as Intellection (intuition at its heights), reasoning, and sense. Correspondingly, the perceiving subject at these three levels is termed the spiritual subjectivity, psychical subjectivity, and bodily subjectivity. (AD, 7/6/83)

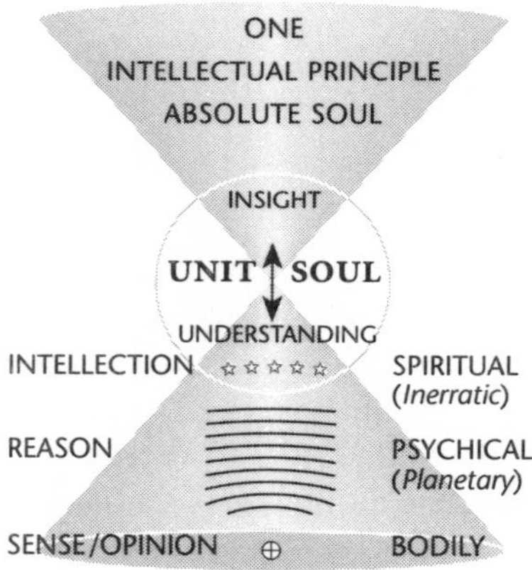

This conception of Soul or Mind may be likened to a transparent crystalline sphere of life-radiating consciousness, which is a reflex or emanation from the Absolute Soul. The vision of the pure soul in the nous is held within the boundless consciousness and this is represented by the inerratic sphere. The planetary spheres represent our rational soul, the discursive form of the abiding wisdom of the soul in the nous. And finally, the individual mind contains within it the realm of body, the medium in which the two priors are expressed and which provides the means that the Soul may come to know the reason principles through its experience of the sensible world. (AD, *Astronoesis*)

NIRVIKALPA AND SAHAJA: MYSTICAL VS. PHILOSOPHIC GOALS

The mystical path culminates in the experience of *nirvikalpa samadhi,* a state of mind characterized by the total absence of all thoughts and appearances. The philosophic realization is a stage beyond this mystical peak because it involves next assimilating the experience of the world and ego as ideas into the experience of oneself as real. This assimilation discovers the World-Idea in a different relation to the soul than that described in mystical schools as the relation of embodying soul to adventitious vehicles.

> *Nirvikalpa samadhi* means precisely that you have become the unit soul, soul per-se, void of the World-Idea as a content. On the other hand, the development of the second knower brings about the individuation. Or let's say, what God had in mind for this individual soul to become is being ac-complished through the medium of the World-Idea, so that each unit or individual soul is being individualized according to the World-Idea. (AD, 7/20/83)

> SAHAJA SAMADHI is the awareness of Awareness, whether appearing as thoughts or not, whether accompanied by bodily activities or not. But *nirvikalpa samadhi* is solely the awareness of Awareness.
> (Paul Brunton, *Notebooks* vol. 16, 25:2.140)

> Your awareness can be solely preoccupied with itself and nothing else. That is awareness of awareness. That is *nirvi-kalpa samadhi.* That is complete subjective introversion. No World-Idea. Nothing else exists—if I can be outlandish and say this—except you. It is the highest kind of solipsism that is available, although actually the truth will

be that it itself is placed in reality so it can't be really solipsistic. But in a sense it is the highest solipsism that's available to us. It is, so to speak, being that I AM principle. Where nothing else matters.

On the one hand, we're speaking about *nirvikalpa* as a kind of psychological introversion. On the other hand, we're speaking about *sahaja* as a kind of penetration into the metaphysical reality. But reality, the ultimate reality, is the same in both. We're bringing about this clarification in order to help us understand. (AD, 9/19/83)

PSYCHOLOGICALLY the world-transcending trance is deeper than the world knowing insight, but metaphysically it is not. For in both cases one and the same Reality is seen.

(Paul Brunton, *Notebooks* vol.15, 23.7.301)

Suppose I find that in principle, in essence, I am pure consciousness. Within that pure consciousness there manifests the world. That means thoughts. What would be the next requirement in order for me to be complete and to become a philosopher? You have the World-Idea being expressed, and the substratum of that World-Idea is your consciousness. The first achievement—not the harder one, but the easier one, according to this quote—is the recognition that in your essence you are consciousness. The more difficult achievement is the reconciliation that this pure essence is the substratum of the manifested universe, and that the two points of view are to be kept simultaneously alongside each other. This will make you a philosopher.

The philosopher is both: the double knower. In other words, for PB, the philosopher-sage is one who is poised in both positions, and includes both positions: that of recognizing his essence as pure consciousness, and the entirety of the manifestation of that pure consciousness, which maintains itself as a principle not separate from but distinct from the consciousness. (AD, 9/19/83)

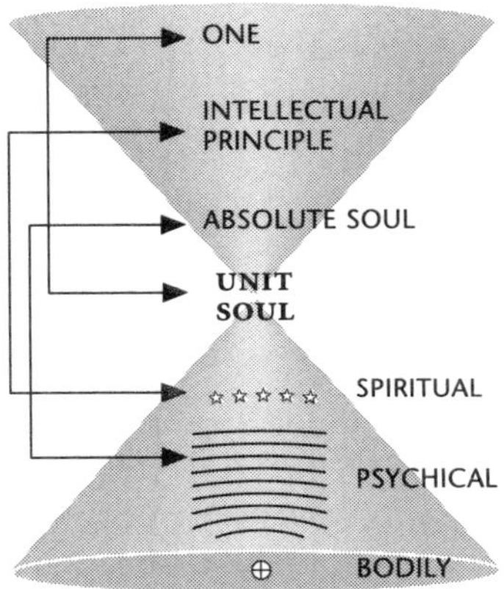

RELATION OF THE EXPERIENCE OF THE VOID AND MANIFESTATION

PB makes this remark: the philosopher who has developed insight can penetrate into three deepening initiations. He speaks psychologically about the three initiations, or levels of inwardness or penetration of insight, corresponding to the penetration, or presencing of the three primal aspects of Mind (which Plotinus describes) to the amazed gaze of the soul. If we imagine that he has achieved a status where he has come to the recognition of his own I-AM, the god within himself, his own Overself, now he can achieve identification with the supreme. Soul, being of the essence of Mind, is open inwardly to the grace of the Divine Mind revealing to it the nature of soul or life, of the Nous, and even of the One. Both Plotinus and PB speak of insight having these degrees of penetration, and getting to know something about the Void, besides that It is. Back in the world, insight can perceive that the substratum of the world is also Mind or consciousness. (AD, 10/14/83)

How does the knowledge/assimilation of the experience of the world as idea relate to the deepening experience of the soul as a particle in the void? The realization of the World-Mind as source of the unit soul is parallel to the realization that the World-Mind is the source and ultimate ground of the World-Idea. Soul/Overself is not the ultimate reality or source of the universe, and must realize its relation to the World-Mind in order to shift its relation to the world. Plotinus says that the Nous (World-Mind) is the higher knower in us: either soul knowing itself by means of the World-Mind, or the World-Mind knowing itself in the soul. Ultimately, the deeper realization completely annihilates the attachment to the ego, and turns the relation to the World-Idea inside out.

At an earlier stage of the journey to spiritual maturity, the freedom of the soul may be felt as a possibility of detachment from the ongoing World-Idea. This freedom inheres in the inviolable nature of consciousness, which is imagined to have put itself in association with the system of nature, the ongoing karmic continuity of the universe. A deeper exploration of this consciousness in relation to Divine Mind reveals the same Mind to be the source of the World-Idea. An entirely different order of freedom results from the realization that the whole world is a manifestation of one's own very being, not something imposed from or by an alien source. Freedom is not only detachment from the ongoing circuit of life's evolution, but the cosmic circuit seen as the free expression or emanation of one's own essence. Therefore, there is no longer a dualism of purpose. One consents to and expresses the World-Idea because it is inseparable from the law of one's own self.

Glossary

Here are "working descriptions" of a few key terms in *Living Wisdom* for readers unfamiliar with how Anthony Damiani used them. They are not meant to be exhaustive, only to give readers easier access to passages in which these terms appear before they have been adequately developed in the text.

AVATAR

An enlightened being who incarnates in human form from a higher order of existence. Each brings a special and unique presence or impulse into the evolution of humanity.

INTELLECTUAL-PRINCIPLE

See Nous.

LOGOS

A term for the intelligence of the World-Idea. It is both universal and present within the depths of the individual. In some traditions it is the idea and underlying purpose of the individual, guiding the individual's entire life and unfoldment.

MENTALISM

Mentalism as used in this text maintains that the natural universe is mental, and traces its creative thinking principle to

Mind as the unique reality. It upholds both the existence and the marvelously intricate detail of this universe, but denies the materialistic view of it. "It refuses to attribute to matter a creative power to be found only in life, an intelligent consciousness to be found only in mind." (*Perspectives*, p. 282) It encompasses the relation of the individual mind to its world of experience, the World-Idea as the source of world existence, and Mind as the ultimate nature of both the world and the individual.

MIND

Paul Brunton's term for the ultimate mystery of Reality. It is not only the transcendent Reality in itself, but also Reality as the nature of all that is authentic: "Mind alone is."

Mind, World-Mind, and Overself are not conceived as separate entities, but as three aspects of One Reality. Mind is Reality per-se. World-Mind is the reality of the universe, active in and as the Universe. Overself is the reality of the individual, the individual's indissoluble inner connection to Reality.

NOUS

A term from Neoplatonic philosophy that enjoys a stimulating variety of interpretations. Anthony generally uses it for the Divine Mind itself, for its divine Wisdom, and for the higher Self-knower. The Neoplatonic terms One-Nous-Soul, when used by Plotinus as three aspects of Reality transcending the universe, convey the same meaning as Brunton's term "Mind." From the individual perspective, we may also think of One, Nous, and Soul as parallel to Mind, World-Mind/World-Idea, and Overself.

OVERMIND

See Solar Logos.

OVERSELF

The inner and ultimate reality of the individual, the individual's participation in the universal intelligence from which the world arises. Overself, where the human and the divine meet and mingle, is both universal and individuated. As Brunton writes, "Overself is the true inner self . . . reflecting the divine being and attributes. The Overself is an emanation from the ultimate reality but is neither a division nor a detached fragment of it. It is a ray shining forth but not the sun itself." (*Perspectives,* p. 296)

SAHAJA

The sage's permanent realization of the natural, intrinsic nature of Mind. In Anthony's view, *sahaja* realization follows upon the full development of the mystical entry into the void, combined with the assimilation of the world as idea.

Sahaja samadhi is contrasted with *nirvikalpa samadhi.* In *sahaja,* the world continues to appear within the experience of Reality, while *nirvikalpa* is the experience of Reality without thought. A student adds to this, and Anthony seems to agree, that "*nirvikalpa* would be the penetration into the soul as life-principle, and *sahaja* would be more fully the experience of the whole soul plus the World-Idea within it."

"*Sahaja samadhi* is the awareness of Awareness, whether appearing as thoughts or not, whether accompanied by bodily activities or not. But *nirvikalpa* is solely the awareness of Awareness." (Paul Brunton, *Notebooks,* v16, 25:2.140)

SAMADHI

Rapt contemplation. When the individual mind becomes so thoroughly absorbed in the object of its contemplation that the object shines forth as it is in its own right, uncolored by the ego-subjectivity of the contemplator, one has attained a state of *samadhi.* In yoga philosophy this state is the culmination of a three-step process that begins with concentration (*dharana*) and continues with an intermediate state called meditation (*dhyana*). If the object is a form of or within the World-Idea, then this absorption is called *savikalpa* (with appearance) or *sabija* (with seed). If the absorption is into the formless Mind or Overself, without the appearance of any form of the World-Idea, then it is called *nirvikalpa* (without appearance) or *nirbija* (without seed).

SOLAR LOGOS

Neoplatonism presents the universe as a living, sympathetic organism which is manifest within a confluence of individual and universal soul (or mind). The soul or mind of the actual sun of our solar system is the Solar Logos, transforming divine intelligence into the universe. The soul or mind of the Earth is called the planetary mind or Overmind. Various planetary and cosmic souls may all be viewed as aspects of the World-Mind, or each may be referred to as a World-Mind in its own right.

UNDIVIDED MIND

A term for the deeper mind which is not "cut up" into subject and object. It suggests experience in which subject and object, ego and world, higher and lower selves are not split apart in consciousness. Anthony sometimes uses it as equivalent to the Mind of the World, that is the Earth Mind, which is the most immediate source of the World-Idea for individuals here.

VASANAS

Vasanas are traces, or residues, of the mind's activity. They are emotionally charged memories that persist as dynamic tendencies or thought habits in the mind. They comprise what modern psychologists call the unconscious. We are normally unaware of the extent to which our ego experience is constituted by the totality of these traces. Mircea Eliade, in *Yoga, Immortality, and Freedom* writes that "life is a continual discharge of *vasanas*." In the mentalist view, as the mind projects a world for the individual by transforming itself into experience, it also has the dynamic power to retain a memory of these experiences. All life experiences thus leave traces within the individual (and cosmic) mind which has them—feelings, sensations, habits, language, actions, etc.

WORLD-IDEA

The Idea of the world, or the world as known to and produced by the Mind of God. It is both a stable archetype, and also the creative energy of the mind which manifests as the world. It is the World itself, experienced in its inner nature as a living intelligence. Anthony refers to it variously in these dialogues as "the master plan of the universe," "an ordered, intelligent whole which is manifesting according to wisdom principles," and "the entire potential of all circumstances, situations, events, bits and pieces of knowledge that can be brought together."

See *Perspectives,* chapter 26.

WORLD-MIND

The active aspect of Reality or Mind, the aspect which thinks the world into existence and within which the entire world appears. It is Mind as associated with the world. See *Perspectives,* chapter 27